# Ask a Mufti
# Vol 1

INTRODUCTION

ABOUT THE AUTHOR

BELIEF

KNOWLEDGE

SUNNAH

INNOVATION

PURITY

## By
## Shaykh Mufti Saiful Islām

JKN Publications

© Copyright by JKN Publications

Published in December 2014

ISBN 978-1-909114-06-7

British Library Cataloguing in Publication Data
A catalogue record for this book is available from the British Library.

Publisher's Note:

Every care and attention has been put into the production of this book. If how-ever, you find any errors they are our own, for which we seek Allāh's ﷻ for-giveness and reader's pardon.

Published by:

JKN Publications
118 Manningham Lane
Bradford
West Yorkshire
BD8 7JF
United Kingdom

t: +44 (0) 1274 308 456 | w: www.jkn.org.uk | e: info@jkn.org.uk

Book Title: Ask A Mufti (Vol 1)

Author: Shaykh Mufti Saiful Islām

"In the Name of Allāh, the Most Beneficent,
the Most Merciful"

# Contents

5

# Preface

بِسْمِ اللهِ الرَّحْمٰنِ الرَّحِيْمِ

All praises are for Allāh ﷻ, the Lord of the worlds. May peace and blessings be upon the beloved Messenger of Allāh ﷺ, upon his noble family ﵇, his Sahābah ﵃, and upon those who follow the true path until the Day of Judgement.

Throughout history, Allāh ﷻ has blessed and guided many of His servants from the time of Sayyidunā Ādam ﷺ, until the present day to show His true path to mankind whether it is through their lofty character, speeches or writings.

Allāh ﷻ states in the Holy Qur'ān:

"**Allāh is the Walee (Protector) of those who believe. He brings them out from (the depths of) darkness into the light. As for those who disbelieve, their friends are the rebels. They bring them out from the light into (the depths of) darkness. Those are the dwellers of the Hellfire wherein they shall remain forever." (2:257)**

The true believers are those whom Allāh ﷻ has chosen to revive and propagate His Deen (Islām) throughout the world. All praises be to Allāh ﷻ, amongst those servants of Allāh ﷻ is my beloved teacher, friend and spiritual mentor Shaykh Mufti Saiful Islām, who at this very young age has embarked upon the same path as those of the pious predecessors.

Jāmiah Khātamun Nabiyyeen, commonly known as JKN was established in June 1996 from the residence of my beloved Shaykh, Mufti Saiful Islām. Alhamdulillāh, through the Infinite Grace, Mercy and Help of Allāh ﷻ JKN has become a prominent institution both in the UK and internationally, through which many brothers and sisters have acquired the true understanding and knowledge of Islām, the teachings of the Holy Qur'ān and the Sunnah of the Holy Prophet Muhammad ﷺ.

Allāh ﷻ has granted my beloved Shaykh the zeal for knowledge in which he has strived and acquired for many years. He is the founder and Principal of our Institute Jāmiah Khātamun Nabiyyeen and the director of numerous JKN projects and activities. He is also the Editor of the popular family magazine Al Mu'min and he has published many books and literature in the field of Islām. It is due to his great efforts and sacrifices that today we are witnessing and reaping the rewards of his achievements.

As time is passing by and we are drawing closer to the Last Day (Day of Judgement), we are witnessing our Ummah in a state of crisis. Ignorance has prevailed and the misguided "so-called scholars" have emerged in great numbers issuing incorrect verdicts (Fatwas) and misleading people. Therefore, Fitnah (corruption) is spreading at an alarming rate.

Taking all the above matters into consideration as well as to fulfil the aspirations of many brothers and sisters, my beloved Shaykh, Mufti Saiful Islām, with the Help of Allāh ﷻ has compiled this valuable book, *"Ask A Mufti"* with the spiritual regeneration of the

Ummah in mind. I pray to Allāh ﷻ that He makes it a means of removing ignorance and spreading the true and correct teachings of Islām to a wider audience.

This book, which is before you is an evidence of his great work and sacrifice for Deen. I am very grateful to Allāh ﷻ that He has given me the ability to take part in this noble work.

I pray to Allāh ﷻ that He keeps me steadfast in the service of Deen and He keeps me in the pious company of my beloved Shaykh, Mufti Saiful Islām.

This book, titled *"Ask A Mufti"* is an outstanding, very comprehensive, yet simple Fatāwa book compiled by my beloved Shaykh with the hope that it becomes a source of guidance and reaches out to a wider audience i.e. the English speaking Muslims and non-Muslims alike.

Based on Islamic Laws, this book will answer commonly posed questions relating to beliefs, knowledge, Sunnah, pillars of Islām, marriage and divorce as well as other contemporary issues.

Alhamdulillāh, this is the first volume of the many to be published in the near future, Inshā-Allāh. May Allāh ﷻ increase my beloved Shaykh's blessed knowledge and give us all the ability to benefit from it. May Allāh ﷻ accept my beloved Shaykh's efforts and make it a means of his and our salvation in the Hereafter. May Allāh ﷻ give my beloved Shaykh the ability to continue and increase in the service of Deen and make it a means of guidance for the Muslim Ummah of our beloved Prophet Muhammad ﷺ.

I pray to Allāh ﷻ that He protects us all from the evil whispers of Shaytān and from the mischief of the society we live in. I further pray that Allāh ﷻ gives us the ability to carry out the work of Deen with full sincerity only to please Him and that He grants us Jannah.

Finally, I pray with tearful eyes and a weeping heart that Allāh ﷻ showers His Mercy upon the Muslims around the world who are suffering from the oppression of the oppressors.

**"They conspire but Allāh ﷻ also plans and indeed Allāh ﷻ is the best of all planners." (3:54)**

I pray that Allāh ﷻ keeps us steadfast upon His Deen and unite the Muslim Ummah, Āmeen!

*Maulāna Ismāeel Aziz*
*Graduate of JKN*
*December 2014/Safar 1436*

# Introduction

بِسۡمِ اللّٰهِ الرَّحۡمٰنِ الرَّحِیۡمِ

All praises are for Allāh ﷻ, the Lord of the worlds and may peace and blessings be upon the beloved Messenger of Allāh ﷺ, upon his noble family ﵃, his Sahābah ﵃, and upon those who follow the true path until the Day of Judgement.

By the Infinite Grace of Allāh ﷻ we humbly present before you *"Ask A Mufti."* Since the publication of *"Your Questions Answered"* in 2010, Alhamdulillāh we have received a positive response and feedback from many people, scholars as well as non-scholars. The publication of *"Your Questions Answered,"* has become considerably read and widely purchased by many people. Very recently a number of requests have been made by the general masses to Shaykh Mufti Saiful Islām (may Allāh ﷻ preserve him and prolong his life) to publish a separate yet comprehensive book dealing with general Islamic queries, especially those that are relevant today. This compilation is aimed to educate the laypeople and to facilitate for them the practicing of the Deen.

Ever since the publication of *"Your Questions Answered,"* our Fatāwa department has become increasingly busier and gained more recognition nationally. By the Grace of Allāh ﷻ, we have received questions and Fatāwa more extensively via post, email and phone in our department than ever before. From amongst them, there are many that need addressing to the general masses which were not published in *"Your Questions Answered."*

18

In view of the above, we have made additions to this new publication by inserting some of our recent and relevant Fatāwa, some of which have been elaborated at length for the benefit of the general public. In addition to this, we have included queries pertaining to Islamic medical issues and other contemporary issues answered by Maulāna Doctor Rafāqat Rasheed in detail.

We sincerely hope that our inquisitive readers will benefit immensely from this and it becomes accessible for a wider readership. May Allāh ﷻ bless and reward Shaykh Mufti Saiful Islām immensely for his enormous efforts for the preservation and propagation of the Deen and prolong his life so that we can acquire more beneficial knowledge from him, Āmeen!

*(Mufti) Abdul Waheed*
*Teacher of Fiqh at Jāmiah Khātamun Nabiyyeen & serving JKN Fatāwa dept*
*December2014/Safar1436*

# Some Principles Regarding Fatwa

## Introduction

Although the religion of Islām has been completed, the responsibility of enjoining what is good and forbidding what is evil still remains an obligation until the Day of Judgement. The Holy Prophet 🕌 foretold that a group amongst this Ummah will continuously strive to uphold the truth and guide the Ummah to the right path until the Day of Judgement. In order to be included in that promised group it is incumbent to fulfil this great responsibility to prevent the Ummah from goining astray. This Ummah has been privileged to be the best nation ever to evolve for mankind on the account of enjoining what is good and forbidding what is evil. Allāh 🕋 states in the Holy Qur'ān;

**"You are the best of nations emerged for mankind (because you) enjoin what is good and forbid what is evil and believe in Allāh." (3:110)**

Nevertheless, there are many modes and forms of fulfilling this responsibility from which amongst them is issuing Fatwas. This is because when issuing a Fatwa(legal verdict), the Mufti distinguishes for the people what is Halāl and Harām and what is permissible and what is prohibited. One of the instrumental factors of the corruption of the previous nations was that people became unaware, as a result, neglectful of what was Halāl and Harām. Their influential leaders and scholars altered the religion of Allāh 🕋 and concealed many of His Divine teachings due to worldly gains. Issuing verdicts inevitably falls into the category of enjoining what is good and forbidding what is evil which preserves the pure traditional Islamic teachings as taught by the Messenger of Allāh ﷺ and the generations that followed.

## The Meaning of the Term Fatwa

The term 'Iftā' or 'Fatwa' literally means to clarify something (Qāmoosul-Muheet). The Fuqahā have given different interpretations to its technical meaning, however one of them is, "To issue a ruling from the command of Allāh ﷻ in response to a question of a particular issue or event (that is related to the Shariah) in light of the Shar'ee evidence" (Kitābul Fatāwa).

The role of a Mufti is to respond to a query that has been posed to him and to clarify its verdict in light of the Shari'ah sources. A Mufti cannot issue a verdict which is contrary to the fundamental principles of the Shariah or that which opposes the consensus of the Ummah.

## Issuing Fatwa (legal verdict) is a very delicate matter

It is very unfortunate that today issuing a Fatwa is taken very lightly and used inappropriately. Many incompetent people are taking the roles of scholars and issuing Fatwas without acquiring the necessary expertise. Such incompetent people, rather than doing good, are in reality jeopardizing their own faith and the faith of others and incurring the wrath of Allāh ﷻ and the burden of other people's sins on their shoulders. The Holy Prophet 鷺 said in one Hadeeth, "Whosoever is issued with a legal verdict without knowledge then the sin will be on the one who issued it."

(Abū Dāwood)

Allāh 鷺 has attributed the term Fatwa to Himself in the Holy Qur'ān. Allāh 鷺 states; **"Say, Allāh gives you a legal ruling (Fatwa) in regards to them." (4:176)**

This is why Imām Ibnul Qayyim Al-Jawzi 鷺 states, "A Mufti should be conscious of who he is representing (when issuing a verdict)." (I'lāmul Mooqi'een)

Imām Nawāwi 鷺 a renowned Hadeeth master states, "A Mufti represents Allāh 鷺 ." (Sharhul Muhadthab)

The above statement suggests that a Mufti, who delivers an Islamic ruling of a particular matter to the general public, actually represents Allāh 鷺 . So this illustrates that to issue Fatwas is not something that can be taken lightly, nor would it be permissible for an incompetent person to take this responsibility without acquiring the necessary skills. It has been the practice of our pious predecessors that they would always exercise caution when issuing Fatwas inspite of having the qualification to do so. Imām Ibn Abi Layla 鷺 a famous Tābi'ee, states, "I have seen 120 Sahābah 鷺 and have witnessed the fact that if one of them was posed with a question then he would refer it to the second person and that second person would refer it to the third person and this question continued to circulate until that same question returned back to the initial person." (Sharhul Muhadthab)

The state of the Sahabāhs ﷺ was such that inspite of memorizing many Ahādeeth directly from the Holy Prophet ﷺ and having the eagerness in relating them, they preferred others to do so. It is also reported that the four great Imāms would exercise caution when issuing verdicts. Imām Mālik ﷺ on one occasion was posed with 48 questions out of which 20 questions he refrained from answering and said, "I do not know." The questioner said, "The questions are simple." He then replied furiously, "Knowledge is no small matter." Imām Shāfi'ee ﷺ once said, "The most competent person for issuing Fatwas is Sufyān Ibn Uyayna ﷺ since I have not seen anyone exercising more precaution in issuing Fatwas than him." Imām Ahmad Ibn Hanbal ﷺ would frequently say, 'I don't know' due to his precautionary measures in issuing legal verdicts.

This was the level of their precaution inspite of their competency and level of expertise. Unfortunately today every person is eager to answer every question posed to him without reflecting. If a person attempts to answer every question on the spot without prior research, then he is putting himself at serious risk. Sayyidunā Abdullāh Ibn Abbās ﷺ and Sayyidunā Abdullāh Ibn Mas'ood ﷺ would say that if a person attempts to answer every question posed to him (without prior investigation) then he is insane.

## Historical Development of Fatwa

### a) The Noble Era of the Holy Prophet ﷺ

In the history of Islām the very first Mufti and Jurist was the Holy Prophet ﷺ. Imām Ibnul Qayyim Al-Jawzi ﷺ states, "The very first

person who established this noble task was the Holy Prophet
![](I'lāmul Mooqi'een)

The Holy Prophet ![] would issue verdicts in accordance with the
divine revelation inspired to him. His statements and actions,
known as the Sunnah, were a commentary of the Holy Qur'ān and
his way of life was an illustrious guide for all of mankind. Allāh ![]
states , **"And whatever the Messenger gives to you then accept it
and whatever he prohibits you from then abstain from it" (59:7).**
In another place He states, **"But if you dispute in any matter then
refer it to Allāh and the Messenger." (4:59).** If the Holy Prophet
![] did not receive any divine revelation then he would issue a ruling based on his Ijtihād (analogical deduction). If a particular ruling based on Ijtihād did not conform to the judgement of Allāh ![],
then the Holy Prophet ![] would instantly receive a revelation from
Allāh ![].

Although the Holy Prophet ![] possessed the mandate of issuing
verdicts, he also appointed certain Sahābahs ![] as governors in
different regions and permitted them to issue verdicts and make
Ijtihād when necessary. One such governor was Sayyidunā
Mu'ādh Ibn Jabal ![] who was appointed as a governor in Yemen.
Apart from him other Sahābahs ![] were permitted by the Holy
Prophet ![] to issue verdicts and make Ijtihād such as Sayyidunā
Abū Bakr ![], Sayyidunā Umar ![], Sayyidunā Uthmān ![], Say-
yidunā Ali ![], Sayyidunā Zaid Ibn Thābit ![], Sayyidunā Ubay Ibn
Kab ![], Sayyidunā Abdur Rahmān Ibn Awf ![] and others.

## b) The Era of the Sahābahs ؓ

After the demise of the Holy Prophet ﷺ the responsibility of Fatwas was transferred into the hands of the Sahābahs ؓ. They exerted every effort in fulfilling its responsibility in order to benefit the future generations. However, there were only a handful of them who were dedicated in this field. According to the analysis of Ibnul Qayyim ؒ there were just over 130 Sahābahs ؓ who would issue Fatwas. Apart from the aforementioned those that would issue verdicts prolifically included Sayyidunā Abdullāh Ibn Mas'ood ؓ, Sayyidunā Abdullāh Ibn Abbās ؓ, Sayyidunā Abdullāh Ibn Umar ؓ, Sayyidah Ā'ishah ؓ and others. Whatever initial training they acquired from the Holy Prophet ﷺ was imparted to their students.

## c) The Era of the Tābi'een and Tabi Tābi'een

The mandate of Fatwas did not come to a halt but continued within the generation that followed them. They also took great care in preserving it and utilizing it in accordance to the methods illustrated by the Sahābahs ؓ. The later Jurists used and adopted their Fatwas to formulate the principles of Ijtihād and Fatwa. Towards the latter period of the Sahābahs ؓ, many lands were conquered and subsequently became part of the Islamic Empire. The Muslim Jurists (Muftis) subsequently were no longer restricted to one region but were spread throughout the empire. In every region there were designated and recognized scholars on whose Fatwas the people of that region would rely on, for instance, in Madeenah there was Sa'eed Ibn Musayyib ؒ, Urwah Ibn Zubair ؒ, Qāsim

Ibn Muhammad ﷺ and other scholars known as the Fuqahā Sab'ah (the seven renowned jurists of Madeenah) as well as Imām Mālik ﷺ. In Makkah there was Imām Mujāhid ﷺ (a great Qur'ān commentator), Ikrimah ﷺ and Atā Ibn Abi Rabāh ﷺ. In Kufā there was Alqamah ﷺ, Ibrāheem an-Nakha'i ﷺ, Hammād ﷺ, Masrooq ﷺ and Imām Abū Haneefah ﷺ. In Basra there was Hasan Al-Basri ﷺ, Muhammad Ibn Sīreen ﷺ and Qatādah ﷺ. In Yemen there was Imām Tāwoos Ibn Kaisān ﷺ. In Syria there was Imām Makhool ﷺ and others. Many of their Fatwas can be found in many books of Fiqh, Tafseer and Hadeeth.

**Some Rules When Issuing Fatwas**

The scholars have outlined a set of integral principles that are mandatory for any scholar who wishes to pursue this field. Some of those principles are as follows:

1) He must have studied Fiqh in depth under the supervision of an expert and recognized scholar and have a good understanding of the sources of Shari'ah.
2) Has developed a profound perception and insight of Fiqh and Usool of Fiqh.
3) Good analytical and research skills.
4) To be aware of the multiple juristic views and differences of the Jurists on a particular issue.
5) To issue verdicts based upon the authentic juristic works only.
6) Knows how to interpret the juristic text correctly.

7)     Prioritize the preferred views that have been expressed in the text or given by those scholars from the category of Ashābut-Tarjeeh (those that give preference to one view from the multiple views on a particular matter).

8)     In the case where the Ashābut-Tarjeeh have not preferred any views then to adopt the view of Zāhir-ur-Riwāyah.

9)     Acquired the necessary training of issuing verdicts under the supervision of an expert and recognized Mufti.

10)    Possesses a wide range of reading around the subject area of Fiqh and Usool of Fiqh.

The classical and contemporary scholars have enumerated much more, however I have deliberately sufficed to the above to avoid a lengthy discussion.

**The Necessary Qualities of a Mufti**

It is necessary for a Mufti to be a Muslim, sound minded, mature, reliable, upright, practicing, adherent to the Shariah laws, implementing the Sunnah into his life, God fearing, abstinent from the love of worldly materials, abstaining from major sins, not perpetual upon committing minor sins and have the ability to analyze and infer rulings from a text. Women can also issue verdicts as long as they fulfil the necessary qualities and criteria as outlined above.

(Ādābul Mufti wal Mustafti & Kitābul Fatāwa)

# ABOUT THE AUTHOR

## Foreword

In the name of Allāh ﷻ the Most Gracious, the Most Merciful. Praise be to Allāh ﷻ the Lord of the worlds and may peace and blessings be upon His final Messenger Muhammad ﷺ, upon his noble family ؏, his Companions ؆ and upon those who follow their path until the final hour.

Alhamdulillāh, being a student and Mureed of Shaykh Mufti Saiful Islām Sāhib is an honour and a privilege for me which I feel I can never show enough gratitude to Allāh ﷻ for. I am one of the many thousands of people whose lives are impacted in a beneficial way on a daily basis by Mufti Sāhib and his services to Islām and the Muslim Ummah.

Mufti Sāhib's generosity knows no bounds. Around the clock he is constantly engaged in some form of Deeni Khidmat, be it through teaching, writing, delivering speeches or providing invaluable help and guidance to the general public, just to name a few of his duties. Whilst most of us can barely cope with one occupation in our daily lives, almost every day Mufti Sāhib takes on the role of principal, writer, Masjid chairperson, public speaker, teacher, shopkeeper, events organiser, counsellor, magazine editor, community leader - the list can go on and on.

This introduction provides just a brief glimpse of the life of our beloved Shaykh but in his autobiography you will find a more detailed account of Mufti Sāhib's life to date. Originally it was intended to be written as a biography from the 3rd person's perspective. However, after consultations it was decided that we keep
Mufti Sāhib's original text in 1st person perspective because it was
felt that this would incorporate a more personalised approach and
the reader would feel more connected with the story and the author. Inshā-Allāh in the future we are looking to provide a complete book version of this autobiography which will include much
more extra information. In addition, we are hoping to write another exciting book in which Mufti Sāhib's beautiful words of wisdom
and teachings will be included Inshā-Allāh.

Those of you who are story lovers would agree that a good story is
the one that makes you reflect and ponder, it keeps you drawn in
by its twists and turns and it has the ability to kindle your emotions – one minute you will be laughing, the next minute you will
be reduced to tears! Being the editor of this autobiography, I have
found all of the above points to be true about Mufti Sāhib's story.
Many a time whilst editing this work, I have either been left
astounded, thought-provoked, laughing or with tears strolling
down at the emotional moments. So if this is how the story has
made its editor feel – the person who is critically analysing and
rectifying its content – then I am certain that the reader will be so
engrossed in it that they will not be able to put it down (Inshā-
Allāh)!

I would like to conclude by thanking my respected teacher and
Shaykh for granting me the honour and privilege of being in-

volved in such a special and noble task. I would also like to thank my family for their support in this work particularly my beloved niece Juma Ā'isha who put in hours to help me. May Allāh ﷻ grant my family contentment and Āfiyah (safety) in the Dunya and in the Ākhirah. Ameen!

Finally, I pray that Allāh ﷻ preserves and bless the life of our beloved Shaykh Mufti Saiful Islām Sāhib and allows him to continue with the great work he is doing in His path. May Allāh ﷻ accept all of the tireless efforts and sacrifices of Mufti Sāhib and all those working with him for the sake of our beautiful Deen and may He reunite us all in Jannatul-Firdaus with our beloved Shaykh. Lastly, may Allāh ﷻ make this, the story of Mufti Sāhib's life a source of inspiration and motivation for the Muslims and many more to come. Āmeen!

*Sister Sahla Begum*
*Student of Jāmiah Khātamun Nabiyyeen*
*December 2014/Safar1436*

# About the Author
## Part 1-Birth, Family, Early Life, Education, Employment

### Early Days

On the outskirts of Biswanath, a town in the famous district of Sylhet in Bangladesh, there is a small village called Duhal. A few decades ago, my grandfather, Sayyid Ali used to live there who was a very famous and prominent person in his tribe and locality. The ancestral home of my grandfather was Duhal where he had lived all of his life.

### My Grandfather

My grandfather, Sayyid Ali was from a noble family. He first married Teraban Bibi (my respected grandmother) with whom he had 4 sons and 2 daughters. From his second marriage he had 4 sons and 3 daughters. So altogether he had 13 children. My grandfather was a very pious person who was punctual in his daily prayers. He was also very keen on fasting and performing Nafl Salāh.

The people accepted him as a judge to solve their family issues. He was also very experienced in exorcisms; helping those afflicted with Jinn related illnesses. An incident, which my respected mother narrated to me regarding him, is mentioned below.

Once my uncle Monuhar Ali, was possessed by a Jinn which troubled him a great deal. He was walking around the yard semi-consciously due to the possession of the Jinn. Fortunately for my uncle, my grandfather, Sayyid Ali came to his rescue. He immediately recited some Du'ās and ordered the Jinn to leave. The Jinn replied, "Do not harm me or else I will harm your son, move away from my path and I will leave your son alone." My uncle was a smoker but out of fear of grandfather he would never smoke in front of him therefore my grandfather was not aware of his smoking. Here in the yard, my uncle was smoking a cigarette and he offered one to my grandfather for him to smoke it! My grandfather who felt pity upon my uncle was angry to discover that he smoked. But it was the Jinn to be blamed as it was controlling his body and making him behave out of character. Finally when everyone moved from his path, the Jinn left my uncle's body. My uncle having regained his senses hid all of his cigarettes. A troublesome incident initially, became a story to laugh at in later gatherings!

## My Father

My beloved father Muhammad Ali was born in 1935 (approximately). He was the eldest son of Sayyid Ali (from his first marriage). He was a person of high calibre. He was educated in one of the local schools where he studied for five years. Although he did not gain any religious education, he was constant in prayers and fasting. He deeply regretted his lack of religious education in his later life when he educated me in the religious field.

Being the eldest in the family was a big responsibility for my father. He could not attain higher education and instead had to work hard all day in looking after the crop field and cattle. He was a person who utilised all of his time in hard labour and bringing up the family.

In 1963, many people travelled to England seeking work to sustain their families back in Bangladesh. My father joined them and after obtaining a visa, he came to England via Karachi, Pakistan. He was in his late twenties and he worked long and hard hours in the mills of Bradford to earn a living for himself and to send money for his relatives back home in Bangladesh. My father married my mother 7 years later in 1970.

## My Mother

My mother, Asdaqun-Nisā was born in 1953 in the village of Akil Pur, Birahimpur, Sadr, Sylhet, Bangladesh. My mother was also from a noble family. My maternal grandfather, Abdul Jabbār was a well-known and eminent person in his village and he was honoured by his contemporaries. One of his most remarkable qualities was his bravery. Nobody would dare to speak against him or his relatives! My mother was about 16 when she got married to my father. She was a quiet, clever and busy woman who was engaged virtually all day in domestic work.

## My Elder Brother

My elder brother, Nazrul Islām was born on the 6th of June 1971, the year when Bangladesh gained independence from Pakistan.

Due to the great turmoil and upheaval in the country, many people lost their lives in the battle for Independence. My father was at that time residing in England. After hearing of the birth of his first child, he rushed back to Bangladesh to celebrate the occasion. My brother received his elementary education from the local school for five years and also gained religious education at home before we came to England in 1981.

## My Birth

I was born on the 6th of August 1974 in the small village of Duhal in the town of Biswanath, Sylhet. I am the second eldest child in my family. My mother has narrated that I was unable to speak a word till the age of 4. Everyone in my family and village were very concerned and anxious that I was not speaking because usually a child learns to speak at the age of 1. They took me to various scholars and doctors in search for help and treatment. They also sacrificed many animals in the path of Allāh ﷻ in the hope of the alleviation of my problem.

Alhamdulillāh, their efforts bore fruit when Allāh ﷻ bestowed His Infinite Mercy upon me and one morning I automatically starting speaking. The previous night one of my cousin brothers was sleeping next to me, so when I spoke my first word: "Mother", everyone initially thought it was he who was speaking but with a different tone of voice! However to their utter amazement, it was truly me, speaking my very first words! Everyone chanted praises out of happiness and rejoiced at this miraculous incident. It was the best moment of my life!

## My Name

Regarding my name, my elders chose various names. I was initially called Shamsul Islām – 'The Sun of Islām' and then after a few months it was altered to Saiful Islām – 'The Sword of Islām'. My second eldest uncle chose to keep this name which eventually became my permanent name.

## My Siblings

In addition to my elder brother, I have 2 more brothers and 3 sisters. After me, I have one brother Amirul Islām. Thereafter one sister, Rasheeda Khātun. The four of us were all born in Bangladesh and later after coming to the UK three more siblings; Sājida Khātun, Moinul Islām and finally Rehāna Khātun were born.

## My Early Education

As far as I could remember, in my early years I attended the local school with my elder brother and cousin brothers and sisters for only a number of days. I remember that I did not like attending school because I found the discipline to be too strict. Likewise, I didn't attend the religious classes in my local village punctually resulting in my lack of progress in both the educational fields.

## Near to Drowning

Bangladesh is a tropical country with vast amounts of vegetation and crops. The second largest and longest river, the River Ganges flows through Bangladesh from India. Many a time, excessive rain would lead to the occurrence of severe floods in Bangladesh. I was only 2 years old when a similar flood swept through virtually all of the country. The water level began to rise considerably. People started to panic and many lost their valuable lives. Children were supervised and monitored very closely, in case they would be swept away by the dangerous floods. The water gradually reached the houses and was slowly rising, when suddenly a violent storm occurred. To my horror I was swept away into the floodwater. I started drowning and panicking frantically as blood-sucking leeches started to attack me in the water! Alhamdulillāh, by the grace of Allāh ﷻ, someone from my family came to my rescue and saved my life. I will always be grateful for that because without the help of this person I may not be here today.

## A Great Robbery

Bangladesh being a very poor and highly populated country, was unfortunately prey to many vices and evils. Killings and robberies were common in the local villages of Bangladesh. As I mentioned earlier my respected father was in the UK earning a livelihood for everyone in Bangladesh. For this reason we were considered by the people as being wealthy and noble. Hatred and malice gradually stirred in the hearts of some of our relatives and local village dwellers, which ultimately resulted in the robbery of our wealth.

It was in the deep portion of the night while I was asleep, that suddenly noises of cracking doors echoed into my ears. I swiftly sat up and to my utter shock, discovered that about 30 to 40 burglars and robbers had encircled our entire village. There was no escape! My father who came for a visit to Bangladesh from U.K. was also in the house. After a quick consultation with my mother, he decided to leave the house through the back door, which ultimately saved his life, Alhamdulillāh, as the robbers had in fact come with the intention of murdering him.

At that moment, we heard the terrifying sound of axes pounding on our bedroom door. Then a frightening voice shouted, "Open the door or else, if we break in we will kill every one of you!" My mother, thinking of her small children, opened the door and came running to me and my younger brother Amirul, drawing us towards herself and grasping us tightly.

The first thing they asked was regarding my father, "Where is he?" My mother told them that he had gone to his in-laws. Then they started searching for every valuable item in the house and gathered everything in a huge pile in the yard. The scene of all our belongings being taken away so ruthlessly angered me and I began to swear at them! In response to my cries one of them pointed a knife at me and scolded: "If you do not observe silence we will slay you!" In an effort to suppress my shouts and screams, my mother had to cover my mouth with her hands whilst they took away all of our furniture, clothes and valuables. The robbery was at its final hurdle when help was on its way and the firing and shouting from the adjacent village was heard. However by then it was too late, the robbers galloped away, taking away all of our belongings which they had secured in their hands.

## Decision to Move to the UK

After this horrific incident, my father decided that we move to England with him. After the necessary documents and paperworks were obtained, we went to apply for our entry to England which was granted swiftly without any complications. This was the sheer grace of Allāh ﷻ upon my family that a procedure which was often a great obstacle for others, was so easily accomplished by us.

## Migration to England

On the 1st of March 1981, my father, mother, two brothers, sister Rasheeda Khātun (then only 3 months old) and I, set off for our fateful migration to England. My father booked the tickets with Bangladesh Biman Airlines and we set off from Sylhet Airport by a domestic flight to the capital city Dhaka and from there we reached our destination, Heathrow Airport in London via Dubai. My uncle, Mohram Ali, who resides in Coventry, was at the airport with all of his family to welcome us. From there we were escorted to his home and we remained his guests for a few days.

## City of Bradford

United Kingdom was a completely unique and new place for every member of my family. After the few days of hospitality at my uncle's house, my father set off with us to our new home in Bradford. Accompanied by my uncle Mohram Ali, we safely reached 46 Peel Square, which was to become our first stop and first home in Bradford.

Purchasing homes at that time was a very difficult task due to the fact that many of the elders were single without their families in England. Therefore they lived as tenants and three to four families would be crammed into one house. We also experienced the same situation; the house we lived in was the accommodation of 3 to 4 families. As a young boy of 6, I was unaware of all the pain and hardship my parents must have gone through in one house with a variety of people.

## My First School in the UK

Education is essential and soon it was time to commence our school life. My brother Nazrul attended Drummond Centre which catered especially for children with language difficulties and I was admitted to Belle Vue Infant School. My first non-Muslim teachers were Mrs Myers and Mrs Bithell and then Mrs Hill.

Alhamdulillāh, I quickly settled into the school and began to enjoy the amusing and interesting atmosphere. The teachers, staff and especially the pupils were very understanding and friendly. I stayed in the school for 2 ½ years and in that time I became a prominent pupil, well known by the other pupils and teachers.

## My Interest for Religious Knowledge

Islamic education was not an important issue in those days and for that period of 2 ½ years, I was left in the darkness regarding Qur'anic teachings. Many a times, I would ask my school friends regarding what they studied in their local Masjid. When I discovered that they had read the Qur'ān and I was still illiterate and couldn't even read the Arabic alphabet, I felt a deep sense of sorrow and regret in my heart and I eagerly wished to learn about Islām.

## Moving from House to House

In the meanwhile, we moved many houses from 46 Peel Square Bradford 8, to 16 Cornwall Terrace, to 14 Cornwall Place and from there we moved to a flat given by the Council at 28 Green Lane. This happened in a period of two years leading to no substantial progress for me in Islamic education apart from the memorisation of a few Sūrahs, which I had learnt from an old person in Number 3 Cornwall Place.

## Admission to Maktab (Elementary Religious School)

I was nine years old, attending Manningham Middle school in December 1983, when we moved to 35 Lupton Street, a house purchased by my father for a grand sum of £10,000. By the grace of Allāh ﷻ, Tawakkulia Masjid was just a few steps from the house my father had bought. Deep in the heart of my father was a feeling of anxiety and restlessness because of not being able to educate his children in the religious field and it was this one vital factor which compelled him to purchase a house near a Masjid. After we moved in, the first and foremost thing my father did was to admit us into the Maktab of the Masjid.

## Tawakkulia Islamic Society

Due to the growing and increasing population of the Bangladeshi community in the area, a large premise was purchased on Cornwall Road for a purpose built Masjid. The existing Masjid was initially at 40 Cornwall Road established in 1970. After the completion of the first floor work and ablution facilities, the Masjid was officially opened in 1983.

## Commencing of Islamic Learning

I started punctually attending the evening class held at the local Masjid, Tawakkulia Islamic Society from 5pm to 7pm. I began with the basics and my first teacher was Hāji Mukhlisur Rahmān, well known by the people as Qāri Sāhib. Under his supervision, I studied Qā'idah and Sūrahs and Alhamdulillāh, within a few months I completed my Qā'idah etc – something other students took up to 4 or 5 years to learn.

## Qāri Mukhlisur Rahmān Sāhib

Qāri Sāhib was a very humble and sincere person who never interfered in other people's business. Many a time, I observed that even in trouble spots, he avoided controversy with others. He lived nearest to the Masjid in 23 Lupton Street and he regularly attended the Masjid for prayers. One of his sons, Maulāna Habibur Rahmān went on to study in Dārul Uloom Bury with me and later graduated with me in January 1995. His humbleness was to such an extent that when I was still studying, he showed respect for me and always tried to commence the Salām before me. I also admired his conduct and character and always expressed my respect and honour to him. He had 3 sons and 2 daughters.

## Qur'anic Teaching

After passing my test for the Holy Qur'ān with other pupils of the class, I commenced my Nāzirah. I was 10 years old and Alhamdulillāh, was one of the youngest and amongst the bright ones from the 40 students in the Qur'anic class. Soon I started to progress and I read about 7 Juz (parts) under the supervision of the Principal of the Maktab and the Head Imām of the Masjid, Maulāna Ashraf Ali Sāhib.

## Maulāna Ashraf Ali Sikder Sāhib

Maulāna Ashraf Ali was a teacher of great excellence. He was a fully graduated Ālim and also a Master of Arts in Accountancy and Commerce. He combined both the secular and the religious education. As I was a student of his, he narrated to me many incidents of his life, which if written will become a big volume of its own. Due to the fact that his close relatives were worldly educated, he achieved both types of knowledge demonstrating to his friends and relatives that a person who has achieved one type of knowledge can also gain the other with great ease and excellence. Alhamdulillāh, he became successful in both the fields. He came to England in 1983 and after a fortnight in London, he came to Bradford for his permanent post of Imāmat and Principal of the Maktab and by the grace of Allāh ﷻ, he is still steadfast on his duty of Deen till this very day.

It was his affection and love which moulded me and turned me towards Islamic knowledge and till this day his valuable sayings, opinions and suggestions gives me great confidence in my life and Khidmat of Deen.

## Introduction of Hifz Class

After learning the Holy Qur'ān for a few months by the great scholar Maulāna Ashraf Ali Sāhib, we were blessed with a new Hifz class teacher Hāfiz Jalāl-Uddin. He came as a visitor to the UK through his maternal and paternal uncle Haji Abdus-Salām in 1985 to commence the Hifz class. The teachers and committee leaders chose the students who were capable of memorising the Holy Qur'ān. By the grace of Allāh ﷻ, I was chosen for this auspicious class which started with approximately 25 students in the summer of 1985.

## Hāfiz Jalāl Uddin Sāhib

Hāfiz Jalāl Uddin Sāhib was a very kind and loving teacher who treated me as his own son or even better. I was blessed to have the opportunity to memorise the complete Holy Qur'ān with him over a period of 3 years. I could remember when I was afflicted with Chicken Pox in 1986, he even took the trouble of coming to my house and listening to my Sabaq (lesson) daily. I can never forget his favours bestowed upon me. On a regular basis, he would make Topees (hats) for me and present gifts to me, and many a times, when I lost all confidence and made a firm intention of giving up Hifz, he put a new zeal and interest in me to continue. He always obliterated all the different doubts that were lingering in my mind. I think today that if it was not for him and his assistance, I would have never completed my Hifz. May Allāh ﷻ reward him immensely for his great pain and efforts in inculcating in me the greatest gift and treasure of Hifz and may Allāh ﷻ preserve the Holy Qur'ān in my heart till the last day. Āmeen!

## My Sincere Friend

From the first day I started the local Masjid, I met my sincere class-mate called Suhel (official name Azād Ali). It was wholly the Infinite Mercy of Allāh ﷻ that this friend studied Qā'idah with me, then after passing the test for the Holy Qur'ān stayed with me in the Qur'anic class. We then went on to commence the Hifz class together and finished this together also. All through the 3 years, we had the same Sabaq and we always stayed together in memorising our daily Sabaq. Amazingly after the completion of Hifz, we commenced the Ālim class the same day and Alhamdulillāh, went on to finish this together also! May Allāh ﷻ enter us to Paradise together also. Āmeen!

Maulāna Azād Ali was a very clever and knowledgeable person. All through his academic years, he would mostly finish at the top of the class and his Qur'anic recitation was of such standard that it was always worthy of envy.

## My Completion of Hifz

After completing Hifzul-Qur'ān, my respected teachers and the committee of the Masjid decided to hold a Hifzul-Qur'ān completion ceremony. Posters and leaflets were distributed everywhere and many scholars from around the country were invited to this auspicious gathering. The ceremony took place on the 13th of May 1988 in the local Jāmi-Masjid, Tawakkulia Islamic Society.

Hundreds of people gathered for the blessed occasion and the programme lasted all day with various scholars addressing the gathering with speeches regarding the virtues of knowledge and the excellence of memorising the Holy Qur'ān. At the completion of the ceremony, Azād Ali and I were told to recite some Sūrahs of the Holy Qur'ān and then we had the honour of having the turban put around our heads by Maulāna Luqmān, the Head Imām of Jāmi-Masjid, Rochdale as well as other scholars. We were also presented with copies of the Holy Qur'ān, gifts and money along with the certificates of Hifz in English by Tawakkulia Islamic Society.

It was a memorable moment in my life and I praise Allāh ﷻ for this tremendous gift which He bestowed upon me through His Infinite Mercy and Grace. After the ceremony, friends and relatives were invited to our house for food.

## Visit to Dārul Uloom Bury

After becoming a Hāfiz, I continued with school education along with my revision of the Holy Qur'ān in the local Masjid. As I was now in the senior school, Belle Vue Boys, I was proceeding towards taking my GCSE Examinations. Thus my father was eager to see me doing well in school also. But Allāh ﷻ had decided something else.

At that time, Maulāna Abdul Jalil Sāhib, the Imām of Tawakkulia Masjid, came to my father and informed him of a boarding Madrasah in Bury, Manchester where I could study and qualify as an Ālim. Initially my father was very reluctant, but then he left the choice to me. I readily agreed, thinking that Allāh ﷻ would fulfil my dreams of becoming an Ālim as well. After the decision was made, Maulāna Abdul Jalil Sāhib, my father, Azād Ali, his father and I went to visit the grand Dārul Uloom in Bury, Manchester. It was there when I got the opportunity of meeting the great Shaykh Yūsuf Motāla Sāhib (Principal of Dārul Uloom, Bury), who listened to our recital of Sūrah Yāseen.

After successfully passing the Hifz test, we were told to learn Urdu in our local Masjid so that we could be enrolled into the first year of the Ālim course.

## Urdu Studies

Alhamdulillāh, Maulāna Abdul Jalil Sāhib took his valuable free time to teach us Urdu Ki Pheli Kitāb, Taleemul Islām, Etymology, Rahmat-e-Ālam, and a few basic books of Sarf and Nahw. By the grace of Allāh ﷻ, in a short period of time we learnt basic Urdu and prepared for our admission into the historical Islamic College Dārul Uloom Bury.

## Admission into Dārul-Uloom Bury

It was Monday the 1st of August 1988, the memorable day when I bid farewell to my mother, brothers, sisters, relatives, and neighbours to attend Dārul-Uloom Bury. Azād Ali, Maulāna Abdul Jalil

Sāhib, our parents and I travelled to Dārul Uloom Bury with our duvets, pillows and necessary items.

Shaykh Abdur-Raheem Sāhib (Senior Lecturer of Hadeeth, Dārul Uloom Bury) took our test and commented that our Urdu was still very weak and that we should go back and learn more Urdu. We became very sad and upset. I foolishly pleaded, "O' Ustād, you know that we are Bangladeshi, our Urdu will be very poor, please give us the opportunity to study. We have even brought our belongings as well!" Shaykh Abdur-Raheem Sāhib and the other senior students around him burst into laughter! Eventually he gave us the admission temporarily, on condition that we study properly. We were overwhelmed with gratitude and thanked him immensely for this discretion.

## My First Year at Dārul-Uloom Bury

Azād Ali and I were a couple of months late in our enrolment, therefore we were placed in a separate class – Oola Jeem with other new and weak students. In the 1st year of Ālim Class there were 3 classes- 1st: Oola Alif for the over 16's, 2nd: Oola Bā for the under 16's and 3rd: Oola Jeem for the newcomers and weak students. In our class there were about 15 students, from various towns and cities around the UK and abroad. The following are the Kitābs (books) that we were taught and their respective teachers:

(1)     Muallimus-Sarf - Maulāna Ziāul-Haque Sāhib
(2)     Nahwameer - Mufti Abdus-Samad Sāhib
(3)     Qasasun-Nabiyyeen - Maulāna Ibrāheem Badāt Sāhib

(4)     Safwatul Masādir - Qāri Fārooq Sāhib
(5)     Behishti Samar - Maulāna Abdullāh Sāhib
(6)     Rahmat-e-Ālam - Maulāna Abdullāh Sāhib
(7)     Duroosul-Lugatul-Arabiyah - Hāfiz Ahmad Sāhib
(8)     Das Sabaq - Maulāna Ziāul-Haque Sāhib
(9)     Al-Arabiyatu-Linnā-Shieen - Maulāna Imrān Miah Sāhib

Initially we commenced our studies from Oola Bā and we had various teachers for the various books, but later, as mentioned, we
moved to Oola Jeem. In the Sehmāhi exams (after the first Semes-
ter), by the grace of Allāh 🌟 , I came first in my class. My family,
teachers, friends and classmates were very surprised but happy to
see my progression.

As mentioned earlier, one of my teachers, Shaykh Abdur-Raheem
Sāhib after taking our admission test commented that my Urdu
was very weak, and my admission would be temporary. However,
after seeing my results, he was overjoyed and he stated, "Now you
are a permanent student of Dārul-Uloom Bury!"

In the beginning when Fajr was early, approximately between 4
and 5 o'clock, I would remain awake after Fajr to catch up with all
the lessons I had missed. The 24 hour routine initially seemed difficult to follow, but Alhamdulillāh, I soon became adjusted to it. I
was staying in boarding in the 1st floor, last room with another 11
students in bunk beds. My room-mates were very friendly and
helpful and soon I became an active member of the room.

Staying in boarding meant that I needed to be mature and intelligent. I had to wash my own clothes, clean the room on my turn, and make sure I looked after my valuables, goods and health. By the grace of Allāh 綱, Madrasah life became my nature and I started to love my Dārul-Uloom, my teachers and my classmates.

## Leading My First Tarāweeh Salāh

The following Ramadhān, I was appointed to lead the Tarāweeh Salāh, alongside my respectful and honourable teacher Hāfiz Jalāl-Uddin and a senior student of Dewsbury Markaz, Hāfiz Hāmid Ali. It was a beautiful and challenging experience, being the first Hāfiz graduate in our locality to lead the Salāh.

My parents stressed that I recite and learn my Juz properly so that I was fluent in my recitation. By the grace of Allāh 綱 and my parents Du'ās, I hardly made any mistakes throughout the Holy Month of Ramadhān.

My beloved father was overjoyed with my progress which was clearly evident from his attitude and affection towards me. Seeing my progress and achievement, my father began to consult with me regarding various family issues and other delicate matters. I felt privileged and put forward my opinion regarding particular subjects that I thought to be relevant.

## My Second Year of Ālim Class

After passing my first year exams with distinction by the grace of Allāh 綱, I progressed to the 2nd year– Thāniya Bā. In that year the following books were taught by the following teachers:

(1)     Sharh Miat Āmil – Maulāna Abdullāh Sāhib
(2)     Hidāyatun Nahw – Maulāna Ibrāheem Badāt Sāhib
(3)     Ilmus Sega – Maulāna Ibrāheem Badāt Sāhib
(4)     Qudoori – Maulāna Yūsuf Kāra Sāhib
(5)     Jamālul Qur'ān - Qāri Ismāeel Sāhib ﷺ
(6)     Noorul Idha - Maulāna Yūsuf Kāra Sāhib
(7)     Qasasun Nabiyyeen Part 2 & 3 - Maulāna Yūsuf Kāra Sāhib

During my first and second year of Ālim class, I was also studying the final two years of the national curriculum. Only four subjects were taught after Zuhr till 4pm. The subjects taught were:

(1)     English – Mr Ibrāheem
(2)     Maths – Mr Sābir
(3)     Science – Mr Nāsir
(4)     Urdu – Maulāna Shuaib Nākuda

In Year 5B – Year 11, I managed to take only 3 GCSE's in Maths, Science Modular and Urdu. Unfortunately in English due to unforeseen circumstances, the class could not take the exam.

## My Beloved Father's Hajj

My beloved father once came to visit me in my boarding room and asked me about getting my older brother married. He also wanted to hear my opinion with regard to whether he should perform Hajj in the current year or get my brother married. I replied neither; first you should consider keeping a beard and then perform the Hajj. He remained silent and turned away from me. I feared that he was not pleased with my reply. To my surprise and pleasure, after a couple of months, my father came to the Madrasah and Subhān-Allāh, he had a full beard and he was smiling towards me! I praised Allāh ﷻ in my delight and requested my father to proceed for Hajj.

My father alongside many of the locals performed Hajj that year in July 1989. He was so concerned about me and my well-being that he wrote a letter to my mother from Saudi Arabia to look after me well when I come home for the Eidul Adhā holidays; to ensure I was given some jackfruit to eat which was one of my favourite fruits. When he came back from Hajj, he presented me with many gifts including a Seiko 5 watch.

## Disapproval of Meelād Gatherings

Unfortunately, due to the ignorance of the people, customary Meelad gatherings were prevalent in our local Masājid without any exception in Tawakkulia Masjid. One day in the Madrasah holidays, I was present in the Masjid for Zuhr Salāh when an announcement was made for Meelād. I stood up after my Sunnats and made my way to the exit, my father followed quickly in my pursuit and asked, "Why don't you sit for the Meelād Mahfil?"

I replied, "O' my beloved father, you sent me to the Madrasah to learn what is right and what is wrong. I have come to know that this customary Meelād is against the Sunnah, hence I left." My father, Subhān-Allāh, remained silent and also left with me. Later on, my father's friends and associates reprimanded him for forsaking

Meelād - a tradition which had been coming down for many generations. My father remained firm and declined to carry on. May Allāh ﷻ reward him immensely for his strong faith. Āmeen!

## Sunnat Method of Eating

Once when I came home for my holidays, I took my plate of food and sat on the carpet instead of dining on the table with the rest of my family. Much to my surprise, my father witnessing this scene, stormed out of the house from the back door! I felt worried by this, thinking he may have been offended but he soon came back with a beautiful and elegant rug and told me to use it when I eat on the floor. From then onwards, I would sit on the floor and eat my food in the Sunnat method. This rug became so precious to me that I even took it to the Madrasah and used it till my graduation. May Allāh ﷻ bless my beloved father and enter him into Paradise without reckoning. Āmeen!

## Chādar of Madeenah

My beloved father bought me a Chādar (shawl) from Madeenah Munawwarah which was so dear to me that whenever I wore it in class, I always remained successful and happy, Alhamdulillāh. I would wear it all the time regarding it as a Sunnah and a blessing from Madeenah Munawwarah as well as a gift from my beloved father. Many students borrowed my blessed Chādar in order to receive Barakah from it and it remained with me for many years.

## Discarding the Television

One day I questioned my father as to why he had sent me to Dārul Uloom. He replied, "So you know the truth about Islam". I spontaneously replied, "I have learnt that the TV is not Islamic". He immediately commented, "Take it out from the front room." Alhamdulillāh, my respected father, though not educated in the Deeni field, was an open-minded person and he accommodated any necessary rectifications in himself without thinking himself too superior to be offered advice from his own son.

## Third Year Ālim Class

Our first two years of Ālim class were part time with school in the afternoon. In our third year of Ālim class, it became full time with many extra lessons, senior teachers and advanced Kitābs. The following Kitābs were taught in the 3rd Year:

1.      Muallimul Inshā – In the beginning - Shaykh Hāshim Sāhib then Mufti Ibrāheem Rāja Sāhib
2.      Zādut Tālibeen - Maulāna Yūsuf Kāra Sāhib
3.      Qasasun Nabiyyeen - Qāri Fārooq Sāhib
4.      Riyādhus Sāliheen - Maulāna Saleem Dhorāt Sāhib
5.      Kāfiyah - Maulāna Ziyāul Haque Sāhib
6.      Qur'ān Translation - Mufti Abdus Samad Sāhib
7.      Duroosut-Tāreekh - Maulāna Ziyāul Haque Sāhib
8.      Al-Ikhtiyār - Mufti Ismāeel Vānia Sāhib
9.      Al-Qirā'atur-Rasheeda - Mufti Sadr Uddin Sāhib
10.     Usūlush-Shāshi - Maulāna Abdur-Raheem Sāhib

11.    Al Qirā'atur Rāshidah - Maulāna Imrān Miah Sāhib

12.    Kanzud Daqāiq - Maulāna Tāhir (commonly known as Sūfi Sāhib)

It became a predicament towards the end of the year because we had a combination of part time and full time students in the class which interfered with our timetable. The full time students were looking forward to moving on to the 4th Year, the following year, but it was not to be...

Alhamdulillāh, I achieved 100% in my final oral exam and achieved the top marks in the whole class and Madrasah, alongside another two students. However, despite this achievement the decision was made for the class to stay behind and re-take that year. In our aid, many of our teachers signed a letter confirming to the management that we were competent enough to be allowed to progress to the next year. The matter came to its peak when I, being the spokesman of my class, alongside my colleagues, approached our beloved Principal - Shaykh Yūsuf Motāla Sāhib and informed him regarding our predicament. Addressing me and my colleagues, our beloved Shaykh said the following words, which to this day, still echo in my ears:

"Re-take this year again and Inshā-Allāh you will excel your contemporaries."

After listening to these words of wisdom, my colleagues and I, having complete trust in our beloved Principal, became happy to re-take the year again.

## Third Year Re-Take

Though we were re-taking the same year, we were taught different Kitābs by different teachers which Alhamdulillāh, enhanced and increased our knowledge and insight immensely. The following were the books taught in that year:

(1)    Alfiya- Ibn Mālik - Maulāna Ziyāul Haque Sāhib
(2)    Al-Adabul Mufrad - Maulāna Saleem Dhorat Sāhib
(3)    Al-Mukhtārāt - Maulāna Saleem Dhorat Sāhib
(4)    Mueenul Mantiq - Hāfiz Ahmad Sāhib
(5)    Usūlush-Shāshi - Mufti Ismāeel Vānia Sāhib
(6)    Talkheesul Miftāh - Maulāna Fazlul Haque Sāhib
(7)    Sharhul Wiqāyah - Maulāna Noushād Sāhib
(8)    Jazri - Mufti Ibrāheem Rāja Sāhib

In my third year, I decided to put extra effort into my Nahw, hence I began studying the book Kāfiyah in depth. I utilised the Hāshi-yah (marginal notes) Sharh-Jāmi, and other commentaries and my-self wrote a commentary of Kāfiyah. Alhamdulillāh in the final ex-am of Kāfiyah I attained 52 out of 50 due to bonus marks. Students from other classes began to come and learn their Nahw from me and thus I became known as Sāhib 52!

All of this demonstrated to me that Allāh ﷻ helped me immensely in my re-taking of the 3rdYear, true to the words of my beloved Shaykh and Principal. Though initially it felt like a setback, it even-tually became a great blessing in disguise for me. Sometimes Allāh ﷻ works in mysterious ways but the success and victory is always the end result for those who put their trust in Him and in His Infinite Wisdom.

## Dream About Shaykh Zakariyya ﷺ

From all the subjects I was studying, Tajweed was my weakest. Hence, I was very worried about the final exam, because that was to determine our Qirāt Sanad and certificate. Prior to the exam, I was studying Aap Beeti – the autobiography of Shaykh Zakariyya ﷺ and Allāh ﷻ blessed me with seeing him in my dream.

I did not get the opportunity to see the honourable Shaykh in my life. However, I dreamt that I saw the Shaykh come to our class and call me to come to him so that he could teach me Jazri (Tajweed Kitāb). I came out and my classmates followed. Shaykh Zakariyya ﷺ was so humble in the dream that firstly he sought permission to teach me from our teacher, Mufti Ibrāheem Rāja Sāhib and then in the corridor he again asked permission from the supervisor Qāri Yaqūb Sāhib. I could remember Qāri Sāhib granting permission with great zeal and encouraging us to go with him. The dream ended with Shaykh taking us to a place.

In the following days, I took the exams including Jazri, in which I achieved full marks and overall came top in my class, Alhamdulillāh. In addition, by the grace of Allāh ﷻ and through the blessings of the dream, I was identified as the top student in the whole of the Madrasah, having my name on the top of the results paper on the notice board. I was overwhelmed with happiness and praised Allāh ﷻ for this most unexpected blessing and gift.

## Fourth Year Ālim Class

4th year Ālim class was an important year, with many important Kitābs and senior teachers. It was a challenging year, due to the fact that two classes merged into one big class - Thālitha Alif and Thālitha Bā. In total, 30 students were in the 4th Year, bringing together many competent and intelligent students.

The 4th Year also became the first year in which we had the opportunity of being taught by our beloved Principal, Shaykh Yūsuf Motāla Sāhib, not only for one Kitāb, but for three Alhamdulillāh. The Hadeeth Kitāb At-Tajreedus Sareeh - a summarised version of Bukhāri Shareef, was taught by Shaykh Yūsuf Motāla Sāhib - and I had the privilege of reading out the forward text to the class. The following books were taught in the 4th year of Ālim Class:

(1)     Hidāya Awwal - Maulāna Tāhir (Sūfi Sāhib)
(2)     Hidāya Thāni - Maulāna Fazl Haque Sāhib
(3)     Qur'ān Translation - Mufti Shabbir Sāhib
(4)     Maqāmāt - Maulāna Abdur-Raheem Sāhib
(5)     Tajreedus Sareeh - Shaykh Yūsuf Motāla Sāhib
(6)     As-Sab'ul Muallaqāt - Shaykh Yūsuf Motāla Sāhib
(7)     Mukhtārāt Thāni - Shaykh Yūsuf Motāla Sāhib
(8)     Mirqāt - Maulāna Umarjee Sāhib ﷺ
(9)     Mukhtasural Ma'āni - Sūfi Sāhib
(10)    Noorul Anwār - Maulāna Bilāl Sāhib/Maulāna Junaid Desai Sāhib
(11)    Tajweed - Maulāna Zākir Sāhib

## Naseehat Class

In the Madrasah, there was a system of teaching the youngsters (under 16s) in a programme called Naseehat. Senior students from the final two years were chosen to teach the youngsters. Though I was in the 4th Year, I was nominated to take a class for Naseehat. Tutoring the Naseehat group was a privilege and a boost to my confidence. It increased my knowledge and created a strong bond between the students.

In those days, all the Naseehat teachers got together and organised the Naseehat with a set curriculum including Seerah, Social Etiquettes, Fiqh, Hadeeth and the 99 Names of Allāh ﷻ and there were exams set in the mid-year and end of year. After the arrangements and first exams, we sent a copy of the results to Shaykh Yūsuf Motāla Sāhib, who was at that time residing in Madeenah Munawwarah. He expressed his intense happiness to see the great progress of the Naseehat system.

## My Own Room

Till my fourth Year of Ālim class I had been staying in boarding with other students, initially in the last room of the 1st floor with 11 other students for the first two years and then in the central boarding, famously known as the 'black hole'. I stayed in the 'black hole' with students of various classes and towns. At the end of my 3rd Year (re-take), one of my friends who was graduating passed me keys for his room and said, "I have allocated you this room. Just confirm it with the senior students who are in charge of boarding."

After Ramadhān, I moved into my new room and confirmed my seat with the management. After years of sharing I finally had my own privacy. My friends decorated the room with new wallpaper and curtains which I had brought from my home. I also brought a fridge, sandwich maker, kettle and other essentials for my room. In addition, I had bookshelves and a cassette player in the room. I praised Allāh ﷻ for this blessing which I did not even dream of.

## Fifth Year Ālim Class

The following books were taught in the 5th Year:
(1)     Mishkāt Awwal – Maulāna Fazl Haque Sāhib
(2)     Mishkāt Thāni – Mufti Shabbir Ahmad Sāhib
(3)     Hidāya Thālith – Sūfi Sāhib
(4)     Hidāya Rābi – Maulāna Umarjee Sāhib ﷻ
(5)     Tafseer Baydhāwi – Maulāna Abdur Raheem Sāhib
(6)     Sharhul Aqāid – Shaykh Yūsuf Motāla Sāhib
(7)     Mueenul Farāidh – Maulāna Umarjee Sāhib ﷻ
(8)     Sharh Ma'āni Al-Āthār - Sūfi Sāhib
(9)     Jalālain Awwal – Mufti Shabbir Sāhib
(10)    Jalālain Thāni – Shaykh Hāshim Sāhib/Mufti Ibrāheem Rāja Sāhib

## Pledging the Oath of Allegiance

Near to the end of the 5th Year, I decided to take the oath of allegiance to Shaykh Yūsuf Motāla Sāhib. Hence, one evening I proceeded towards the library where he usually occupied himself with research and studies. I explained my case to him and Alhamdulillāh, without any further comments, he immediately accepted me for Bai'ah and the brief ceremony concluded with a short Du'ā. Alhamdulillāh, my life gradually began to change and higher objectives in life became my goal. I punctually started performing the Dhikr and Ma'moolat (daily practices) prescribed by my Shaykh. Before I retired to bed I would perform Dhikr – 200 times 'Lā ilāha illallāh' and 500 times 'Allāh'. I also became punctual in my recitation of the Holy Qur'ān.

## My Father's Last Tarāweeh Behind Me

Towards the end of the fifth year Ālim class, our teachers gave us the opportunity of performing Tarāweeh in a foreign country or at least in a different town. Many of my classmates accepted this wonderful opportunity. I had the intention to accept also but my father was reluctant and he expressed his wish that I lead the Tarāweeh in Tawakkulia Masjid. I complied with his wishes and led the Tarāweeh in Bradford. Who was to know that this would be my father's last Tarāweeh behind me? On the 27th night of Ramadhān, it was also the Khatm (completion) of the Holy Qur'ān. I was appointed to finish the Holy Qur'ān and also to perform the Du'ā. I became emotional and burst into tears. All of the attendees of the Masjid cried excessively and the Du'ā lasted for over 20 minutes. My father was delighted and he expressed his joy and happiness to everyone, exclaiming that his son had become the coolness of his eyes. All praise be to Allāh ﷻ.

## Final Year

I was looking forward to my final year especially of getting the opportunity to study Saheeh Bukhāri with the senior scholar, Shaykh

Islāmul Haque Sāhib 🌸. The Kitābs taught were:

(1)      Bukhāri Shareef - Shaykh Islāmul Haque Sāhib 🌸
(2)      Muslim Shareef – Shaykh Yūsuf Motāla Sāhib
(3)      Abū Dāwood Shareef – Shaykh Hāshim Sāhib
(4)      Nasai Shareef – Shaykh Bilāl Sāhib
(5)      Tirmizi Shareef – Mufti Shabbir Sāhib
(6)      Ibn Mājah Shareef – Maulāna Abdur Raheem Sāhib
(7)      Muwattā Mālik – Maulāna Noushād Sāhib
(8)      Shamāil Tirmizi – Maulāna Ismāeel Rāja Sāhib

Extra lessons of Bukhāri Shareef were taught in the evening and Muwattā Mālik was taught after Fajr Salāh. Initially, I read the text of Bukhāri, Muslim and Muwattā Mālik. In fact, I read the text of the entire Muwattā Mālik from the beginning to the end, Alhamdulillāh.

## Shaykh Islāmul Haque Sāhib's 🌸 Affection

When I would read the text of Bukhāri Shareef, the Shaykh would provide the commentary. In those days I used to wear a black turban. After explaining a Hadeeth in detail, he would look towards me and say, "O, the one with the black turban, have you understood?" I would reply with joy and happiness, "Yes Hadhrat." Allāh 🌸 knows best why his concentration was focussed towards me in this way. Maybe it was because I would be teaching these very same Ahādeeth in the future that he was inspired by Allāh 🌸 to give me that extra attention. All praise is due to Allāh 🌸.

## Shaykh Hāshim Sāhib's Attention

Shaykh Hāshim Sāhib, one of the disciples of Shaykh Zakariyya Sāhib ﷦, would frequently ask my name. One day in class he posed a question, and by the grace of Allāh ﷻ, I was the only student who put up his hand to answer. He graced me with beautiful Du'ās and prayed that Allāh ﷻ make me excel over my contemporaries. He stressed to everyone in the class to say "Āmeen!" on the Du'ā. I was overjoyed by his kindness and generosity and from then onwards, he paid extra attention towards me, Alhamdulillāh.

## Dream of the Holy Prophet ﷺ

In my final year, I saw a vision of the Holy Prophet ﷺ. He was dressed similar to the way my beloved Shaykh Yūsuf Motāla Sāhib dressed. In the dream, I saw that I was seated in the position of Tashahhud and our beloved Prophet ﷺ was seated on something like a chair or Mimbar. I asked him about success and progress. He replied, "You will achieve success and progress; make a lot of effort." Immediately I saw a ladder going towards the Heavens, and the Holy Prophet ﷺ said, "You will reach the top, make the effort." I was very pleased and then asked, "Where will I see you on the Day of Judgement?" He replied, "The fountain of Kawthar. I will meet you there." I remember him mentioning that Jābir ﷺ will be there, referring to his Companion Sayyidunā Jābir ﷺ. I was overjoyed with this comment and after this, I woke up. I narrated this dream to my Shaykh and he commented, You have been guided towards the right path and the right person.

## Dream Regarding Shaykh Ashraf Ali Thānwi ﷺ

I was studying the biography of Shaykh Ashraf Ali Thānwi ﷺ, 'Ashrafus-Sawānih' during my final years when one night, I dreamt of the great Shaykh.

In the dream I saw that the Shaykh was seated on a chair, his face was glowing with Noor and he was smiling towards me. Having read his biography I learned that he was of a strict temperament so I asked him, "What would have happened to me if I was in your time? You are so strict; you would have taken me out of your Khanqah." He smiled and said, "How could I? You are my beloved." I became extremely happy. I then said, "You became lenient towards the end of your life." He replied, "Yes, what could you do when all sorts of people come to you?" I woke up with great happiness in my heart.

## Forty Days I'tikāf

It became a routine in the last few years at Dārul-Uloom that the final year students would observe I'tikāf for forty days before graduating. The I'tikāf routine commenced from the year 1992 when all the students of the final year would seclude themselves in the lower Jamāt Khana (Masjid) for forty days. Classes would take place as normal with extra lessons in the evening.

In our final year, during September 1994, we performed our I'tikāf. Alhamdulillāh, the I'tikāf benefitted me immensely and I still feel the spirituality of those blessed days. By the grace of Allāh ﷺ, my colleagues and I adhered to the following Ma'moolāt on a daily basis:

- Observing fast
- 10 Juz of the Holy Qur'ān
- 500 times Durood Shareef
- 1 Juz in Tahajjud
- Tā'leem
- Meditation before retiring to bed
- Dhikr after Ishā Salāh
- Studies of the Sihāh Sitta (6 authentic books of Ahādeeth)

These daily practices gave us so much benefit in realising the value of time. May Allāh ﷻ forgive my sins and give me sincerity and steadfastness on Deen. Āmeen!

## My Marriage

After I'tikāf finished, I came out of the Masjid and immediately felt a huge change in my spirituality which made me deeply saddened. For a few days I could not sleep or eat properly.

Then suddenly one day, my respected teacher, Maulāna Abdul Jaleel Sāhib phoned to share the news that my honourable father was intending to arrange my marriage. I was surprised as well as reluctant to proceed with marriage before my graduation. My father however, insisted that it goes forward and within a few days after giving the proposal, it was accepted.

The following week on Sunday 20th November 1994, the marriage ceremony was solemnised by my father-in-law Shaykh Mufti Tālib Uddin Sāhib ☼, the student of Shaykh Mufti Rasheed Ahmad Ludhyānwi ☼. The marriage was performed in Tawakkulia Jāmi Masjid, Bradford in front of a full congregation. Dates were served after the Du'ā.

When I was performing I'tikāf, I decided to observe 60 days Kaffārah fasts consecutively as a precaution for any previous Ramadhān fasts broken deliberately. Due to the marriage taking place unexpectedly, I was actually fasting on my wedding day! It was quite an embarrassing situation and I decided to keep the matter discreet. On the morning of my wedding, I was offered tea and breakfast which I gave to my friend and colleague, Maulāna Zubair Sufi to consume!

After the ceremony, I went out for a walk with my friends and I told everyone that I would eat after Maghrib Salāh because some of my friends would arrive at that time (which I had intentionally arranged). This remained a secret until the next day when I had to go to my in-laws house. I had to break the news to my wife. Alhamdulillāh, she accepted it with happiness and joy. Before Sahree, she prepared my food and we ate together. It was an unusual experience!

Even though, I was given one week holiday from Madrasah, I returned back the following day so that I would not miss my Bukhāri lesson. Teachers and classmates were surprised and began to question whether I had actually got married or not!

## Graduation Ceremony

Our graduation ceremony was organised on the 25th of January 1995. It was a dream come true for me to be graduating from such a blessed institute which had been blessed by the likes of Shaykh Zakariyya ﵀, Qāri Muhammad Tayyib Sāhib ﵀, Shaykh Abul Hasan Ali Nadwi ﵀, Mufti Mahmood Hasan Gangohi ﵀ and many other high profile scholars and saints.

On this particular ceremony, Shaykh Talha Kandhalwi (son of the great scholar Shaykh Zakariyya ﵀) and Shaykh Salmān Sāhib (the son-in-law of Shaykh Zakariyya ﵀) were the chief guests. We were honoured to have the turbans presented to us by these pious personalities.

Thousands of people attended the gathering including my respected father and all of my brothers, relatives and local community members. My father was so excited and proud that he personally invited many people to be part of my graduation ceremony and he even hired a mini bus to accommodate them all!

After the ceremony, my father hugged me emotionally and began showing the turban to all the guests. I embraced and hugged everyone and requested their Du'ās. It was one of the best moments of my life!

## Death of My Respected Father

My beloved and respected father was severely ill in hospital for a few weeks. He was suffering from cancer. The doctors decided to operate on him to remove the cancer, but unfortunately it did not prove successful. His health deteriorated drastically and on Friday 3rd of February 1995, the nurse phoned us from Leeds General Infirmary to inform us that he was in his last moments. I was preparing for my Tarāweeh for the night but I had to rush to the hospital. When I reached there, he was in his last moments. My wife and I held both his hands and started reciting Sūrah Yāseen. Just as we reached the last verses, his Rooh (soul) left his body. We were all devastated. The news spread like wild fire and after Tarāweeh prayers, everybody rushed to the hospital.

It was a coincidence that on this same day, my father's best friend, Al-Hājj Abdul Musawwir also passed away. The funeral prayer was organised for Monday for both of them and I led the Janāzah Salāh. I was so grieved that I did not even realise that I had raised my hands whilst reciting the four Takbeers. There was an ocean of people. Tawakkulia Masjid very seldom witnesses a Janāzah so large. My beloved father was then put to rest in the Scholemoor Cemetery, Bradford.

**Turmoil in My Community**

Many incorrect and un-Islamic customs existed in the local community after a death. At the death of my beloved father, many of my relatives, neighbours and colleagues insisted on practising these customs. I declined vehemently which provoked severe debates in the community. Many called me misguided, evil and disobedient to my parents. The matter was even brought forth to my Shaykh, Maulāna Yūsuf Motāla Sāhib, and I was summoned to him to explain the situation.

After hearing the full scenario, he became pleased and remarked, "If scholars will not prevent these wrong and baseless customs, then who will?" Then he narrated that he was in a similar situation when his father had passed away which made me feel comforted and relieved.

## Vision of Glad-tiding

During that time one particular night, I dreamt of my beloved father. He was very happy and jubilant and he consoled me saying, "O my beloved son, don't worry (about the Fitnah that has spread like wildfire) whatever you send me, I receive it." I was overjoyed with this vision and praised Allāh ﷻ for this consolation in my time of hardship and grief.

## My First Employment

Whilst in my final year, I wrote to my Shaykh, Maulanā Yūsuf Motāla Sāhib when he was residing in Madeenah Munawwarah, asking him for advice with regards to what I should pursue after my graduation. I put forward three options:

(1)    Imāmat
(2)    Iftā Course
(3)    Madeenah University

My honourable Shaykh replied, "I will give priority to Madeenah

Munawwarah because of its sacredness and blessings." In response to my beloved Shaykh's advice, I made the intention that I would continue my studies in Madeenah Munawwarah. However, Allāh ﷻ had another plan for me. As my father had recently passed away and I had also recently got married, I had responsibilities at home and my family to consider. Therefore, I could not afford to go abroad to study and hence I chose the next best thing – both of the other 2 options combined!

I stayed on at Dārul-Uloom Bury to study the Iftā course under one of the senior Muftis in the UK, Mufti Shabbir Ahmad Sāhib. However rather than boarding there full time, I would travel to Bury on Monday and stay there until Thursday after which I would return home overnight on Thursday.

To support my family financially, I also accepted a post of Imāmat and teaching at a Masjid in Huddersfield. Before Jumu'ah Salāh on Friday I would travel to Huddersfield where I would stay the weekend and return to Bradford on Sunday evening to spend the night at home. In this way I was able to manage my time around my studies, work and home life, by the Grace of Allāh ﷻ.

# Part 2-Travels, Establishment of JKN and Teaching

## My First Visit Back to my Birthplace in Bangladesh

After moving to the UK at the age of 6, I did not get the opportunity to visit Bangladesh for a very long time. It was only 15 years later, in the year 1996, after I had completed my studies, that my mother expressed to me her yearning to visit Bangladesh. She had also not visited Bangladesh in that interim so she was very keen to reunite with her family after all those years, especially her father as he was unwell at the time.

Hence, we made our preparations and on Wednesday 7th January 1996, myself, my beloved mother and my youngest sister who was 5 years old at the time, travelled to Bangladesh. For the journey, we had organised to travel together from Manchester Airport with my father-in-law and the rest of my in-laws. My wife did not travel with us as my son Naeemul Islām was only two months old at the time.

We commenced our journey at 6:00am on Wednesday 7th January 1996 from Bradford with our local taxi driver, brother Abdul Khāliq. On the way we stopped for breakfast in Oldham and picked up my in-laws. After reaching the airport, we bid farewell to our well-wishers and relatives, being completely oblivious at that point as to how challenging our journey would turn out to be!

We travelled via Royal Dutch Airlines but due to treacherous weather conditions, the plane could not land at its scheduled destination, Amsterdam Airport and instead it landed at Rotterdam Airport. From there we were escorted to Amsterdam Airport via coach so that we could catch our second flight. But it was not destined to be! By the time we reached Amsterdam the plane had already left.

There was a large number of passengers with us who had also missed the flight and the next flight was not due until after 3 days. After long hours of consultation with the officials, it was decided that we would travel with British Airways instead. However, in order to do that we would have to travel back to Heathrow Airport in the UK. We had no choice but to accept.

That night, we stayed in one of the hotels of Amsterdam and the following day we travelled back from Amsterdam to Heathrow Airport via Royal Dutch Airlines. By that time everybody was extremely tired and frustrated.

In the midst of all this chaos, whilst waiting for our flight, my elder brother called me to inform us that my beloved maternal grandfather Abdul Jabbār had passed away. I was very saddened to learn of his death. I was looking forward to seeing him after so many years but now this would not be possible.

I decided not to break the sorrowful news to my mother at this particular juncture because we were already under so much stress; thus I intended to tell her at a more appropriate time. However, she could detect from my facial expression that something was not right. I explained to her that grandfather was at rest, there was nothing to worry about and that we should concentrate on our journey.

In the evening at 9.45pm on Thursday, we set off for Bangladesh. Our flight initially stopped at Delhi and then proceeded to its final destination, Dhaka where we stayed overnight because it was too late to travel any further. My wife's maternal uncle, Abdul Hamid came to pick us up from Dhaka and on Saturday we travelled to our hometown Sylhet. My in-laws were dropped off on the way.

Due to my grandfather passing away, we immediately went to my maternal grandfather's village, Akil Pur to visit what was now sadly, only his grave. My mother was utterly grief-stricken when she came to hear the heart-breaking news. Her primary objective for the trip was to visit her beloved father due to his severe illness, so she was bitterly devastated. I alongside all of our relatives sympathised and consoled her.

## Reunion in Bangladesh

Coming to Bangladesh after such a long time brought back many memories of my childhood. It had been so long that I could not recognise my relatives and nor could they recognise me! In fact, on meeting my eldest uncle, I asked him about his whereabouts and well-being, not knowing that I was in fact speaking directly to him! Out of sheer happiness for my concern, he shed tears and exclaimed, "I am your eldest uncle!" For the next few weeks, I was acquainted to all the relatives and neighbours of my village. It was a special experience being reunited with everybody after a long time.

## Tested by Scholars

News spread like wildfire that a young man, aged only 21 years, who is a qualified Hāfiz, Qāri, Ālim and Mufti, had arrived in Bangladesh! Scholars approached me and in order to test my knowledge, they put forward many intricate Mas'alahs. I initially declined, explaining that I was only a student and anything they had heard about me regarding any qualifications and high status was not true. However, they would not have any of it!

One night some scholars came and began asking me questions regarding the Tafseer of the Holy Qur'ān. One particular question was: Why is 'Bismillāh' not mentioned before Sūrah Barā'ah? I gave them a few reasons mentioned in the books of Tafseer which I had studied. They were surprised and impressed and they requested me to lead Jumu'ah (the Friday prayer) the following day.

I accepted the invitation and the next day I was privileged to lead Jumu'ah in one of the local Masjids. As I was delivering the Khutbah (sermon), people stood up all of a sudden from the back to find out who I was. After the prayer, people flocked around me and hugged and embraced me. Thereafter, requests flooded in from all corners for me to visit different Masjids and Madrasahs.

## Tarāweeh Salāh in Bangladesh

During my stay in Bangladesh, I visited many of the famous institutes there. One of these was Dārul-Qur'ān in Banyachong which was run by my father-in-law, Mufti Tālib Uddin Ahmad Sāhib ﷺ.

It was the month of Ramadhān, and because I was Hāfiz-e-Qur'ān (memoriser of the Holy Qur'ān), everyone was eager to listen to my recitation.

I was requested to lead the Tarāweeh Salāh in the Masjid of Banyachong. I remember reciting the 15th Juz (part) and by the grace of Allāh ﷻ, I managed to complete it without any mistakes. In spite of this, there was, unfortunately, a Hāfiz who wanted to make the people think that I had made a mistake. Thus, he corrected my recitation by reciting an isolated verse. This incident brought to light the fact that if I was to continue in this manner, there would be a degree of jealousy building up in the hearts of some of the people. Hence it helped me to be more aware and conscious of this potential danger. After the Tarāweeh Salāh, people crowded around to shake hands with me and to request for Du'ās.

### Salāh In Jamā'at – An Amazing Incident

As mentioned earlier, in my final year at Dārul-Uloom Bury, all of the Bukhāri students performed I'tikāf. In that 40 days spiritual course, we would strive to perform our 5 daily Salāh with Takbeer-Oola (the opening Takbeer of the Imām). Alhamdulillāh, I had continued this noble practise after my graduation also.

During my visit to Bangladesh, I was once travelling to my uncle's village in a taxi with my grandmother, mother, maternal aunt and uncle. Whilst on the journey, the time for Asr Salāh approached and I requested the driver to stop nearby a Masjid so that I could perform my Salāh but to my surprise, he declined. As the time of

Asr Salāh approached its end time, I feared that I would miss my Salāh so I insisted that he stopped. However, this message just fell on deaf ears.

All of a sudden the car abruptly stopped! The driver tried his best to re-start the car but to no avail. I could not believe it, but when I looked around I noticed a Masjid nearby and the locals were performing their Asr Salāh! Hurriedly, I left the car and joined the congregation with the opening Takbeer. I was overjoyed and expressed my gratitude to Allāh ﷻ for allowing me to continue upon my practise of performing the Salāh with the Takbeer-Oola. After the Salāh, there was a Janāzah (funeral) and the people appointed me to perform the Janāzah Salāh.

When I completed the prayer, I came back to the car to find the driver still occupied in trying to repair the car. I got in and requested him to drive on. He tried the engine once more and to our utter amazement the car restarted! I just smiled at him and praised Allāh ﷻ. When we arrived at my uncle's village, the news had already reached his ears that I had performed a Janāzah Salāh in a miraculous way! I seized the opportunity to explain to my uncle about the importance of Salāh.

Whilst in Bangladesh, I would deliver lectures in the Bangla language which was something new to me. I was encouraged and motivated by my relatives to speak and guide the people in matters of Deen (religion). I realised sadly, that many of my own relatives did not even know the basics of Islām and I tried to explain to them the importance of seeking knowledge. I gathered all my cousins and encouraged them to study the Deen and assured them that I would financially back them if they wanted to enrol into an Islamic institute.

## Political Unrest

During our travels one day we got caught in a rally of two of the main political parties – BNP and Awwami League – who were stood face to face in a confrontation. Suddenly, to our horror, violence erupted and stones and bricks were being thrown all over the place! We swiftly had to take refuge in a nearby Hindu village for safety and remained there until the violence subdued. Alhamdulillāh, without any further delay we returned back to our village safely. However, due to the political unrest in the country, there were frequent strikes and we could not fly back home at our fixed date. Our departure date was delayed by 10 days due to these political problems.

## My First Hajj

From my childhood I always had the intense yearning and aspiration to perform Hajj. I consistently supplicated to Allāh ﷻ to bestow me this opportunity as soon as possible. Alhamdulillāh, my Du'ās were heard. I was overwhelmed with happiness and joy when I told my mother that we could perform Hajj as she was also longing to see the House of Allāh ﷻ. The local residents advised me not to travel because firstly I had just returned from Bangladesh and secondly I was too young. Nevertheless, I was determined to go.

After graduating from Dārul-Uloom Bury, I received a post of Imāmat in a Masjid in Huddersfield called Shāh-Jalāl. I had saved up enough money for my Hajj from the small wage I earned from this job. It might now seem laughable and petty but I even saved pennies to prepare for this auspicious journey.

I can remember the bus fare being 34p from Manningham Lane to Bradford Interchange, and then I would catch the X6 bus to Huddersfield Interchange which was 60p off peak, and a further 34p bus fare from Huddersfield Interchange to Victoria Road which was next to the Masjid on Fenton Road. My return journey to Bradford at night after leading the Ishā Salāh would be the same.

However, at that time, rather than taking 3 buses, I would walk from my house to Bradford Interchange and then when reaching Huddersfield Interchange, I would walk from there to the Masjid. Similarly at night, I walked from the Masjid to Huddersfield Interchange at night and then when reaching Bradford Interchange, via X6, I would walk from the Interchange to my house. In this way I managed to save £1.36 a day and after some time this accumulated to a couple of hundred pounds.

In addition to this, I scrutinized my daily expenditure and only spent on that which was necessary. This may seem insignificant, but by the Grace of Allāh ﷻ, due to these savings I was ready to proceed for my first Hajj. Therefore I was able to make my firm intention to travel to the Holy Sites with a group of elders from my local Masjid.

In 1996, there was no package system for Hajj, therefore it was very economical. I paid my ticket fare, visa and draft money, which came to a total of £700, to the travel agent, Riaz Travel, Lumb Lane, Bradford. The hotels were also very economical at the time, being 400 Riyals for the 8 day stay in Madeenah Munawwarah and 1,800 Riyals for the accommodation in Makkah, which came to a total of just under £400. Hence my first full Hajj was performed with only £1100.

We set off from Tawakkulia Masjid in Bradford to Manchester Airport and then from there we travelled via Saudi Airlines direct to Jeddah. I was delighted to know that a few other youngsters who were of similar age to me, were also travelling with their parents including Maulāna Abdus-Salām, Maulāna Abdullāh and Mufti Noorullāh. As it was my first time travelling to the Holy Lands, I was over-excited with passion, love and anticipation to see the historical sites.

**Madeenah Munawwarah**

We began our illustrious journey by visiting the blessed city of our beloved Prophet ﷺ, Madeenah Munawwarah. When I visited the sacred grave of the Holy Prophet ﷺ it left me speechless and wonderstruck. The Seerah of the Holy Prophet ﷺ and Islamic history flashed through my mind as I sobbed and cried, thinking about the great gift bestowed upon me by Allāh ﷻ. I could not describe in words my jubilance and joy. It was my life-long yearning and desire to visit the sacred grave of my beloved Prophet ﷺ and that day my dream had become a reality! All praise is due to Allāh ﷻ.

In our 8 days stay in Madeenah Munawwarah, I was fortunate enough, by the grace of Allāh ﷻ, to fulfil the Hadeeth of the Holy Prophet ﷺ in which he mentioned, "Anyone who performs 40 Salāh in my Masjid will get his sins forgiven and he will be free from hypocrisy."

In Madeenah Munawwarah, I also had the opportunity to meet my close friend and colleague, Maulāna Fazl Dād who was studying in Madeenah University at the time. He kindly and affectionately showed me around the city and shared with me valuable infor-mation and knowledge regarding the blessed city.

## Establishment of JKN

It was in Madeenah Munawwarah, that my colleague Maulāna Ab-dus-Salām who had also gone for Hajj with his mother, ap-proached me with another colleague Maulāna Abdullāh. They in-formed me that they were interested to study the Deen and that they wanted me to teach them. Initially, I excused myself saying that I had a full-time Imāmat job but I was inspired by their enthu-siasm and zeal, so I conceded and promised them that I would teach them on weekends when we returned back to the UK. Who would have thought at that time that this meeting would be the initiation of the great JKN Institute? And who could wish for a more noble city in which this initiation would take place? I prayed to Allāh ﷻ that He accept our intentions and that He transforms them into reality.

After our stay in Madeenah Munawwarah, we travelled via coach

to Makkah Mukarramah and we halted on our way at Dhul Hu-
laifah in order to don our Ihrāms.

## My First Sight of the Holy Ka'bah

In the Ahādeeth we are informed that any Du'ā made at the time
of sighting the Holy Ka'bah is readily accepted. Keeping this in
mind, I looked forward to my first sight of the Holy Ka'bah with
great anticipation.

The wait was more than worth it! It was one of the most emotional
and passionate moments of my life. I focussed my eyes towards
the Holy Ka'bah and cried till my heart was content and I supplicated for everything that I could think of at that time.

One particular Du'ā I made was, "O Allāh! You have given me the
Tawfeeq (ability) and strength to visit Your Holy House. Please
give me the Tawfeeq again and again to come to Your House at
least once every year, whether it is through Hajj or Umrah." Allāhu
-Akbar – Allāh ﷻ has truly fulfilled this aspiration of mine by allowing me to continue visiting His blessed House for many years,
Alhamdulillāh. How can I express my gratitude to my Allāh ﷻ? I
pray to Allāh ﷻ that He allows me to continue in this way until I
depart from my temporary abode. Āmeen!

By the grace of Allāh ﷻ, I have seen the fruits of my Du'ās many
times and often very swiftly. I prayed for my son Naeemul Islām
to become a Hāfiz and Alhamdulillāh, he completed his Hifz. I
prayed for my wife to become an Ālimah and Allāh ﷻ fulfilled this

wish. I prayed for a Madrasah and Allāh ﷻ made this happen also. O Allāh ﷻ I could go on and on – You have fulfilled all of my Du'ās. I have never been deprived from Your Benevolence and Kindness!

O my beloved friends and students! I request to you from the bottom of my heart - never underestimate the power of your Du'ās! Make a habit of supplicating to the One Who provides for us without limits. It is the essence of worship, so never lose hope of the acceptance of your Du'ās. May Allāh ﷻ fulfil all of our Du'ās. Āmeen!

## The Initial Stages of JKN Institute

After returning back from Hajj, I continued with my duty of Imāmat in Huddersfield. As promised to Maulāna Abdus-Salām, I commenced classes with him in his residence of 23 Springfield Place. I was inspired by how the great Dārul-Uloom Deoband was established with one teacher (Mullāh Mahmood) and one student (Shaykh Mahmood). Alhamdulillāh, the same scenario occurred with the JKN Institute when there was only one teacher (my humble self) and one student (Maulāna Abdus-Salām Sāhib). It was a historical day on Saturday 1st June 1996 at 11am that this blessed class began. Who knew that this humble class would blossom to become a great institute of learning in the future?! Subhān-Allāh!

Initially, Maulāna Abdus-Salām was the only student but soon afterwards, another handful joined the classes due to his encouragement. May Allāh ﷻ reward him for his efforts. Āmeen!

My first students were:

1.  Maulāna Abdus-Salām
2.  Maulāna Abdullāh
3.  Al-Hājj Abdul Mateen
4.  Al-Hājj Abdus-Samad
5.  Al-Hājj Moynah Miah (deceased)

For the next 10 weeks the classes were held on weekends at the residence of Maulāna Abdus-Salām but then on the 17th August 1996, we moved to my residence at 25 Spring Gardens. Initially I taught the Holy Qur'ān, Urdu and Fiqh and then, later I introduced the Arabic language and Arabic Grammar.

Slowly and gradually more students enrolled and within the first few months, I was teaching a good 20 students. My Imāmat continued as normal and I taught in the weekends. Later on, I began teaching the students on weekday evenings also after coming back from work in Huddersfield.

## The Eagerness of the Students to Study Deen

In their thirst for knowledge, the adult students were not content with the hours of study hence we decided that they travel to Huddersfield every day for more lessons. Tāj Uddin (one of my students) was a van driver and he volunteered to bring everyone. I would finish my Maktab classes at the Masjid at 7pm and then teach the students who had travelled from Bradford.

Soon the class numbers began to rise and one van was no longer sufficient! Subsequently, I decided to travel back to Bradford after my Maktab classes every day to teach them in my house at 25 Spring Gardens. The students would arrive at 7pm at my residence, whilst I would reach home at approximately 8pm from Huddersfield. For the supervision of the students in my absence, I appointed Maulāna Abdus-Salām to take care of everything.

By the time I reached home, the Qur'ān class and Hifz class students would be ready to recite their Sabaq (lessons). After listening to their Sabaq and giving them more Sabaq to learn, I would teach the Ālim class students. These lessons would last until between 10pm and 11pm and I taught up to 15 different books in that time. This system of teaching continued until we took time off for Ramadhān in 1997. In the month of Ramadhān I lead the Tarāweeh Salāh in Huddersfield with my student Hāfiz Shafiqur-Rahmān. We travelled daily to perform Maghrib, Ishā and Tarāweeh and returned back after the Tarāweeh Salāh.

## Management of Shāh-Jalāl Masjid

Shāh-Jalāl Masjid was situated in the area of Lockwood in Huddersfield in which there was a small community of predominantly Bangladeshi and Pakistani background. There were two groups of people who maintained the Masjid – one from the local area in Lockwood and the other from another area in Huddersfield called Newsome.

It so happened that the day I left for Hajj in 1996, there was a friction in the committee. To my dismay, when I returned back from Hajj, I found the community to be utterly divided. I tried my level best to reconcile between the two parties but to no avail. However, the people of the town had a great deal of respect for me, Alhamdulillāh, so they suggested that I take on the responsibility of the management committee. They made it clear that should I accept they would be happy and they considered it as a good solution to eradicate the problems of the Masjid. Though I was very reluctant to take on such a post of responsibility, I felt that I had no choice but to accept, bearing in mind the welfare of the Masjid and the community.

I began by arranging an emergency meeting in which everyone would need to agree that they would abstain from any interferences in the day-to-day management of the Masjid, by signing a document. For a year, I undertook the responsibility of the executive committee as well as my original duty of Imāmat and teaching. It was a tiring and rigorous responsibility but by the Grace of Allāh ﷻ, everything ran smoothly and the people were content.

The radical changes that occurred in my new management role were within the Maktab system. I introduced an official uniform for the boys and girls whereas previously children would attend with their school uniforms. I also established a new syllabus consisting of sessions on Islamic studies, Seerah, Fiqh and Etiquettes.

I was responsible for the welfare and teaching of a total of 40 students, from the age range of 5 years to 16 years. The pupils were all at different stages, therefore it was a difficult task to manage and maintain the classes. However, within a few weeks, everything was organised and the children and parents were overjoyed with the changes and the progress of the Maktab, Alhamdulillāh.

## My Accommodation and Food

My living quarters were on the upper floor of the Masjid for when-ever I needed to stay in Huddersfield. In my quarters, I would uti-lise my time in research and studies. When I first arrived at the Masjid, the committee informed me that I would have to prepare my own food and they showed me the kitchen! They advised me to buy essential items like rice, onions, potatoes and Masala (in short, everything that a kitchen should have!). I had no idea of how to cook or prepare food, nevertheless, I just replied with a smile and said, "No problem, everything will be ok."

In the evening the person in charge invited me to his house and said that I could eat there that day and from the following day I could start my own cooking. The next day was Saturday and I was teaching in the morning from 11am till 1pm. The Masjid secretary who lived next door sent breakfast over to the Masjid for me. After the class it was Zuhr time and the Masjid officials were all present. They all approached me, and I was surprised to learn that they were all eager for me to be their guest on a permanent basis! Hav-ing accepted their kind offers, I expressed my gratitude to them and gave them the following decision as to where I would eat and when:

1. Breakfast – next door at the secretary's house at 10.30am.
2. Lunch – after Zuhr Salāh at the cashier's house at 10 Bland Street.
3. Supper – after Ishā Salāh at one of the executive member's house at 27 Fenton Road.

Everyone agreed and expressed their happiness and I expressed my immense thanks to Allāh ﷻ for providing me these great facilities. I cried out of happiness and joy, "O' Allāh ﷻ! How sinful a servant I am and how Merciful You are. You have provided the means for this weak and disobedient servant of Yours. Indeed O' Allāh ﷻ, You provide sustenance to whomsoever You wish without any account."

This routine continued whilst I remained in Huddersfield and in that whole period, I did not have to make even a cup of tea! Nor did I need to wash my clothes or carry out any other household chores, by the Grace of Allāh ﷻ. Additionally, I began to build a deep attachment with the Musallies (worshippers) of the Masjid and now and then they would invite me to their houses for food or a snack also.

### My Dear Friend Dr. Fareed

Whilst in Huddersfield, I met an eye surgeon called Dr. Fareed who became a very close friend of mine. He expressed an eagerness for me to teach him the Holy Qur'ān. I taught him from the basics of the Qā'idah to the Holy Qur'ān. Māshā-Allāh, though he was in his seventies, he managed to memorise Sūrah Yāseen and other key Sūrahs of the Holy Qur'ān.

One day, he approached me and said, "I have one request which I would be obliged if you could fulfil." He became emotional and repeated his request. I replied that I would try my best and told him to put forward his request. He exclaimed, "You are a Hāfiz-e-Qur'ān and Ālim and you can take a lot of people to Paradise. Will you take me?" Tears filled his eyes and he paused. I looked down and replied, "O' Dr. Sāhib, only Allāh ﷻ knows. It is not so easy. But I have high hopes in my Allāh ﷻ that if He grants me Paradise, I will Inshā-Allāh not forget you." Out of joy and happiness with my response, he embraced me in a big hug.

Once Dr Sāhib narrated to me that he was invited by the British Government to work in the UK as an eye-specialist. However, the working hours did not permit for him to perform his Salāh, so he declined the offer and returned home. A week later they rang him to inform him that he could work according to his convenience. He told me that Alhamdulillāh, he had not missed any Salāh or fast since reaching the age of puberty. I was left spell-bound and inspired to hear this amazing achievement in this day and age by a doctor. It was a great lesson and an eye-opener for me.

After leaving my post in Huddersfield, I made it a point to call Dr. Sāhib or visit him whenever I had the opportunity. He maintained a close relationship with me until he passed away. May Allāh ﷻ forgive the sins of Dr Sāhib and elevate his ranks in Paradise. Āmeen!

## My Resignation from Shāh-Jalāl Masjid

Everything was running smoothly both in Huddersfield and in my home town Bradford. The number of my students in Bradford increased to 40 and the requests and pleas for more teaching time from students and parents intensified. At this point, I had to make a decisive choice as to whether I would continue with my duties in Huddersfield or take on the growing responsibilities back home in

Bradford. It was a difficult choice. Huddersfield had become my second home. The Musallies, parents and students had a deep love and respect for me and my heart was also attached to them. However the choice would have to be made. It was May 1997 and after a long thought out decision, I made the choice to focus my attention towards my hometown Bradford.

One night I had a dream in which I saw my father performing Hajj and coming to meet me. He was very happy and jubilant. I woke up thinking that my father has passed away and he can no longer perform Hajj, therefore, I will perform a Hajj as a Sadaqah Jāriya for him. Hence I intended to perform Hajj the following year in 1997, taking my wife with me so she could perform her Fardh (compulsory) Hajj. As I was going for Hajj, I took the opportunity to give in my resignation at Shāh-Jalāl. It was one of the most difficult steps in my life but I felt that it had to be taken.

In order to cause the least disruption at the Masjid which I had grown to love, I appointed one of my colleagues – Maulāna Saeed Abbās, a graduate of Dārul-Uloom Bury, as my replacement before approaching the people with my resignation. They were deeply shocked and saddened by the news. I reassured them that I would always keep contact with them and that I would always try to assist them in whatever way I could. I explained my dilemma and the need to establish a permanent institute in my hometown Bradford. They reluctantly conceded and prior to my Hajj, I bid farewell to Huddersfield and its warm community with tearful eyes and a weeping heart.

## Preparations for Hajj

My wife, at the time was 5 months pregnant with my daughter Aneesa Islām so when I decided to take her for Hajj, it became an uproar within my family. Even the nurse refused to give her the Meningitis injection. I decided to consult Dr. Fareed Sāhib regarding the matter and having researched upon it for me, he gave me a green light to go. He informed me that it is perfectly normal to take this injection whilst pregnant. Consequently, after signing a declaration form, my wife was given the injection and we were ready to proceed.

We decided to travel with a group from Oldham which my father-in-law was in charge of. We processed our essential documents and on the 13th of April 1997, we travelled via Cyprus Airlines, first to Larnaca Airport in Cyprus, where we donned our Ihrām and then to Jeddah.

## Generosity of My Father-in-law

My father-in-law Mufti Tālib-Uddin Sāhib ⚜ was a great scholar and a close student of Mufti Rasheed Ahmad Ludhyānwi Sāhib ⚜. He himself narrated that there are over 100 Fatāwa of his in the book Ahsanul-Fatāwa. In this Hajj journey, he paid a big portion of the expenses of both myself and my wife.

His generosity knew no bounds! He would give without hesitance! He continuously spent on all the pilgrims throughout the Hajj. It was a Hajj never to be forgotten due to the emotional Du'ā of Mufti Sāhib ⚜, the kindness of my beloved wife, the soft heart of brother

Afruz Ali (Babul), a close colleague from Oldham, and the co-operation and kindness of all the brothers and sisters in the group. All of this left a permanent mark of love in the depth of my heart. Even till this day whenever I visit Oldham, the brothers make a point to see me and request for Du'ās. May Allah ﷻ bless everyone and bestow everyone of us the goodness of this world and the Hereafter. Āmeen!

## In the Company of Shaykh Mufti Tālib Uddin ﵾ (1361-1431 AH/1942-2010 CE)

Mentioning my father-in-law Mufti Tālib-Uddin Sāhib ﵾ, I thought it befitting at this point to attach the article I wrote after his demise, regarding his great legacy. It will hopefully give us all a brief glimpse of his amazing life:

Shaykh Mufti Tālib Uddin Ahmad ﵾ was amongst the many pious scholars of Islām who became successful through seeking knowledge and propagating it. He was born in the year 1942 in the village of Shataihal, Dinarpur, Nabigonj in the county of Habigonj, Bangladesh. His father Qāri Alā-Uddin Ahmad was a prominent Qāri of his community, well respected by the elders, famously known as 'Boro Miah Sāhib'. His mother was the Rābiya Basriya of her time, well known for her Ibādah, good morals and character.

Shaykh Mufti Tālib-Uddin Ahmad ﵾ received his primary Deeni education at home from his respected father. He went further on to study in the famous Islamic institutes known as Jāmiah Qāsimul-Uloom Bohubal and Jāmiah Arabiyah Dinarpur Balidara,

Habigonj.

To quench his thirst of knowledge, he travelled to Pakistan in 1962 and studied in the institute Darul-Uloom Tendwala, established by Khateeb Pakistan Shaykh Ihtishāmul Haq Thānwi ﷺ. There he studied under great luminaries; the likes of Shaykh Zafar Ahmad Uthmāni, Shaykh Idrees Kandhalwi, Shaykh Jamsheid and Shaykh Abdur-Rahmān Kāmilpuri ﷺ.

In the year 1964, he studied Mishkāt Shareef in Jāmiah Fathiyya, Lahore. He gained the privilege of learning from great scholars like Shaykh Habibur-Rahmān Lāhori and Shaykh Ghulām Mahmood.

In 1965, he studied his final year of Hadeeth under the world renowned Hāfizul-Hadeeth Allāma Abdullāh Darkāsti ﷺ in Markazul Uloom Wal-Fuyooz in Raheem Yār Khān. His other great teachers include Shaykhul-Hadeeth Shaykh Ibrāheem ﷺ and Shaykh Mufti Ghulām Haydar ﷺ.

In the year 1966, he did the Iftā course under the supervision of Shaykh Mufti Rasheed Ahmad Ludhyānwi ﷺ in Ashraful-Uloom Nāzim-Ābād, North Karachi. During his Iftā course, he benefitted from the company and knowledge of the Grand Mufti, Mufti Shafee Sāhib ﷺ. He would go and attest and verify Fatāwa and Masā'il from him. Occasionally he would also attend the Majlis of Shaykh Mufti Mahmood Sāhib ﷺ, Mufti Abdullāh ﷺ and Shaykh Ghulām Gaus Hazārvi ﷺ.

After his graduation as a qualified scholar and Mufti, he was immediately chosen by his seniors to commence teaching at the institute where he originally once studied, Qāsimul-Uloom Bohubal. There, he was promoted to the post of senior teacher. In the following year, he moved to Al-Arabiyah Husainiyah Dhaka Dakhin. He was assigned to teach the senior Kitābs of Fiqh and Hadeeth in that institute.

After six years of Deeni Khidmat (service) he was invited to take the role of principal in the institute Al-Arabiyah Husainiyah Boytakhal. After a decade of Deeni Khidmat as a principal in the institute, he migrated to Saudi Arabia. Meanwhile, a group of people from England went to perform Hajj. They realised the potential and expertise of Mufti Sāhib and thus invited him to migrate to England so they could benefit from his knowledge and company. Hence, he moved to England as an Imām after staying 14 months in Saudi Arabia. He became the main Imām in Jāmi Masjid, Middleton, Oldham.

In the Masjid he commenced the Dars (discourses) of Tafseer, Hadeeth and Fiqh and soon became recognised for his sharp knowledge and inspirational talks. He was invited across the country for lectures and for the resolving of intricate issues of marriage, divorce, inheritance, domestic violence etc.

In 1994, Shaykh Mufti Tālib Uddin ﷺ was appointed the principal of Dārul-Qur'ān Madrasah, Banyachong, Habigonj. With the grace of Allāh ﷻ and Mufti Sāhib's persistence and hard work, the Jāmiah became a well renowned and credited Madrasah for knowledge and Tarbiyah (upbringing). Many chose it as a first choice for study. During his time as principal, the Jāmiah progressed rapidly and underwent numerous construction and expansion works providing more space and facilities for the students. There are currently 710 students studying in the departments of Hifz and Ālim classes.

In 1997, Mufti Sāhib founded and established the famous Markazi Masjid, Al-Khazrā in Oldham. This soon became the central point for the work of Da'wah, spirituality and knowledge. Many leading Islamic Scholars have paid a visit to this place to witness the hard work of Mufti Sāhib.

Izhār Haq is an organization which was founded by Mufti Sāhib and is currently run from the Masjid. Izhār Haq as understood by its name was established to proclaim the truth and eradicate evil and Bid'ah (innovation) from the Deen. It was the tireless effort and sacrifice of Mufti Sāhib which progressed and promoted the work of Izhār Haq throughout the UK.

In order to complete his thirst of knowledge and spirituality, Mufti Sāhib took Bai'ah (the oath of allegiance) to one of the leading disciples of Shaykhul-Islām Shaykh Husain Ahmad Madani ﷺ, Shaykh Abdul Mannān Ghunoy. He progressed through the path of spirituality very rapidly and was awarded by his Shaykh with the mantle of Khilāfah and Ijāzah in the year 1978. Mufti Sāhib for quite a number of years had been ill and bed ridden. Nevertheless, he continued to impart the knowledge and wisdom which Allāh ﷻ bestowed upon him.

It was Saturday evening on the 3ʳᵈ of July 2010 when the health of Mufti Sāhib seriously deteriorated. His family members were called to the hospital and in their presence, he read out a few couplets expressing his long desire to meet his Creator and then breathed his last. Innā lillāhi wa-innā ilayhi-rāji'oon. The news of his demise spread like wildfire across the UK and abroad. I, alongside many of my colleagues, immediately arrived at the hospital and within minutes it became overcrowded with relatives, friends and scholars.

The funeral prayer took place on the following day after Zuhr Salāh in the Millennium Centre, Oldham. Mufti Junayed Ahmad Sāhib, the eldest son of Mufti Sāhib lead the funeral prayer. Thousands of people from across the UK attended the funeral prayer. May Allāh 🕌 have mercy on Shaykh Mufti Tālib-Uddin 🕌, elevate his status in Jannah and bless his family and everyone associated with him. Āmeen!

Mufti Sāhib was well known to everyone and was classed as one of the senior Muftis of the UK. Intricate and complicated issues would be referred to him and he always came out with a solution. I was very fortunate to be acquainted with Mufti Sāhib due to being his son-in-law. I have witnessed many great qualities and attributes in the life of Mufti Sāhib, the most prominent being his generosity and kindness. Volumes could be written about his lofty character and attributes and I hope that a detailed biography will be available in the near future.

He has left behind 4 sons out of whom 3 are qualified scholars and

7 daughters, out of whom 4 are qualified Ālimahs. All of his six son-in-laws are scholars who are engaged in the work of Deen. They will all, Inshā-Allāh, be Sadaqah Jāriyah for him alongside the institute Dārul-Qur'ān, Al-Khazrā Markazi Masjid and the thousands of students and disciples who have benefited from this ocean of knowledge.

I pray to Allāh ﷻ that He gives us the ability and strength to follow in the footsteps of Shaykh Mufti Tālib Uddin ﷫ and our pious predecessors. Āmeen!

**Purchasing a Building for JKN**

After performing Hajj, I continued teaching the students at my residence. By that time I had 5 classes:
1. Qā'idah Class
2. Nāzirah Class
3. Hifz Class
4. Urdu Class
5. Arbi Awwal

I would teach Qā'idah, Nāzirah and Hifz between 5pm to 7pm and from 7pm till 10pm I would teach approximately 15 Kitābs to the other classes. At that time, due to the growing number of students, we began to look for a building to accommodate everyone. We searched around Bradford and its outskirts, visiting various estate agents and talking to scholars and businessmen seeking their advice. We were searching far and wide but who was to know that the building destined to become the JKN Institute was just next door in the same street! Furthermore, it was previously a synagogue! Subhān-Allāh! How Allāh ﷻ works mysteriously!

Brother Hushiar Ali who lived in 19 Spring Gardens approached me saying that he had heard that I was intending to purchase a Madrasah. When I confirmed this, he informed me that the businessman who lived next door may be ready to sell his building. We approached the businessman and Alhamdulillāh he agreed to the sale. We accepted with the terms subject to planning permission being granted. He agreed and simultaneously we submitted our plans and began raising funds for the purchase. It was an uphill struggle to raise the money.

### Struggle and Hardship in Establishing JKN

My student, Maulāna Abdus-Salām and I prepared a list of potential donors who we thought would assist us in this noble task. Thereafter, I arranged meetings with the local scholars and friends to emphasise the importance of establishing a Madrasah in the area. These meeting took place at my residence, 25 Spring Gardens. Being young and naïve, I did not realise or understand the politics of many of the elders. They raised issues such as who would be the trustees of the Madrasah? Who would be in the management committee and who would be the main chairperson? etc. Considering these issues as being secondary at that time, I explained that we primarily  need to raise funds and establish the Madrasah before worrying about these things. Despite all my efforts, it was an uphill struggle to make them understand. Unfortunately, many of them declined to help us financially and there were several times during this hardship and struggle that I almost lost hope and gave up.

I eventually realised that the two main reasons behind the difficulty in raising the funds were; first being my age which made people reluctant to support me and secondly, the sectarianism in the Muslim community. Many offensive and disheartening slogans were being chanted by the people. I was called a Wahābi, a dictator, and too young to be trusted with people's money as well as other offensive remarks. How dejected all of this made me feel! My supporting helper throughout this turmoil was my beloved student and colleague, Maulāna Abdus-Salām who stood by my side through thick and thin. May Allāh ﷻ raise his ranks. Āmeen!

There were times when we visited an individual with the expectation that he would donate a generous amount, instead he would turn us away empty-handed. There were other occasions when individuals mockingly gave us bags of bronze coins, saying sarcastically, "Count them and give us a receipt!"

How disheartening all this was! Nevertheless, Allāh ﷻ took me through this hardship and struggle to test me and make me strong. How Mighty and Wise He is! Allāhu-Akbar, I cannot praise Him enough!

Despite the negative response from the community, those brothers who assisted us tremendously and encouraged us were many, Alhamdulillāh. May Allāh ﷻ grant them the best of rewards. Āmeen! Due to this invaluable support, we managed to raise the sufficient amount needed for the exchange of contracts, Alhamdulillāh.

## Difficulties in Obtaining Planning Permission

Whilst we were going through the hurdles of raising funds, we also had problems in obtaining planning permission. Initially, we were refused permission mainly due to insufficient parking space for an institute. I wrote back with an explanation, using the aid of a map of the catchment area from which the majority of our students were expected to be from. It showed that the students would be within a one mile radius, hence they would be able to travel without cars and there would be no need for a big car park. Alhamdulillāh, after consultations and much reassuring, they accepted. All praise be to Allāh ﷻ.

## Fundraising Event

On the 25th of December 1997, I invited an eminent scholar of Bangladesh, Shaykh Abdul Ghani Jakigonji, to help us to raise funds for the new Madrasah. Alhamdulillāh, hundreds of brothers and elders attended the gathering and a great amount of donations and Qardh Hasanah (interest free loan) was pledged. This became the stepping stone for us to gather a lump sum of the purchase price. We continued having events and gatherings to raise funds and Alhamdulillāh they became very instrumental in the collecting of funds as well as promoting the institute.

## Grand Opening of JKN

Although the Madrasah was already purchased, we did not move into the new premises until August 1998. Prior to the classes, we invited Shaykh Noorul Islām Sāhib, the general secretary of Khat-me-Nabuwwat Bangladesh, to the opening and also to help with fundraising.

Though Shaykh Noorul Islām Sāhib was very busy with the Khat-me-Nabuwwat movement, out of kindness and affection for me, he assisted us in every way possible, Alhamdulillāh. He even decided the name Jāmiah Khātamun Nabiyyeen for the institute. He would deliver very influential speeches in which the hearts of the masses would be moved. Even to this day, he keeps regular contact with us to enquire about the welfare of the institute. Whenever he visits the UK, he makes it a point to visit our institute and pray for its well-being. May Allāh ﷻ bestow him with the best of rewards of this world and the Hereafter. Āmeen!

### The First Classes in the New Premises

After moving to the new premises, there was a need to employ more teachers because by then JKN had 7 classes which I was sin-gle-handedly catering for. I approached a very close friend of mine from my student days at Dārul-Uloom Bury, Maulāna Abdul Wāhid to assist me in teaching the classes and Alhamdulillāh, he readily accepted my invitation.

The Madrasah picked up momentum and students from all corners of Bradford began to attend. Initially, we accommodated a few adult students in the Madrasah for boarding. However, this only lasted for approximately two years after which it was terminated due to financial difficulties and shortage of staff.

## My Beloved Shaykh MaulānaYūsuf Motāla Sāhib's Visit

After the Madrasah work and teaching began to settle, I invited my beloved teacher and Shaykh, Maulāna Yūsuf Motāla Sāhib to attend the institute and bless it. He readily accepted and one evening he came to the Madrasah. I showed him around and I was delighted to see that he was immensely pleased with the Madrasah. He raised his hands in supplication and he showered us with his Du'ās and kindness.

As he was leaving, my beloved Shaykh said to me words that I will never forget, "I am leaving for Madeenah Munawwarah hence I am very busy. Your love and kindness brought me here. Others also invited me but I could not go." I became overjoyed by this and felt incredibly fortunate. I requested him to make Du'ā for me when he goes to the Holy Lands and to send my salutations and Salām to the beloved Prophet ﷺ.

## Dream of My Shaykh and My Performance of Umrah

It was December 1999, just after my beloved Shaykh's visit that I dreamt I saw him calling me to come for Umrah. I replied, "I have made my intention to perform Umrah but I will have to come after closing the Madrasah for Ramadhān Holidays." He insisted that I come and said out of kindness that he would pay for my expenditure. I expressed my gratitude to him but stood by my decision explaining, "Alhamdulillāh, Hadhrat I have the money and I will come in the holidays after closing for Ramadhān." He smiled and said, "Fine."

I woke up with a great sense of happiness and joy. Though I had already made the intention of performing Umrah that year, the dream strengthened my intention. So that year, I went to Umrah for the first two weeks of Ramadhān with Maulāna Abdus-Salām and another colleague from Bradford.

## Miracle of My Shaykh

When I visited Makkah Mukarramah, I made a point to meet my beloved Shaykh. I made enquiries and reached the hotel where he was staying. After Zuhr Salāh, I went to Dar-Ridhwān where he was taking part in a Dhikr Majlis. When the Majlis had finished, I approached him and put my hands forward to shake his hands. Whilst placing my hands into his, he smiled and to my utter amazement he said, "Madrasah ki Chutti Dhe kar Ageye (Have you given holidays for the Madrasah and come)?" I was astonished that he was also aware of my dream and conceded that it must be an inspiration from Allāh ﷻ to His Auliyā (friends of Allāh ﷻ). I replied with a big smile, "Yes, Hadhrat!" Hadhrat's kindness knew no bounds. He asked me where I would be having my Iftār and requested that I have it near King Fahd Gate with him. I eagerly and happily accepted.

## Khilāfah and Ijāzah (Permission to Take Bai'ah)

It was after Asr Salāh when I was trying to determine the exact location for my meeting with Hadhrat. I saw him with one of our colleagues Maulāna Yūsuf Lorgat preparing to do Dhor (revision of the Holy Qur'ān). He saw me and called me to one corner. Then

101

holding my hands, he asked me about the Madrasah, and my daily Ma'moolat and spirituality. Thereafter, he took me in front of the Holy Ka'bah and began to say the words which I thought were a dream.

Hadhrat said in a calm voice, "I have for a considerable time been thinking about you. Due to the fact that we are in the blessed land, in the blessed month, at a blessed time, I hereby grant you Khilāfah and Ijāzah (permission)" I was dumbfounded! I did not know what to do! My feet became stuck to the ground and I could not feel or move my legs! My hands would not separate from Hadhrat's. My beloved Shaykh just kept telling me to praise Allāh ﷻ and perform Tawāf to express my gratitude. I left with tears in my eyes and completed a Nafl Tawāf and concluded with an emotional Du'ā.

The next day I woke up feeling very guilty and sinful. The thought repeatedly came to my mind that I should approach Hadhrat and have this responsibility taken away from me because, by Allāh ﷻ, I am never worthy of it! I know how sinful I am and I feel totally unworthy of this post. However, I comforted myself with the hope that through the blessings of these pious saints, Allāh ﷻ will shower His mercy upon me also.

I would like to reiterate this statement that I am never worthy of any high position. Only Allāh ﷻ and I, know how sinful and evil I really am. I always pray to Allāh ﷻ to conceal my faults in this world and the Hereafter. My beloved brothers and sisters and students who are reading this, please pray for this humble and sinful servant. I would have never mentioned this but as a token of gratitude I mentioned it briefly. May Allāh ﷻ forgive all of my sins and shortcomings. Āmeen!

## Launch of Al-Mu'min Magazine

After establishing JKN, I had a longing desire and yearning to launch an Islamic magazine which would be the backbone of the institute. I had already gathered articles from my Madrasah days with the intention of compiling books and magazines in the future. Whenever I came across any interesting articles in Arabic, English or Urdu, I would note them or photocopy them and keep them safe for future reference. I gathered a few students and colleagues and put the idea of the magazine forward and Alhamdulillāh, they all agreed. One local brother Shams-Uddin Ahmad, a police officer and a pilot, actually donated a full PC set for the publication of the magazine and other literature. May Allāh ﷻ grant him the best of rewards. Āmeen!

Until then I had no idea what we would name the magazine. We thought of various names and eventually decided to write them on pieces of paper and then draw lots to determine the name of the magazine. Some of the names put forward were:

1. Ad-Da'wah
2. An-Naseehah
3. Al-Haq
4. Sawtul-Haq
5. Al-Islām
6. Al-Mu'min
7. An-Noor

After drawing lots, Al-Mu'min was chosen and we all agreed to call the magazine Al-Mu'min. An editorial board was appointed which included:

1. Maulāna Mujibur-Rahmān
2. Hāfiz Muminul-Islām
3. Hāfiz Sādiqur-Rahmān
4. Hāfiz Yaqūb

It was decided that the magazine would be published bimonthly with 28 pages initially. The first ever edition of the magazine was in January/February 2000. We contacted Impress Printers and ordered 1000 copies in black and white with colour covers. After the magazine was published, we manually wrote the names of the subscribers on the envelopes and sent them by hand delivery. I contacted people door-to-door and via phone to encourage them to subscribe. Alhamdulillāh, we received a tremendous response from the community and it was not long before we reached the 1000 mark in subscriptions within the first year of launching the magazine.

## First English Tafseer in Tawakkulia Masjid

For a considerable amount of time I was attempting to begin conducting the Tafseer of the Holy Qur'ān in our local Masjid – it was a long burning desire in my heart. Though there was a weekly Bangla Tafseer taking place on Sundays, there was a pressing need for the Tafseer to be in the English language to accommodate the needs of the local community.

I believed that to further rectify the community, Tafseer was a must. I was inspired to commence this commendable act by the historical statement of Shaykhul Hind Maulāna Mahmoodul Hasan Sāhib ﷺ made in a gathering of scholars. After being released from Malta prison, Shaykhul Hind ﷺ remarked, "I have been contemplating over the declining situation of the Muslim Ummah and have come to the solution for this crisis. If the Muslim Ummah hold firmly to two things, then they will be able to overcome this crisis: 1. Muslim unity and 2. Clinging to the Book of Allāh ﷻ! (understanding the Holy Qur'ān and acting upon it)"

Initially, it was not easy to organise. However, after many consultations and meetings with the executive committee, we managed to eventually secure a time for the Tafseer, Alhamdulillāh.

It was a historical day in my life when I had the privilege to commence the Tafseer of the Holy Qur'ān in English. Before the programme, colour posters were put up on the notice boards of all the Masjids in Bradford and an announcement was made in the local Masjids and Madrasahs. Then, on Saturday 7th April 2001 after Maghrib Salāh, the gathering took place. Hundreds of brothers and sisters attended the programme, Alhamdulillāh. Many youngsters were attracted because the Tafseer was conducted in English and there was a question and answer session at the end. Sisters were also able to attend on the second floor of the Masjid.

In the first week, I discussed about the miracle of the Holy Qur'ān and in the second session I mentioned about the revelation of the Holy Qur'ān. These two talks were then transcribed and made into a book form and distributed nationwide for all to benefit, Alhamdulillāh. Also 1000 audio copies of each speech were made and sold in many Islamic bookstores. By the Grace of Allāh ﷻ, the Tafseer session proved to be very beneficial and soon it became a centre for seeking knowledge for many youngsters.

Alongside the Tafseer, I would also invite well-known scholars to enlighten the gathering each month. Alhamdulillāh, we were fortunate enough to invite many great scholars. Almost all of the renowned scholars of the UK and abroad visited the Masjid and blessed the audience with their lectures. Some of these pious scholars and speakers included:

1. Shaykh Yūsuf Motāla Sāhib
2. Shaykh Hāshim Sāhib
3. Shaykh Bilāl Sāhib
4. Shaykh As'ad Madani Sāhib ﷻ
5. Shaykh Arshad Madani Sāhib
6. Shaykh Anzar Shāh Sāhib ﷻ
7. Shaykh Muhi-Uddin Khān Sāhib
8. Shaykh Ubaidul Haque Sāhib ﷻ
9. Shaykh Ahmad Shafee Sāhib
10. Shaykh Abdul Mu'min Sāhib
11. Shaykh Noor Uddin Gohorpūri Sāhib ﷻ
12. Shaykh Mufti Shabbir Sāhib
13. Shaykh Abdur Raheem Sāhib
14. Shaykh Muhammad Saleem Dhorat Sāhib
15. Shaykh Muslih-Uddin Sāhib
16. Shaykh Mufti Sadr-Uddin Sāhib
17. Shaykh Riyādhul Haque Sāhib

18. Shaykh Ahmad Ali Sāhib
19. Shaykh Ibrāheem Madani Sāhib
20. Shaykh Noorul Islām Walipuri Sāhib

These are to name but a few of the thousands of other scholars who have attended functions and programmes in Tawakkulia Masjid, making it a centre point for the best of the Ulamā, by the Grace of Allāh ﷻ. The Tafseer sessions are still continuing until this day, Alhamdulillāh, with many other scholars contributing to it. Alongside myself these scholars also deliver the Tafseer in the Masjid:

1. Mufti Shihāb Uddin
2. Maulāna Abdul Aziz
3. Maulāna Dr Rafāqat Rasheed
4. Mufti Abdul Waheed

May Allāh ﷻ keep this Tafseer continuous until the Last Day and make it a means of our salvation and a means of rectification for the Muslim Ummah at large. Āmeen!

## The Opening of Al-Mu'min Primary School

My eldest son Muhammad Naeemul Islām and my daughter Aneesa Islām were attending the local primary school. I was determined to educate my children in an Islamic environment coupled with a strong academic approach. Therefore, one evening, I gathered my colleagues and adult students and put forward a plea regarding opening an Islamic school.

They were utterly surprised and confused! Due to the rigorous regulations involved in an Islamic school, they thought how could we even attempt to open one?! However, I was determined that it could happen with effort and I managed to convince the audience to agree with my pleas. After we all agreed, we managed to prepare an action plan and raise some funds for the necessary equipment and stationary. I appointed two students from the Ālim class, Maulāna Munir Azam and Maulāna Mahbub Khān to be in charge of the school with the co-operation of the other students.

Initially, it was very difficult to convince parents to send their children to an Islamic school which had to be paid for by their own hard-earned money. However, the parents accepted that it needed to be done. In the first year we started with Year 1 and 2 and only managed to enrol approximately 20 students.

In the midst of this struggle, I would keep the advice of Shaykh As'ad Madani Sāhib ﷺ in my mind. He had, for the last 20 years or more, continued to stress the importance of opening Islamic Schools. He would stress, "If you want to safeguard the Imān of your future generation, then open Islamic Schools otherwise if you send them to normal schools and they lose their Imān you will be held responsible."

Though it was a struggle to begin with, Al-Mu'min Primary School now has over 120 students and many on the waiting list, by the Grace of Allāh ﷻ. The school has been inspected several times by Ofsted resulting in good reports, Alhamdulillāh. I am very happy that all of my 3 children attended Al-Mu'min Primary School which opened up for them an Islamic ethos and moral upbringing.

## Introduction to the Ālim Course in the English Medium

A number of university graduates and professional workers approached me asking to be taught the Ālim Class in the English medium. Though I was extremely busy and overburdened with work,
I agreed, seeking the pleasure of Allāh ﷻ. I began to teach them
after the main Madrasah hours at 9pm in my local residence at 25
Spring Gardens. My first Theology course students included:

1. Maulāna Munir Azam
2. Maulāna Amjad Muhammad
3. Maulāna Badruddin Patel
4. Maulāna Yūsuf Māyat
5. Maulāna Hāfiz Azizur-Rahmān

I taught these students all of the books until Mishkāt class on a vol-
untary basis. Alhamdulillāh, this also greatly helped me with de-
veloping my English language. After introducing these classes I
barely had any time for myself.

## Teaching the Sihāh Sitta (6 Most Authentic Books of Ahādeeth)

When the Urdu Ālim class students were ready for their Bukhāri
year, I had intended to send them to Dārul Uloom Bury to be
taught by my Ustāds. However, due to the responsibilities of the
students, it was difficult for them to go all the way to Bury, so they
insisted that they be taught by me. Consequently, I began to search
for teachers to aid me in teaching the Sihāh Sitta, but this was to no

avail. So after consulting with my senior teachers regarding the matter, I began to teach the Sihāh Sitta all by myself. It was undoubtedly the busiest period of my teaching years and I was teaching over 20 different books every day! My typical daily timetable in those days was as follows:

After Fajr: Study and research
12-3.30pm: Teaching the Sihāh Sitta
4-8pm: Madrasah teaching
9-12am: Teaching the Theology Class (English medium)

Alhamdulillāh, Allāh ﷻ aided me in fulfilling this mammoth task with ease. All praise be to Allāh ﷻ.

**First Graduation Ceremony of JKN and the Dream of My Wife**

When Bukhāri Shareef was completed, I wanted to invite my beloved Shaykh for the first ever graduation ceremony of the institute. One morning I went to Dārul Uloom Bury to give the invitation which he readily accepted.

Remarkably, the very same morning my wife narrated to me a dream. She saw in a vision the following: The late Shaykh Muhammad Zakariyya Sāhib ﷺ (the Shaykh of Maulāna Yūsuf Motāla Sāhib) came to visit JKN. He stood outside the building facing the Madrasah then he raised his hands in supplication and prayed for the institute. The Madrasah began to illuminate and brighten up with light. Shaykh then stepped into the institute and called my wife asking her, "Where is Yūsuf?" My wife, thinking he was referring to our youngest son, replied, "He is with me." "Can I have

Yūsuf?" he asked. My wife said, "Let me dress him up properly." After dressing him up she put him forward to the Shaykh. He was very happy adding, "I want to rest with Yūsuf here." My wife then woke up.

When I went to invite my beloved Shaykh, Maulāna Yūsuf Motāla Sāhib, I related the dream to him. He was extremely pleased remarking, "Allāh ﷻ has accepted JKN and my Shaykh ( Shaykhul-Hadeeth Maulāna Muhammad Zakariyya Sāhib ﷫) has come for its graduation, waiting for me weeks in advance! Your wife thought it was her son Yūsuf but my Shaykh had meant his Yūsuf (me)!"

On the auspicious day of graduation, hundreds of people attended from all around the UK. It was a historical day for the people of Bradford. My beloved Shaykh spoke at length and using a subtle and indirect approach, he refuted many of the objections and questions which were raised against JKN and myself.

The four graduates who received the turban by my beloved Shaykh were:
1.   Maulāna Abdus-Salām
2.   Maulāna Qāri Yūsuf Makan
3.   Maulāna Qāri Ibrāheem Māyat
4.   Maulāna Abū Bakr

**Establishment of Olive Secondary School**

After the establishment of Al-Mu'min Primary School, I was constantly in search of a place to open a secondary school. After a long search we managed to secure a place for the school with a 3 year lease at 7 Cuncliffe Villas. Initially we began with Years 7 and 8 for the boys and later introduced the girls using a segregated system. I appointed my student Amjad Muhammad as head of the secondary school.

Along with this temporary building we managed to purchase, at the price of £400,000, what was previously Byron Primary School as the permanent location for Olive Secondary School. We initially attempted to obtain the premises with an Islamic mortgage but sadly, we were declined at the 11th hour. Consequently, we began to approach brothers and sisters seeking their help through Qardh Hasanah. Alhamdulillāh many brothers and sisters extended their funds very generously and what initially seemed impossible became possible! One extremely generous brother lent a grand sum of £125,000! May Allāh ﷻ grant him a great reward for his contribution and may He reward all of the brothers and sisters who donated with the best of rewards. Āmeen!

By the grace of Allāh ﷻ, Olive Secondary School has developed to become a great institute of learning for the young. The beauty of Olive Secondary School is that the Ālim course is offered alongside the National Curriculum subjects. Alhamdulillāh, we now have over 100 boys and approximately 200 girls studying at Olive with over 40 staff members. Many of our staff at Olive are graduates of JKN which helps to make smooth the day-to-day running of the institute.

## Launch of Al-Kawthar Welfare Foundation

After the devastating floods in Bangladesh in 2004 which swept virtually all over the country, I alongside some concerned Ulamā, decided to initiate a charity organisation called Al-Kawthar Welfare Foundation, in aid of the poor. Alhamdulillāh, later in February 2005, the charity became an officially recognised charity, working to alleviate the poverty of the most needy people.

## Trip to Bangladesh

In the year 2004, I had been contemplating visiting Bangladesh myself to observe the condition of the affected areas and the people. However, it was the closing days of the academic year at JKN and Kitābs had to be finished. Hence, taking a break for the trip was difficult to accommodate. I had to make swift preparations.

Initially, I planned to travel on Monday the 13th of September for the two revision weeks prior to exams at JKN, but due to the peak season there were no seats available. Mufti Junaid, my brother-in-law also decided to travel with me, and he booked both of our tickets for Saturday the 4th of September 2004. As it was an earlier date, it meant that I would really have to dedicate my few remaining days in the UK to my teaching. Remarkably, I had to complete 3 and a half Juz of Jalālayn Tafseer in just 2 days!

## Amazing Completion of Jalālayn

On the 30th of August 2004, it was a Bank Holiday and I called all of the Mishkāt students to arrive at 12pm so that we could derive maximum benefit from the time. Thus the class arrived and by the grace of Allāh ﷻ, that day, after over 7 hours, three Juz were complete! The remaining half a Juz was completed the following day. To celebrate this extraordinary feat, one of my students, Dr Ibrāheem Dadibhai invited the class to a lavishing dinner in which samosas, kebabs, keema, chicken, meat, fish, vegetables, salad, drinks and lassi were served! This special dinner was held at my residential place at 118 Manningham Lane at 11pm and it was a wonderful and memorable occasion. Everybody was full of praises of Allāh ﷻ for granting the Tawfeeq (ability) to have completed the entire Tafseer of the Holy Qur'ān in grand style!

## The Journey

As my departure day came closer, I became more and more busy, which had become a norm for me prior to taking journeys. On Friday the 3rd of September I bid farewell to my mother, brothers, sisters, relatives, colleagues, friends, and students and came home to prepare for the trip. However every time I began packing there would be a phone call or a guest arriving to bid me farewell!

Eventually, I managed to complete my preparations and after bidding farewell to my wife, children and close students who had stayed awake all night with me, I set off at 4:30am with Maulāna Abū Tāhir Sāhib, the Imām of Shāh-Jalāl Masjid in Leeds, and one of his Masjid Musallies who were both travelling with me. Then my close colleague and travel companion, Hāfiz Azizur-Rahmān Sāhib took the three of us first to Oldham, where we halted to perform Fajr Salāh in Jamā'at and had a light snack and tea. From Oldham, we travelled to Manchester Airport, taking my brother-in -law Mufti Junaid with us.

We boarded our flight from Manchester Airport to Heathrow Airport at 8:45am. After 35 minutes we landed at Heathrow where there was a waiting period of 4 hours before our next flight to Bangladesh via Bimān Airlines which was due for 2pm. In that duration of waiting I decided to utilize the time by briefly writing about my travel experiences. We boarded onto the plane at 1:30pm and it commenced its journey at its appointed time. Before the departure we performed our Zuhr Salāh in the prayer hall of Heathrow Airport. Asr, Maghrib and Ishā were performed in Jamā'at inside the plane, Alhamdulillāh. The flight lasted for 9 hours and at approximately 11:00pm and 5:00am local time we landed at the Zia International Airport in Dhaka.

Due to the recent floods in the country, we thought that we may experience delays at the airport but Alhamdulillāh, there were no problems. At Zia International Airport we performed our Fajr in the Airport prayer hall and a light breakfast and tea were served to all the passengers travelling by transit flight. We boarded on the plane for the domestic flight to Sylhet at 7:30am and after a short flight of 30 minutes, we landed at Osmani International Airport.

## Arrival in Bangladesh

Many people had come to the airport to welcome us including Maulānā Burhān Uddin, the younger brother of Maulānā Āshiqur-Rahmān - a great Muhaddith, Maulānā Shareef Uddin, an old classmate of Mufti Junaid Sāhib and a talented and hardworking young scholar, Abdul Hamid, my wife's maternal uncle, Monuhar Ali, my paternal uncle, Arab Ali, my maternal uncle, and other scholars, students and well-wishers. Customs at the airport only took a few minutes; thus, we were swiftly out of the airport.

Before setting off for Biswanath, my home town, we briefly stopped at two places: Mufti Junaid's in-laws' residence for some tea and dinner and then it was Maulānā Abū Tāhir Sāhib's stop so we bid farewell to him. Maulānā Shareef and others continued the journey with us to Duhal – the village in which I was born and had spent nearly seven years of my life.

Due to the severe floods, we travelled about 1 mile from the main roads to the village on boats, which was a new experience for me. My aunts, uncles, cousins and especially my paternal grandmoth-er, who was nearly 100 years old, were waiting in anticipation to see me, so when I arrived it was a joyous occasion. After the warm reception, I managed to take some much needed rest. I spent the next day meeting my relatives and enquiring about their health and circumstances etc.

## Visit to Two Great Institutes

On Monday 5th September I visited the two famous Islamic Institutes in Biswanath. The first was Jāmiah Madania which was established over 40 years ago by the great scholar Shaykh Ashraf Ali Sāhib Biswanathi ﷺ, President of Jamiatul Ulamā Bangladesh. We were fortunate enough to meet the principal and also the staff of the Madrasah. The second Madrasah was Jāmiah Muhammadiyah which was established in 1990 by the great scholar Shaykh Sādiqur -Rahmān Sāhib ﷺ. Though Shaykh Sādiq ﷺ was not present at the time, we managed to meet and benefit from the Shaykhul Hadeeth of the Madrasah, Shaykh Abdul Malik Sāhib, and there was a very warm reception from all of the staff. I was taken around both of the institutes and was very impressed by the standard of education as well as the buildings.

## Invitation to All

My uncle Mohram Ali who lives in Coventry, UK was also in Bangladesh at the time, so when he heard of my visit, he invited all the village people to a huge feast on Monday. Hundreds of people arrived at our village from morning till dusk. Mufti Junaid, Maulāna Shareef and I ate with the local scholars.

## Enquiries into Charity Work

One of my main objectives of my visit to Bangladesh was to observe the progress of Jāmia Zakariya Madrasah and Masjid Zakariya which I had decided to establish in my village. I met with the engineer and we discussed the work done so far and the work which was remaining. Alhamdulillāh, I was very pleased with the progress. I then visited the building site and met all of the workers and spoke to them regarding the importance of Salāh and ensuring the correction of their intentions when partaking in the construction of such a noble project.

After this, I had a meeting with my uncle Monuhar Ali regarding the progress and the finances. I was delighted to see the precise and minute detail regarding every penny spent so far for the construction work. In this meeting, I also discussed with my uncle regarding Al-Kawthar Welfare Foundation and about our intention to provide charity for the poor and needy. He generated a list of those people who were in need of help. Out of the 100 families he put forward, he selected a portion of them who were living in extreme poverty, and I requested him to distribute relief aid to them. There were also a few families who needed emergency shelter and clean water so I told my uncle to fulfill their needs with financial assistance.

## Travelling to Various Villages—Akil Pur

Here in Akil Pur, I took the opportunity to visit the grave of my beloved maternal grandfather, Abdul Jabbār and after this we bid farewell to all of the relatives and then set off for Banyachong.

## Banyachong

Banyachong is a huge village which has transformed into a town with 15 unions. It is a beautiful and elegant place and it is the hometown of my wife's maternal uncles. Here in Banyachong, I visited Dārul-Qur'ān, the Madrasah of my late father-in-law, Mufti Tālib Uddin Sāhib ﷺ. By this time the Madrasah had progressed immensely with 550 students and 21 staff members. Dārul-Qur'ān is one of the few Madrasahs in which the students are educated regarding the true spirit of Islām. I had the opportunity to meet the staff and listen to the recitation of the students. I was greatly impressed by the Qirāt, due to their correct Tajweed and beautiful tone.

The staff there were very co-operative, kind and hardworking and the students were busy preparing for their annual exams. I went to each class individually and spoke briefly to all the students regarding their studies, encouraging them to aim for the best. One thing which immensely impressed me was that the students were very dedicated to their books. I was amazed to see that throughout my tour around the institute I did not observe a single student who was messing about or sitting idly.

## Modhukhani

I then went on to visit Modhukhani where I stayed two nights. Modhukhani was the home of the late maternal grandfather of my wife, Qāri Abdul Qādir, a famous renowned Qāri who achieved the gold medal in the whole of the Sylhet division for his recitation. He taught Qirāt to thousands of students over a period of 40 years. He passed away at the age of 95 on the 5th of June 2004. After Fajr on Wednesday 8th September, we visited his grave.

## Satayhāl and Tājpur

The next day, we set off early to Satayhāl, Nabigonj, a town within the district of Habigonj. Satayhal is the hometown of my father-in-law. Here, we visited the graveyard of my father-in-law's father, who was a prominent scholar of his time. From there, our next destination was Tājpur which was about 10km away. Maulāna Abū Tāhir Sāhib had established a Madrasah in Tājpur. It was his earnest wish that I visit his Madrasah and perform the opening of the Masjid. There were many scholars, students and local residents waiting in anticipation for our arrival. I spent the night engaged in lengthy discussions with the Scholars and we slept only a few hours.

The next day I spoke before the Jumu'ah Salāh and then led the Jumu'ah Salāh and Khutbah. Maulāna Rūhul Ameen, a Muhaddith of Golmokafon and an eminent and talented scholar also addressed the gathering. Maulāna Rūhul Ameen is the son-in-law of Maulāna Abdul Aleem - my maternal uncle-in-law. In this way he was my brother-in-law. I deeply admired his character, knowledge and piety.

### Bolorampur

After Jumu'ah and lunch we headed for Molvi Bazār accompanied by Maulāna Abū Tāhir. We reached Bolorampur at about Maghrib time. It was my long yearning desire to visit this place and when I arrived, everyone came out in joy and happiness. Shaykh Muhammad Ali - the great Khalifah of Shaykh Husain Ahmad Madani ﷺ, was there waiting in anticipation for us. Shaykh was physically disabled and partially paralyzed and there were two students assisting him everywhere. He expressed great affection and love for me and he remarked, "My heart was yearning to see you." These words were so emotional that they brought tears to my eyes. Just to shake hands with the likes of pious saints like the Shaykh was a great honour for me. However, he spoke to me for a considerable amount of time, making me overjoyed to be in his honourable company. Food was served and was of many varieties, leaving me spellbound by the hospitality which I will never forget.

## Too Many Invitations!

That evening we were invited to Borūna, a village which became world famous due to the great saint, Shaykh Lutfur Rahmān, an eminent saint and pious sage. He was the great senior disciple of Shaykh Husain Ahmad Madani ﷺ. Shaykh Lutfur Rahmān passed away on Tuesday 17th of May 1977 and from my childhood I had the yearning to visit his village.

At this point it came to my knowledge that the relatives of my beloved teacher, Maulāna Abdul Jalil Sāhib, had sacrificed a goat in our honour which they planned to feed us for supper that evening. However, because we had already accepted the invitation at Borūna, we had no choice but to decline the invitation, although I felt extremely uneasy in refusing their kind gesture.

## Borūna

After bidding farewell to the many scholars and residents, Maulāna Wali-ur-Rahmān, the brother-in-law of Maulāna Abdul Jalil Sāhib, took us to Borūna. The first thing I did was visit the grave of Shaykh Lutfur Rahmān ﷺ. I felt a great spirituality in my heart and Shaykh's youngest son, Maulāna Wali-ur-Rahmān went beyond the limits in hospitality and affection towards us. We also met the other sons of Shaykh, and especially spent some time with his eldest son, Maulāna Khaleel-ur-Rahmān, who is at present the principal and Shaykh in place of his father. Maulāna Khaleel-ur-Rahmān has many disciples in Britain and Bangladesh. One of the Shaykh's sons, Maulāna Saeed-ur-Rahmān, who invited us for breakfast was a personality whom I had known for the last ten years due to his visit to the UK in 1996. Here in Bangladesh, during this visit, he was overjoyed to see me. We also met the Shaykh's prominent son, Mufti Fārooq Sāhib who established Jāmiah Madania, another Madrasah near Borūna. After spending Friday night in Borūna we set off for Banyachong.

On the way Mufti Fārooq Sāhib invited us to his Madrasah. I was deeply impressed by the piety, character and hospitality of Mufti Fārooq Sāhib who honoured us so excessively. Maulāna Abū Tāhir Sāhib, Mufti Junaid and I addressed the students and teachers at his Madrasah and we were able to observe the teaching methods there. Everybody welcomed us with great zeal and jubilance and many honourable words were said to us. After performing Du'ā and writing a short reference for the Madrasah, we continued on our journey to Banyachong.

The next day, I had a much needed rest whilst Mufti Junaid went with Maulāna Shareef and our driver Rubel to Sylhet to confirm our return tickets back to the UK for the 24th of September 2004.

## Sunamgonj

The following day, we had a program exclusively for the scholars in Sunamgonj which was very well organized by Maulāna Bahā Uddin. The program was scheduled for 12pm but due to the damaged roads, we arrived late at 1:30pm. Initially, we performed our Zuhr Salāh, and then Maulāna Abū Tāhir, Mufti Junaid and I addressed the enthusiastic gathering of approximately 200 scholars. I began by expressing my apology for the delay. I then praised and thanked Allāh ﷻ for allowing us to gather and for giving me the opportunity to meet so many scholars. I expressed my inability to speak in Bengali due to my education being imparted in the UK. My speech was concluded by a Du'ā and then food was served. After the gathering in Sunamgonj, we rushed back to Banyachong to stay the night there.

## Mymensingh

Our next destination was Mymensingh, the home town of our colleague Maulāna Shareef Uddin. Maulāna Shareef was a colleague and classmate of my brother-in-law Mufti Junaid and he had taken a three week vacation to host our trip and take us around the various places. It was his yearning desire that we visit his poor district.

Alhamdulillāh, my cousin brother Rubel was a very skilled driver and he managed all our travel needs from the day we landed at Sylhet airport. He was prepared to take us to Mymensingh though he was not certain regarding the route or how long the journey would be.

We set off for our journey to Mymensingh at 9.30am and estimated that we would be travelling for approximately 6 hours. However, we travelled for hours and hours, yet still we had not reached to our destination. Eventually we reached Netrokhuna, the small district of Mymensingh at 6pm. After performing Maghrib Salāh and having dinner, we travelled for a further hour or so. Then we halted and after parking our van in a safe place, we continued our journey by boat. By this time it was very dark and it was a new experience for me to travel for so long. After two hours on the boat we reached dry land. Here two rickshaws were ready waiting for us. We eventually reached our destination, at 11pm after 13 long hours of travelling! Many brothers were there waiting for us and they had been anticipating our arrival since the morning. We met the brothers and briefly spoke to the attendees. After supper and Ishā Salāh, we retired to bed.

The following day we walked around the flood affected area of Sirāmpur, which was the village of Maulāna Shareef. The flood was so severe that it left many houses demolished, wrecked and damaged. We shared the grief and concern with the people and were deeply moved by their love and affection.

After Zuhr, we met the local scholars and briefly spoke to the gathering. The local scholar, Maulāna Luqmān introduced me with a very high profile, which I definitely did not deserve. Nevertheless, I emphasized to them the importance of establishing elementary schools to educate the children from a young age. After the gathering, food was served by the host to all the attendees.

## A Special Wedding

For some time, Mufti Junaid and I were encouraging our colleague Maulāna Shareef to get married. He finally accepted and here in Mymensingh he went to visit his future in-laws with Mufti Junaid and Maulāna Luqmān. Mufti Junaid and I took on the responsibility to assist him financially with whatever was in our capacity to help with his wedding. The Nikāh took place the next morning after Fajr with simplicity and basic food. It was a wonderful and simple wedding to remember!

## Work of Al-Kawthar Welfare Foundation

By the grace of Allāh ﷻ, through Al-Kawthar Welfare Foundation, thousands of people have directly or indirectly benefitted including scholars, students of Deen, men, women and children.

Alhamdulillāh, Al-Kawthar has been able to establish two institutes of learning in Bangladesh. The first being Jāmiah Zakariyya, in my home village, Duhal, Biswanath, Sylhet and the second, Jāmiah Al-Kawthar, in the poor region of Netrokhuna. Alongside these, several Makātib (elementary schools) which are run in the morning, teaching basic Islamic education, have also been introduced in different parts of Bangladesh. Also through Al-Kawthar's student sponsorship project, over 50 students have become Hāfiz-e -Qur'ān, by the Grace of Allāh ﷻ.

Hundreds of small homes have also been constructed for people who had no shelter at all. Furthermore, approximately 100 tube wells were planted around the whole of Bangladesh, providing clean water for those who previously had no access to clean water.

Once, when relief workers were distributing sheets of metal to people to use as shelter, there was a woman who fell to the ground sobbing as she received her sheets. Everyone was shocked to see her so upset. After all, this should have been a moment of happiness! When they enquired as to why she was crying, she replied, "I am crying out of joy! I never dreamt that I will ever live under a proper shelter! Thanks to Mufti Sāhib!" Subhān-Allāh!

In another place, during my visit to Bangladesh, an old woman invited me to her home for a meal. When I entered, she presented me with a single glass of water saying, "This is my invitation to you. It is the first time I am drinking fresh clean water, thanks to Al-Kawthar." How happy I was to be partaking in an invitation which was so basic yet contained so much Barakah! Alhamdulillāh! May Allāh ﷻ reward greatly all of our sponsors and donors and may He give us the ability to continue to do the work for the charity. Āmeen!

### Al-Mu'min Bookshop

When I purchased the house at 118 Manningham Lane, it was a computer shop called Microma Computers. Initially, I considered converting it fully into a home. However, having realised that the former owner had spent £20,000 decorating the shop, I deliberated as to whether I should continue it as a shop, but this time, as an Islamic bookshop. The reason prompting me to open a shop was that it would enable me to engage in business which was a Sunnah of the beloved Prophet ﷺ, the Sahābah ؓ and our pious predecessors ؒ. Thus, I decided to open the bookshop with the intention of following these great personalities.

I was completely illiterate in business, therefore I was faced with many difficulties and hardships in opening up my own shop. Sadly, this lead to me being deceived and fooled by many suppliers and wholesalers due to my naivety and vulnerability. Despite this, I managed to utilise the back room and extension room for my main office, the Fatwa department and Al-Mu'min Magazine. The flat upstairs was used as my home where I lived with my family.

## My Re-Visit to Bangladesh and the Fatal Accident

For a few years we were involved in the work of Al-Kawthar Welfare Foundation in Bangladesh and at the end of March in 2009, I decided to visit the country to observe the charity work taking place there. I set off for this fateful journey from Birmingham Airport via Emirates Airlines accompanied by my colleague Maulāna Zubair Sufi and my student Mujibur-Rahmān. We were to meet my brother in-law, Mufti Junaid, in Bangladesh as he was travelling on a different flight.

When we landed at Dhaka Airport, many colleagues and well-wishers had come to welcome us. We travelled to many places in Bangladesh, visiting and observing the many Islamic institutes over there. During these eventful days, I delivered many lectures, therefore I hardly had any sleep or rest. Nevertheless, invitations were still flooding in from all corners of Bangladesh!

It was the fateful day on Saturday 4th April 2009, when after Fajr, I conducted a Dars (lesson) of Bukhāri Shareef in Dārur-Rashād Madrasah (a famous institute which was founded by Shaykh Abul-Hasan Nadwi ﷺ). After the Dars I was shown around the various departments of the institute. I was especially impressed with the language department in which students were able to deliver speeches fluently in Arabic, English, Urdu and Bangla.

Thereafter, Shaykh Junaid Al-Habib, a prominent lecturer in Bangladesh, invited me to visit his institute Qāsimul-Uloom. Due to the lack of time, this visit was reduced to a mere few minutes, after which I consumed a quick breakfast, then swiftly set off for our next journey to visit Netrokhuna which was a drive of over 8 hours.

**An Unusual Dream**

We began our journey from Dhaka at approximately 10am and then halted at a service station to perform our Zuhr Salāh. The most peculiar thing happened at this service station. My student Mujibur-Rahmān approached me to inform me that his mother had told him that she had seen a dream in which we had an accident. Mujibur-Rahmān suggested to me that we should not travel further, bearing in mind the dream. I pondered over the situation and came to the conclusion that we could not postpone our journey based on a mere dream. Therefore, I replied to him, "Pray to Allāh ﷻ for our safe journey." However Allāh ﷻ, the Best of planners had another plan for us.

We continued with our journey towards our final destination Netrokhuna. Due to extreme fatigue from my busy schedule of the previous days, I fell asleep on the way. I was fast asleep in the van when all of a sudden, to my utter astonishment and horror, I heard my colleagues and people outside shouting and shrieking! I could hear people, with voices full of panic, screaming that we had an accident! I thought it was all just a nightmare as I was still drifting in between sleep and wakefulness. However, with a big jerk, I woke up and looked back to realise with utter shock that we were no longer on the road...

My eyes grew wide and my breath caught in my throat for I was being plummeted around in the van as it began tumbling into a ditch! Everybody was terrified and shocked and there was a strange silence as we were all rendered speechless. My student, Mujibur-Rahmān broke the silence with a fearful voice, "Ustād, we are going!" I turned my face towards him and saw blood gushing forth from his forehead. Seeing his distress, I took my hand and placed it on his forehead and said in an emotional voice, "Don't worry Mujibur-Rahmān, recite the Kalimah and all the rest of you brothers. If we are departing from this temporary abode, then let us go with Imān!" I then recited the Kalimah.

## A Second Strange Incident

At this critical time, a second strange thing occurred. My mobile phone began to ring and as I pressed the button to answer the call, I heard the trembling voice of my beloved mother echoing, "My beloved son, have you had an accident. Are you ok?" I answered,

"Yes mum, we have had an accident but we are ok. But how did you know?" She replied, "I woke up suddenly after seeing a dream in which I saw that you had an accident. So I insisted Rehāna (my youngest sister) to call you." I was amazed at this because in England it was only 9am in the morning of Saturday and this was a very unusual time for her to be phoning. After terminating the phone call, I became unconscious and subsequently, had no idea what was happening. Allāh ﷻ knows best what happened in that interim because sadly, people were seen crowded over us and our mobile phones were stolen from our injured bodies.

## Regaining Consciousness

When I gained consciousness, I thought that I had left this world and gone to the next abode. I could not recognise anything. I thought about what I could present to my Allāh ﷻ, that would gain for me my salvation. I pondered deeply but could think of nothing! I began to cry with regret but then all of a sudden, I remembered something with which I could comfort myself, "O' Allāh ﷻ, I present the JKN institute as my means of salvation. Please accept it!"

After some time, I woke up hearing sounds of sobbing, screaming and shouting. I realised that I was in a hospital bed surrounded by nurses and doctors. My colleagues gazed towards me with tearful eyes. It was a painful encounter.

**My Concern for Salāh**

For the first time, I recognized that I could not move. My bones and ribs were moving from one side to another. I was motionless on my stretcher bed. Suddenly, I asked somebody to bring me a stone. He asked me the reason for such a strange request. I responded, "The sun is nearly setting. I need to perform my Asr Salāh with Tayammum." He looked at me with utter amazement and shock and exclaimed, "Mufti Sāhib, we are worried about your life and you are worried about your Salāh!" I promptly replied, "Yes brother, I do not want to meet my Lord with a Salāh Qadhā (debt) on my head." So they brought me a stone and I wiped my face and hands with it. I then performed my two Rak'ats Qasr of Asr Salāh lying on the stretcher. Only then was I relieved and content.

**A Special Visitor**

Whilst I was in hospital, news of my accident gradually began to spread to every corner of Bangladesh and abroad. One old woman in a state of panic and shock, entered into the hospital and enquired, "Where is Mufti Sāhib Hudhoor? Is he alive?! Is he ok?!" Frantically, she went from bed to bed, searching for me. When she was eventually directed towards my bed, she looked at me with tears in her eyes and taking a deep sigh said, "Alhamdulillāh, everything is ok then."

By Allāh, I had no idea who this woman was or what had prompted her to come! I was told that she was one of our recipients of the

Al-Kawthar Welfare Foundation. I was amazed and rendered emotional by her visit. It reminded me of the time at the Battle of
Uhud, when a woman Sahābi was informed that her father, brother and son had all been martyred in the battle. Her reaction was to
run out to enquire about the safety of the Holy Prophet ﷺ. Though
she had lost so many family members, she was more concerned
about the well-being of the Holy Prophet ﷺ! Subhān-Allāh! When
she saw him she exclaimed, "All calamities are easy after seeing
the Holy Prophet ﷺ!"

## Assessment of Injuries

Out of all the people who had been in the accident, I was the most
severely injured. My student Mujibur-Rahmān had a shoulder injury and he was lying on the bed next to mine. Within hours the
hospital became overcrowded with scholars, students and well-
wishers. There were scholars who had arrived from Dhaka and
they decided that I should be admitted into Ibn Sinā Hospital - one
of the top hospitals in Dhaka.

The doctors took a scan to ascertain the extent of my injuries. The
results were not positive. It was at this point that I realised the seriousness of my wounds. The pain in my body was deeply intolera-
ble and I was actually screaming out of pain continuously. I was
given injection after injection to relieve the pain but it just continued to increase. I was unable to move and my life, for a moment,
seemed to be coming to an end.

At this critical juncture, my colleague and cousin Maulāna Juhair
took care of me. He remained at my side through thick and thin, 24

hours round the clock. His hospitality, care and affection reminded me of the affection of my mother.

## Transfer From Hospital

I was in the hospital ward for a few days but being hospitalised in Bangladesh was not cheap. The bill ran into Lacs. Hence after consultation with the senior scholars of Dhaka, I was transferred to Shaykh Junaid Al-Habib's institute, Qāsimul-Uloom. Though I had left the hospital, the doctors continued to visit me with the relevant medicine and advice.

News, by then had spread far and wide and the Madrasah became a central point for many people to visit me. All of my relatives as well as well-wishers poured into Dhaka. There were extraordinary scenes of mixed emotions, hope, kindness and regret. In addition, 24 hours around the clock, there would be great scholars from around Bangladesh flocking into the institute. The air was filled with emotion, sentiments and affection.

## Restlessness and Confusion of the People

Whilst I was bedridden in Dhaka, some misleading information was being relayed to the people. Not knowing the extent of my injuries, some people spread the news that I had become completely paralysed! Some received the information that I was now wheelchair bound for the rest of my life! During all of this, I would continue to reassure people who rang or came to visit. I would inform them that I was fine, Alhamdulillāh, and that they should continue to pray for me.

One of my close friends and students, Maulāna Ātif Anwar once phoned and begged, "Please Mufti Sāhib, inform me of your actual state of injury. There is so much confusion regarding it in the UK." I comforted him saying, "I'm completely fine. Convey the message to everyone." Unfortunately, the message did not seem to be passed on successfully.

### Far-Sightedness of My Beloved Wife

My wife phoned me unexpectedly. To my surprise, she began asking me a very intricate and contradictory question, regarding a Hadeeth of Bukhāri which I had taught before my accident. I was shocked and bewildered that even my own wife did not seem to comprehend my condition! Though I answered the question to the best of my ability, the thought would continue to dominate my mind that how could my wife be so oblivious, though she is so intelligent! It was only later on when I came back to the UK that I discovered the far-sightedness of my wife…

One day she approached me and announced, "O' Abū Naeem! That day, when I asked you regarding the Hadeeth of Bukhāri, I know for sure that you must have been startled but let me disclose the reason for it. The only purpose was to give me peace of mind that Allāh ﷻ had kept your intellect intact! Due to the fact that many false and mixed rumours had been spreading everywhere, I wanted to reassure myself that you were fully conscious and sober in terms of your intellect and memory! Alhamdulillāh, I cried out in happiness that you were ok!" I stared at her in utter amazement and became lost in deep thought. May Allāh ﷻ bless her life and increase her knowledge and intellect. Āmeen!

## Hospitality and Kindness of Shaykh Junaid Al-Habib

Whilst staying at the institute of Shaykh Junaid Al-Habib, the degree of his hospitality and kindness was immeasurable! Not only was he accommodating a seriously injured patient, but he was also playing host to the multitudes of visitors. On a daily basis, dozens of people would eat from the Dastarkhān (table-cloth) of Shaykh Junaid Al-Habib. There would be a variety of dishes, fruits, vegetables and drinks available there at all times. I was being spoon-fed by his son-in-law Maulāna Kamāl and my colleague Maulāna Juhair and all of this continued for over a fortnight. May Allāh ﷻ grant the Shaykh the best of rewards in this life and the next. Āmeen!

## Arrangements to Return to the UK

After some time, plans were made for me to return home to the UK so that I could receive better treatment and care there. In my current state, there was a concern that I would not be allowed to travel. Therefore, I booked business class tickets on an Emirates flight, costing me over a thousand pounds. I was very apprehensive about travelling in my condition and it felt like it would be a mission impossible for me. I was completely unable to move by myself but my colleague Maulāna Zubair Sufi reassured me that he would assist me all the way home.

On the planned day of the journey, an ambulance was booked to take me to the airport. But to everybody's shock, at this critical juncture, all of a sudden my condition severely deteriorated! I was in acute pain. I could not tolerate it and I was fearful that travelling would be too difficult for me, so I refused to take the journey. I requested my brother-in-law to call my wife Marzia to Bangladesh so that she can look after me.

There was chaos amongst my colleagues and well-wishers. Although they were saddened to part with me, they knew that it was for the best that I go home. They began to cry, pleading with me, "Please Mufti Sāhib! Try your best! You need to go to the UK for your treatment!" I was in severe pain and I was completely confused. I did not know what to do. Therefore I did the only thing that I could, which was to place my trust completely upon Allāh ﷻ having hope that He would help me. I indicated to the people to proceed towards the airport.

At the airport, the people bid farewell to me by embracing and kissing my forehead, all the while sobbing and weeping. I was so moved by their sentiments and the demonstration of pure brotherhood, that I could not hold back my own tears and I sobbed out of love and emotion.

### An Unexpected Phonecall

On our way to the airport, there was a sister who phoned my colleague and pleaded to him to pass the phone on to me, so she could speak to me. He explained to her that it was not an ideal time for me to talk. However she persisted, so my colleague held the phone at my ear and I asked who the sister was. The only reply I could hear was the sound of sobbing from the other end. After some time she withheld her sobs and answered, "I am that unfortunate woman who could not fulfil the hospitality of a scholar of your calibre." Tears began to roll down my cheeks and I consoled her, explaining that she had done more than I ever expected or dreamt of. Suddenly, another sister took the phone and a similar conversation was exchanged. I asked them both repeatedly who they were and eventually they replied, "We are the two wives of Shaykh Junaid Al-Habib." Subhān-Allāh! How much they did for me and how humble they were regarding their tireless support! They ended the call requesting repeatedly for Du'ās. May Allāh ﷻ bless their lives and keep them both happy always, and may Allāh ﷻ give them a befitting reward for their hospitality. Āmeen!

## My Journey Back to the UK

When the airport officials saw me in a wheelchair with a neck collar and braces on my body, they took pity upon my condition. They immediately put me on the plane and throughout the journey, I was lying on a sofa, in the business class section, with very caring staff who took good care of me, Alhamdulillāh.

When I landed at Birmingham Airport, many colleagues came to receive me and a special car was hired by my two students – Maulāna Rizwān and Maulāna Irfān to take me back to Bradford as comfortably as possible. On reaching Bradford, it was past midnight but many people were still awake, waiting anxiously to see my condition. My beloved mother caught one glimpse of me in the wheelchair and she immediately fainted. But when she regained her senses, she sobbed uncontrollably, whilst grasping me in a hug. Everybody was incredibly grieved to see me in my condition.

I was taken to my bedroom on top of the shop and when news spread of my return, people began to flock. Due to the crowd of visitors, an announcement was made in the Masjid the next day, regarding visiting times. There was one time for the general public and one for scholars and students. Emotional and sentimental scenes were witnessed throughout the day.

My father-in-law was also critically ill at the time but despite this, he arrived in the morning to visit me. Seeing my pitiful condition, he cried like a child. Scholars, students, friends, colleagues and the general public could not hold back their tears during their visits. The whole time I would comfort everyone, hiding my own tears, though deep down, my heart was also tearing.

**Admission into Hospital**

After consulting with my GP and colleague Maulāna Dr Rafāqat Rasheed, an ambulance was called on Thursday morning and I was admitted into the Bradford Royal Infirmary. All the necessary scans and medical checks were carried out, revealing the extent of my injuries. The reports showed that bones in my neck, ribs and back were broken and damaged. Furthermore, there were also major problems with my internal body. I was strictly instructed not to make any movements until surgery would take place.

That night, the doctors and surgeons were discussing the seriousness of my condition with the specialists at St. James Hospital in Leeds. They were trying to arrange a slot where they could carry out an emergency operation on my bones to re-structure them. Throughout the night I could hear them on the phone but nothing was finalised.

The following day, the consultant came and assessed my reports. He was not happy with what he saw, "This is a serious accident. We cannot say whether you will survive or not. It is possible that you will have a blood clot or develop Pneumonia. Your condition is very serious. Do you want us to call a Muslim Chaplain to sympathise with you?"

I took a deep sigh as it seemed that my life would be coming to an end. I pondered over my situation and remarked, "It's ok, I will sympathise myself. All my life I have sympathised with people. It is time that I, for once, sympathise with myself. I have my God, Allāh ﷻ Who will look after me. But one thing I would like to mention is, this accident took place nearly 3 weeks ago. If anything drastic or critical had to happen, it would have happened then. But I have high hopes in my Allāh ﷻ, that I will be ok."

The consultant stared at me in amazement and paused. He then exclaimed, "Yes, this is a brilliant point! You seem very intelligent." Then he scribbled down a lot of information on his file and told me to rest for the remainder of the day.

After Jumu'ah Salāh that day, special Du'ās were made for me in Tawakkulia Masjid and other Masājid across the UK. After the Jumu'ah Salāh, immediately people began rushing towards the hospital. There was a wave of people who had come from all across the UK including many relatives from London, Coventry, Oldham and Leeds. The hospital staff became uneasy and frustrated with the masses of people so they had to restrict the number of visitors. Many people who had travelled a long way to see me, were only afforded a quick glance and a wave of their hands, before having to leave due to the restrictions. I was still in bitter pain, so I would just look at everybody whilst replying to their Salāms. My wife and other relatives would take turns to remain by my side until night time.

## Back Home

The next day, a nurse came and I was very unexpected to be informed that I would be sent home that day, after having my neck collar and braces put on. I was utterly amazed that I would be allowed home so soon, without needing surgery! I praised Allāh ﷻ and after the necessary care, I was driven home by an ambulance. My family, relatives, friends and local residents were astonished and they asked why I was sent home so quickly. I replied, "I do not know. Only Allāh ﷻ knows!"

During my stay in the hospital, it was a unique experience to be staying with people who suffered from Dementia as I was unable to sleep throughout the night. Now I had the opportunity to rest properly. My close friend and colleague Waseem Rāja from Dewsbury (may Allāh ﷻ reward him greatly), kindly gifted me an electronic bed to assist me in my recovery, which I found very convenient, Alhamdulillāh. I would lie down on my bed without a pillow with the neck collar and braces fastened on at all times.

When the people received the news of my return home, it was as though it had become the day of Eid for them! Throughout the day and night there would be continuous visitors coming and sympathising with me.

## Love and Kindness of the Community

I had never experienced so much warmth and affection from my community as I did at that time. People from various backgrounds – elders, men, women, children, scholars and students visited me with gifts, food and well-wishing cards. Brothers and sisters would make it their daily routine to wake up for Tahajjud and supplicate to Allāh ﷻ. Khatm Qur'ān, Sūrah Yāseen, Khatm Shifā, Khatm Yūnus, Khatm Bukhāri and Du'ās in different Masājid were regularly carried out. Brothers and sisters would donate money and gold to charity and sacrifice animals, all for the sake of Allāh ﷻ. All of these were carried out for my speedy recovery. There would be stacks of fruits and vegetables, sweets and flowers surrounding me. Each person consoled and sympathised with me and prayed with a tearful eye and a painful heart.

The beautiful and compassionate attitude of my community and friends, students and scholars kept my spirit high and it made me forget about my critical condition. For the next 6 months I remained bed-ridden performing my Salāh in a lying position.

## Recommencement of Dars and Daily Activities

After a week into my recovery in the UK, I decided to resume my teaching. Though well-wishers and close friends were uneasy with

the idea, they eventually conceded and agreed after seeing my passion and yearning to continue to teach and impart the knowledge
which Allāh ﷻ has endowed upon me. Due to my severe weakness
and lack of mobility, I called the final year students to my accommodation, where they would have to be taught around my bed.
The sisters in the class, including my wife, would sit behind the
veil on one side and the brothers would sit in front of my bed.

I was so weak, that I could not lift or raise anything, including my
Bukhāri Shareef Kitāb. Therefore, I would have the relevant pages
photocopied each day. At night I would instruct my wife to place
the relevant commentaries in front of me on the bed and I would
turn the pages over to study the relevant sections in preparation
for the following day's lesson. This continued until the end of the
academic year. By the grace of Allāh ﷻ, we were able to complete
Saheeh Al-Bukhāri with ease in the most unique of environments,
around my bed! People could not believe it and would enquire
how I did it. I replied, "It is only through the sheer grace of Allāh
ﷻ and nothing else."

In addition to this, editing of Al-Mu'min Magazine, compiling of
JKN books, the Fatwa Department, guidance and counselling,
scholars meetings, Masjid meetings, and local community meetings would all, also take place in the upstairs of my shop. In fact,
marriages were even solemnised around my bed! Subhān-Allāh!
Allāh ﷻ helps in ways we cannot even imagine!

During this period, I would ponder over the life of Sayyidunā
Ayyūb ﷺ, who was afflicted with severe illness for over 7 years

and Sayyidunā Imrān Ibn Husain ﷺ, who was bed-ridden for over 34 years! Subhān-Allāh! This would bring motivation and hope into my life, at a time when I was going through severe hardship.

## Call for a Check-up

In that interim, I made several attempts to contact the hospital for a scan and check-up but I did not receive a response from them. This continued for about 6 months, until the arrival of the holy month of Ramadhān. Then one morning, I unexpectedly received a letter, calling me in for a scan at St. James' Hospital in Leeds. After a scan was taken, it was assessed by a consultant called Mr Rao. He scrutinised my scans, alongside my previous ones, with a puzzled expression. His eyes would go back and forth, from the two scans and then to me. All the while he looked surprised and amazed! I could sense from his behaviour that he was in shock. Finally, he commented, "It seems everything has healed and your bones have come to their original places! You have got away with a light touch!" I could not believe what I was hearing! It could only be a miraculous recovery with the help of Allāh ﷻ! Smiling at the doctor, I praised Allāh ﷻ and exclaimed, "There is a Deity in the Heavens Who did all this. All praise be to Him!" He just smiled and said, "You can live a normal life." I thanked him and left the hospital.

## Back to Normal Life

Although I had a green light from the hospital, I still needed to keep the braces and neck collar on for some time. For a year or more I continued performing my Salāh in a sitting posture at home and in the Masjid. I now look back at my life of those months and it seems like a dream. I cannot thank Allāh ﷻ enough for what He has bestowed me with. As I said then and I say now, this extraordinary recovery was only through the sheer grace of Allāh ﷻ and the exclusive Du'ās and kindness of the thousands of well-wishers and friends from across the globe. Nobody could believe that there would be a natural recovery from my critical condition. It was nothing but a miraculous recovery! May Allāh ﷻ reward my well-wishers immensely for all of their help and Du'ās during my critical illness. Āmeen!

### Move to No. 2 Cornwall Place

I was residing at the top of the Al-Mu'min Bookshop for approximately eight years. Although I had no apparent problems there, it was difficult for my wife and children. There was no lounge or sitting room there. Hence, it was difficult for them to have any real privacy. Many a time, my wife and children would be confined to the bedroom. Consequently to ease the situation, I decided to purchase No.2 Cornwall Place. By the Grace of Allāh ﷻ and with the help of close friends and relatives, I was able to attain an Islamic mortgage.

I moved in to my new residence after refurbishment in Ramadhān 2010. I expressed my gratitude to Allāh ﷻ for enabling me to accommodate my family in a more suitable living quarter. I also marvelled at my wife's patience. Throughout the eight years living on top of a shop, though it was a real struggle for her, she never complained nor nagged. May Allāh ﷻ reward her for her patience and steadfastness. Āmeen!

## Visit to Darul-Uloom Bury and My Shaykh's Desire to Open More Educational Establishments

After my recovery, I visited Dārul-Uloom Bury to meet my respected teachers, especially my beloved Shaykh, Maulāna Yūsuf Motāla Sāhib. It was near the balcony of the prayer hall, that I met him and after finding out about my health, he made enquiries regarding the number of students studying at our schools. I informed him that we had approximately 300 students in our secondary school. He then asked how many were in Maulāna Irshād's girls' school. I reported that he had approximately 100 girls there. Having registered the information, he remarked, "You have provided schools for only 1% of the Muslim children, especially girls. You need to open more schools!"

I excused myself by mentioning the huge amount of Qardh Hasanah we had for Olive and my recent weak health. He passionately said, "This will gradually be paid off! Open more schools and Madrasahs! Utilise all the graduates of Bury and JKN and other institutes. Open as many as you can!" There was a degree of passion and eagerness in his tone, which left a lasting impact on me. During my bed-ridden days, I had made a strong resolution not to proceed towards any new project, as I felt I already had much work to do with the many current projects. However my beloved Shaykh's intentions and views proved to be different, so I knew I would need to reassess my commitments.

## The Miraculous Intervention of Allāh ﷻ and the New JKN Building

After my visit to Dārul-Uloom Bury, I was reflecting on matters, when a close friend and colleague Hāfiz Azizur Rahmān approached me asking, "Are you wanting to purchase a Madrasah or school?" I enquired as to the whereabouts and the price. I was amazed to hear that it was just around the corner from Manningham Lane and the price had been reduced twice for a quick sale. After viewing the premises, I submitted an offer and remarkably the following day, I received a phone call, informing me that my offer had been accepted! I was astonished and began to think about how we would fund it. I immediately made a list of friends, relatives and students and asked for Qardh-Hasanah.

It was an uphill struggle but I continued to pray to my Allāh ﷻ for His assistance. To my delight, many brothers and sisters contributed without me even approaching them! There were even brothers and sisters donating who had previously been against the work of JKN and myself! I expressed my gratitude to Allāh ﷻ for this miraculous help.

Alhamdulillāh, the building on Clifton Street, which was the former Carlton Mills, was eventually purchased and the renovation work of the first three floors have been successfully completed, accommodating the senior students of JKN, who have already been transferred to the new premises.

## Glad Tidings Regarding the New JKN Premises

I was in two minds as to which students would be transferred over to the new premises and which students would remain in the old building at Spring Gardens. In the month of Ramadhān in 2012, a student of JKN saw a dream, in which there was a big gathering for sisters taking place in the new premises. An announcement was made that Sayyidah Khadeejah ﷜ would be arriving at the Jalsa. This ran a spirit of jubilation in the gathering. After hearing about the dream I instantly said, "Allāh ﷻ, through this dream, has made the decision. We will move the senior students to the new premises and the junior students will remain in the old building."

## Hajj 2012

Alhamdulillāh, I have been able to perform my Hajj this year in 2012. It is here in Madeenah Munawwarah, that I decided to complete my autobiography, which I had begun the previous year, when I came to the Holy Lands for Hajj. Alhamdulillāh, I have been sitting here in the serene tranquillity of the Masjid of our beloved Rasūl ﷺ, between Maghrib and Ishā, utilising this time to write my autobiography. I hope that through the blessings of the Holy Lands and the Holy Masjid of our beloved Prophet ﷺ, Allāh ﷻ will make this work a means of inspiration for me and for the Muslim Ummah. I only write this in the hope that it may benefit people and not for any personal glory – Allāh ﷻ forbid. I pray that Allāh ﷻ accepts my humble efforts and I pray for the success of the Muslims. Āmeen!

# Part 3 - Glad-Tidings & Inspirational Incidents

## Dreams and Glad-Tidings

### 1. Encouragement During my Hifz

When I was memorizing the Holy Qur'ān, I was a young boy and at times during this period, the task seemed so great that it felt like a huge mountain to climb. I would feel as though I may never get there, however Allāh ﷻ in His infinite wisdom, knew that it would be achieved though I did not. He showed me signs through dreams, to encourage me to keep striving until I reached my goal.

I began my memorisation with the 30th Juz, which felt a mammoth task in itself! Once I finally completed this, I began from the beginning of Sūrah Al-Baqarah, "Alif Lām Meem..." At this point reaching the end of the 29th Juz, to complete the entire Qur'ān, felt like a lifetime away. It was at that time, when I saw myself in a dream, reading the very last verses of the 29th Juz. I knew that this was a sign from Allāh ﷻ to encourage me that eventually, I would reach my goal.

At another point during my Hifz, I saw another vision in which my house was filled with a magnificent Nūr (light). I was heading up each flight of stairs, trying to reach the source of the Nūr. There were people following me and I was telling them that if they wanted to meet Allāh ﷻ, they should come with me. I woke up feeling a spirit of encouragement and motivation to keep striving hard with my Hifz. Alhamdulillāh, these dreams bore fruit and despite all the hardships and struggles, I managed to complete my Hifz by the Grace of Allāh ﷻ.

## 2. Dreaming of the Holy Prophet ﷺ, Sayyidunā Abū Bakr ؓ and Sayyidah Ā'ishah ؓ Visiting JKN

A student of JKN saw a dream in which the Holy Prophet ﷺ, Sayyidunā Abū Bakr ؓ and Sayyidah Ā'ishah ؓ entered JKN's Jamāt Khāna (prayer hall).

All the sisters gathered around Sayyidah Ā'ishah ؓ. The Holy Prophet ﷺ and Sayyidunā Abū Bakr ؓ sat with the brothers. One of our teachers at JKN, Maulāna Zakariyya Pandor, was instructed by the Holy Prophet ﷺ to recite the Holy Qur'ān. After he read, I was instructed to recite, and then it was the turn of Sayyidunā Abū Bakr ؓ to recite. The recitations were beautiful and melodious. Thereafter, our beloved Prophet ﷺ, himself recited in the most sweetest of voices. He concluded the Qirat Majlis by gifting everyone in the gathering with Itr (perfume). As a token of thanks, and in following the generosity of our beloved Prophet ﷺ in the dream, I gifted all of the students and staff at JKN with bottles of Itr. May Allāh ﷻ bless everyone with His Grace and Mercy and may He enable us to receive the Shafā'at (intercession) of our beloved Prophet ﷺ. Āmeen!

## 3. The Reckoning on the Day of Judgement

I once had a dream that it was the Day of Judgement. The people were divided into various groups. There was a section for businessmen, a section for wealthy people, a section for scholars and so on and so forth. Everybody were sobbing, crying, sweating and trembling. I saw myself stood amongst the group of scholars. We were waiting in rows to be assessed. I was in a state of panic and shock.

Each person was taken individually, into a big hall at his turn, by the angels and a certificate of Maqbool (accepted) or Mardood (rejected) was given to them. I could hear the announcements as clear as the day. Sometimes the Maqbool certificate would be granted and other times it was Mardood. Whenever one of the scholars would receive the Maqbool certificate, his face would light with joy and he would be escorted towards Paradise. If the Mardood certificate was issued, the scholar's face would become overcast with gloom and he would be dragged towards the Hellfire. Seeing all of this made me feel utterly terrified and anxious as all the while, I waited for my turn.

Eventually my turn came. As I went into the hall, my breathing stopped and I began to think about all of my sins. I felt that I would surely fail. An angel pressed a button, on what seemed to be a computer and the screen became completely blank for some time. I closed my eyes out of fear and my breathing became heavier and faster. Suddenly, an announcement was made, "Maqbool! Advance towards Paradise!" I opened my eyes with a deep sigh of relief and ran towards the direction which I was instructed.

I traversed some distance, when I heard a group of people began calling, "Mufti Sāhib! Wait for us!" Without looking back, I replied in a state of panic, "I have no time. I need to go!" They continued to plead with me, "Do you know the percentage you have achieved? It is more than enough to include us in it. Please help us!" I replied nervously, "I don't know anything, let me reach there, then I will see."

At this point I woke up from my sleep in panic and shock. I was completely immersed in sweat and my duvet, bed and clothing were all wet. May Allāh 🕮 save us from the punishment of the grave and the Hellfire. Āmeen!

## 4. Gateway to Paradise

A mother saw a dream that there was a staircase from the JKN Madrasah which extended high into the heavens. The doors of JKN lead people to the heavens and I was near the door, calling people to come towards it.

## 5. Miraculous Dream of a Person Serving in a Prison

Many years ago, a brother who was serving a prison sentence saw a dream whilst he was in prison. He saw himself being directed towards a scholar who was responding to all of his queries and problems. He woke up with no idea of who this scholar was.

After being released from prison, this brother would contact me regularly for guidance and advice. After my fatal accident, he travelled from Birmingham to visit me and it was the first time he actually saw what I looked like. He stared at me for a long time. Then he narrated his dream exclaiming, "The scholar I saw in the dream was yourself! After being released from the prison, I have been constantly in contact with you via phone but never saw you face to face. This is the first time I have seen you and I remembered my dream. Also Mufti Sāhib you are the only Shaykh who answers the call! Jazāk-Allāh for everything!"

## 6. Under the Shade of Allāh's 🕌 Throne

One sister saw a dream in which it was the Day of Judgement. People were all rushing around and Allāh's 🕌 throne descended. The sister saw herself on the right hand side of Allāh's 🕌 throne with my wife, Apā Marzia and my son, Yūsuf and they were all waiting for me. It was said that I was gathering all of my students and friends under the shade of Allāh's 🕌 throne. The three of them were praying to Allāh 🕌 that He gives me the Tawfeeq to collect as many people as possible.

## 7. Dream of the Holy Prophet's 🕌 Generosity

I once dreamt that the Holy Prophet 🕌 alongside many of the great Sahābah 🕌 and scholars were visiting our local area. Everywhere people were talking in anticipation about this great occasion. It seemed that I was not initially informed. However, once I learned of the honourable visit, I rushed to the location and waited there in anticipation to see my beloved Prophet 🕌.

The venue for the illustrious occasion was the park of Springfield Place and Thurnscoe Road. Multitudes of people rushed to the area and many took sleeping bags and packed lunches in preparation for the wait. I arrived with one my friends and told him that he could take rest while I kept watch for the Ziyārat. I assured him that I would immediately wake him when the Holy Prophet ﷺ arrived. Thus my friend rested, whilst I remained awake, and then he woke up and told me to rest. I replied, "I am not going to rest until the Ziyārat."

All of a sudden, the beloved Prophet ﷺ approached amongst a group of scholars. He was simply dressed with a turban on his head and a staff in his hand. I immediately recognised him and ran towards him to become the first to meet him. On reaching him, I looked up into his blessed face and extended my hand, as the Holy Prophet ﷺ drew out his blessed hands. I rushed to shake hands with him. To my delight, he took me to his blessed chest and hugged me! How sweet and soothing his hug was! It cannot be described in words!

The beloved Prophet ﷺ, then made me sit down next to him and a group of people began to distribute food to the people. Due to the great number of people, there were some who did not receive their share of food. Hence, the Holy Prophet ﷺ would stand up, take his blessed hand towards his chest and miraculously withdraw food. He then passed it on to those who had not received their food. I was dumbfounded by his generosity and affection. I woke up feeling a sense of tranquillity and happiness in my heart. May Allāh ﷻ give us all the Tawfeeq (ability) to follow the footsteps of our beloved Prophet ﷺ. Āmeen!

## Precaution in Monetary Dealings

### 1. Coach Fare Incident – A Lesson for All

Once I was travelling home from Oldham to Bradford via coach. At Oldham coach station, I headed for the National Express office to purchase my ticket. However, I was disappointed to find that the office was closed. I headed for the coach stand, hoping that somebody could help me there but I found that the coach had already arrived. I made enquiries with the driver regarding the office closure and my need for a ticket. He replied, "If the office is closed, then there is no other option but to wait." I explained my urgency to travel and offered him the coach fare but he declined and said, "I can't take cash, but there is space on the coach. You can travel. There is no charge for you."

I boarded the coach and travelled to my destination, feeling a great sense of unease at the fact that I had not paid for my journey. Thus, on reaching Bradford coach station, I immediately headed for the National Express office. I purchased a ticket to Oldham from Bradford which cost me £5 and then I disposed of it in the dustbin. When people enquired as to why I had done this very strange and unusual act, I commented, "The driver is not the owner of the coach. He is just an employee. He has no right to pardon me. Only the coach company manager has that right and authority. Hence, by paying for the ticket, I have fulfilled my duty and absolved myself from the debt of the coach company. The money will reach its recipient." People were amazed at this and they were left speechless! I exclaimed, "My brothers and sisters, I do not want anyone demanding their due from me on the Day of Judgement. I am very sinful as it is. May Allāh ﷻ forgive me for my shortcomings. Āmeen!

## 2. Repayment of 1p

One day, I entered a chemist to purchase some medicine which cost £1.99. I gave the cashier £2 and then, having received the change, I hurriedly put the medicine and change in my pocket as I was in a rush. It was only when I returned home that I realised that the cashier had mistakenly given me 2p change instead of 1p.

The next day, I returned back to the chemist and purchased something worth 99p. I was given 1p change but I excused myself from taking it, explaining the incident of the previous day. The cashier looked up at me in surprise and exclaimed, "You are very precautious!" I replied, "This is what our beautiful religion Islām teaches us!"

## 3. School Books Returned With a Letter of Apology

After I completed my Hifz at my local Maktab, I unexpectedly got enrolled into Dārul-Uloom Bury. I was then attending Belle Vue Boys Upper School and I had a number of text books in my possession, which were given to me by the school for homework and research. When I made my preparations to leave for boarding at Dārul Uloom Bury, these books were left at home and I had completely forgotten about them.

After completing my studies at Dārul-Uloom Bury, I returned home and only then realised that the text books were still in my possession. From the teachings of Islām that were instilled in me from my days at Dārul Uloom Bury, I understood that these books were given to me as a trust but they did not belong to me and they needed to be returned to their rightful owners. Thus, I sent them back to the school with a £5 postal order, including a letter of apology explaining my reason for the delay. Having done this, I felt a great sense of relief that I had returned back this trust which was given to me although it was delayed considerably. May Allāh ﷻ give us the true understanding of the importance of Amānat (trust). Āmeen!

## Following the Sunnah of the Holy Prophet ﷺ

### 1. Importance of Using the Miswāk

The Holy Prophet ﷺ would regularly make use of the Miswāk for various occasions. However, sadly nowadays, people have focussed their attention towards using the toothbrush for their oral health. Although this may keep their teeth clean, it does not carry the blessings of following the Sunnah of the beloved Prophet ﷺ. In order to revive this practise, I would always stress the usage of Miswāk and instruct all my students to keep a Miswāk with their toothpaste. To encourage them, I would distribute a free Miswāk from my bookshop for every student at the beginning of the academic year.

## 2. Good Relations with Neighbours

Many a times, our beloved Prophet ﷺ spoke about the importance of kindness to our neighbours. However, sadly, in this day and age, people do not even mingle with their neighbours, let alone be good to them. I wanted to follow the blessed teachings of the Holy Prophet ﷺ, therefore, after moving to 2 Cornwall Place, I invited all of the neighbours of the street for a meal at the JKN institute.

I explained to them that the objective of the Da'wat (invitation) was for us all to acquaint with one other as neighbours and to assist each other in our times of need. I addressed them with affection, letting them know that if they ever needed any help or advice, they should not hesitate to contact me. I stressed to them that they have rights as neighbours and that we should all co-operate with each other. Alhamdulillāh, this gathering was fruitful with positive results, paving the way for a good neighbourhood community.

## 3. Stressing the Importance of Tahajjud Salāh

After all of the compulsory prayers, Tahajjud has been the most emphasised Salāh. It is full of blessings and the Holy Prophet ﷺ would always pray Tahajjud. For this reason, I have always tried to ensure that I perform 8 Rak'ats Tahajjud reciting 1 Juz each night as well as encourage my family and students to do so also.

Once in a conversation with my son, I made enquiries as to which Juz of the Holy Qur'ān he was reciting in his Tahajjud Salāh. He informed me of the Juz and I realised that he was a Juz behind from where he should have been. I made enquiries as to why this was the case and he excused himself explaining that he had been to his uncle's wedding. This upset me and I remarked that even if it was his own wedding he should not miss his Tahajjud Salāh.

## 4. Revival of Tahneek

At the birth of a child, the Holy Prophet ﷺ would perform Tahneek, which involved him chewing a date and taking some of the sweet taste of it from his mouth, with his finger and placing it into the mouth of the baby. In this way, the baby would be blessed by the Holy Prophet ﷺ. This beautiful Sunnah has been disappearing in recent times and even the learned have not been practising upon it. Hence in order to revive this blessed Sunnah, I would raise the subject in speeches on a regular basis, inviting people to do Tahneek. I would also practically carry out the Tahneek at the birth of a child in the neighbourhood.

Alhamdulillāh, this practise became so popular that even before going home, mothers would come to our office for the Tahneek, immediately after being discharged from the hospital after childbirth. By the Grace of Allāh ﷻ, hundreds of children have had their Tahneek done and this has now become a prevalent practise in the community.

## 5. Racing with my Wife

In a display of affection and good conduct with his wife Ā'ishah ﷺ, the Holy Prophet ﷺ would race with her. To fulfil this blessed Sunnah, one day during the early days of my marriage, I had a race with my beloved wife in a park in Oldham.

## 6. Keeping Good Names

It is mentioned in authentic Ahādeeth, that the Holy Prophet ﷺ would change the names of people if they were meaningless or had a bad meaning. This was because he taught that people's names had an effect upon them. Therefore, it is important to have meaningful names, which would have a good effect upon us. Following this Sunnah, I would examine the names and their meanings of each student of JKN at the beginning of each academic year. If I found a name to have a bad meaning or to be meaningless, I would suggest them to change it, following the Sunnah of our beloved Prophet ﷺ.

## 7. Kindness to the Friends of my Father

The Holy Prophet ﷺ said, "Indeed the most virtuous deed is that you show kindness to the friends of your father." In order to act upon these blessed words of our beloved Prophet ﷺ, after the death of my beloved father, I collected all the names of his friends and associates. The number exceeded 50 and I invited them all for a Da'wat (invitation) at JKN. These respected guests were treated to a three course meal, after which each person was presented with a special gift pack which contained a prayer mat, Topee, perfume and Miswāk. To conclude the gathering, I addressed the elders by explaining to them the Hadeeth and my objectives of gathering everybody. They were amazed and many cried out of joy and appreciation for the gesture of good-will. Alhamdulillāh, it had an inspiring effect on everyone.

## Inspirational Incidents and Moral Lessons

### 1. Etiquettes of Teachers – An Eye-Opener for All Students

I was in my Hifz Class, at the age of 11, when one day, my teacher requested me to fetch something from the shop. Without thinking too deeply, I declined his request, making the excuse that it was too dark outside and I couldn't go to the shop at this time. My teacher looked at me and I could tell from his expression that he was surprised and angry.

He took his complaint to the head teacher, exclaiming, "You were saying that this student is very obedient but he has disobeyed my order!" I could hear this exchange of conversation and it made me feel utterly devastated, as though a big rock had landed on me. Sitting there, I felt very remorseful and consequently, I made a firm resolution that I would never ever decline any order or request made by my seniors. Alhamdulillāh, I truly learned my lesson and this practise has remained with me ever since. May Allāh ﷻ keep me steadfast. Āmeen!

### 2. Never Speak Without Verification

It was the month of Ramadhān and we were learning the Holy Qur'ān in the local Maktab. Our teacher had gone to the kitchen for some reason and the students had a little time to gossip. Just then a gentleman approached the class and enquired about our teacher. Thoughtlessly I replied, "He has gone to have some food in the kitchen."

When our teacher came back and was informed regarding what I had said, he became very angry and shouted, "How foolish you are! Firstly it is the month of Ramadhān. Secondly, without any verification you have made a statement. Never do this again!" This telling off hit me like a bullet and I apologised and promised not to repeat my careless mistake again.

## 3. 5,000 Handshakes in One Visit

In year 2007, in my travel to Bangladesh, I wanted to visit the two most renowned institutes of the country – Mueenul Islām Hathazari and Jāmiah Islāmiah Patya. On the way from our stay at Cox Bazār, we halted at Patya Madrasah to pray our Maghrib Salāh. I made it clear to the people there, that the only reason for my stopping was to pray Salāh and I was not there to address anyone. However, little did I know that they had another plan for me! Upon my arrival, the announcement was made that there would be a speech taking place after Salāh, therefore, everybody should remain seated. Then, before I knew it, I was addressing the gathering! I spoke in the Urdu language because my Bangla was very weak. I discussed briefly about the importance of practise with knowledge and the importance of spirituality. My speech was concluded with an emotional Du'ā which brought tears to the eyes of the audience.

After the Du'ā, the stage secretary announced that I was very tired, therefore, rather than having me shaking everybody's hand, he would shake my hand on behalf of the entire gathering. However, the audience would not have any of that! They were about to fall upon each other and injure themselves in order to get the oppor-

tunity to shake my hand! On seeing this, I realised their enthusiasm and love for me. Though I had not intended to stay there so
long, I could not help but be moved by their warmth and affection,
so I announced, "I am more than happy to shake hands with the
guests of the Holy Prophet ﷺ! I consider this my salvation!" These
words lit up the faces of the gathering and they rushed towards me
like moths! I reassured them that I would not leave until I conveyed my Salām and completed shaking hands with everyone.
Subhān-Allāh! What a blessing I felt shaking hands with over 5,000
students! This took me approximately an hour, after which, I was
surrounded by the staff and scholars for further advice.

## 4. Unexpected Nomination for Chairperson of Tawakkulia Jāmi' Masjid

In the year 2003, there was turmoil in my local community regarding the election of a chairperson for Tawakkulia Jāmi' Masjid. A
meeting was held to address these issues. During this meeting a
youngster named Atāur-Rahmān, unexpectedly stood up and gave
an inspirational speech in which he mentioned the need for scholars to run the Masjid. He suggested myself for the position saying,
"Mufti Sāhib has made a difference to the lives of thousands. He
has changed this community towards goodness!"

There were a few people who objected to the idea but he immediately quietened them with logistical answers, which even amazed
me, Subhān-Allāh! Consequently, for the first time in the history of
Bradford, 3 scholars were nominated for the executive committee
of the Masjid:

President: Mufti Saiful Islām
Vice President: Maulāna Abdul Aziz
Secretary: Maulāna Abdur-Raqeeb

## 5. Completing the Holy Qur'ān just Under 6 Hours

It had always been a dream for me to complete the Holy Qur'ān within one day. Thus once, when I was on Umrah in Ramadhān, I decided to fulfil this wish. It was one night, after Tarāweeh, in Masjidul Harām in Makkah, when I began to recite from Sūrah Al-Fātiha. Each time I completed a Juz, one of my colleagues Mansūr Khān would offer me a glass of Zam Zam water. I completed 20 Juz facing the Holy Ka'bāh and the remaining 10 Juz were recited whilst I performed Tawāf. During this interim, I was also asked 5 questions in various languages regarding Fiqh issues, by people who saw me in front of the Ka'bah. Alhamdulillāh, I cannot praise Allāh ﷻ enough, that I commenced the recitation at 9.35pm and completed it at 3.33am. Altogether, it took me 5 hours and 58 minutes. All praise be to Allāh ﷻ.

## 6. Miraculous Invite to a Khatm Bukhāri Gathering

In my journey to Bangladesh in 2004, I was invited to many insti-tutes for speeches and Du'ās. Though there was a devastating flood, which swept over virtually all of Bangladesh, I travelled tire-lessly to many places.

On the day we were returning back to the UK, we set off from our host's residence in Dhaka, heading for the airport. It was only half an hour's journey but we had to check in 3 hours in advance for the sake of customs. On the way to the airport, I was informed that we would be halting for a few minutes at an institute to make Du'ā there. I agreed thinking that it would be on our way to the airport, therefore, no further delays would be expected. Little did I know how long we would turn out to be there...

To my surprise, when we reached the institute, there was a multitude of people including all of the Madrasah students in the hall area. I was requested to come out of the vehicle and meet the teachers, but to my amazement, I was in a graduation ceremony and I was informed that I was the chief guest without any prior notification! I was speechless and astonished that they could take a move of that degree without informing me!

Despite this, the organisers insisted that it would be very brief. Hence I was requested to impart a Dars (lesson) on the last Hadeeth of Bukhāri. All the graduate students were in front of me. I briefly spoke about the Hadeeth and mentioned my chain of narrators. I discussed with them regarding my teacher of Saheeh Bukhāri, Shaykh-ul-Hadeeth Shaykh Islāmul Haq Sāhib 🌸 and about his extraordinary death in Madeenah Munawwarah. I then gave permission (Ijāzah) to the students to narrate Hadeeth from my humble self. After this the senior scholars (Muhaddithoon) also requested me to grant them the Ijāzah. I was full of embarrassment, in light of the fact that they already had the Ijāzah, therefore, I resisted their requests. However, due to their insistence, I could not help but to agree with a nod of the head.

After the Dars, I performed the Du'ā and then put the turbans on the heads of the graduates. By this time our flight was drawing near, so my colleagues became frustrated and pleaded, "Mufti Sāhib, we are going to miss our flight!" I looked at the time and I realised that it was already very late. At this point, it would be very difficult to reach the airport in time. Hurriedly, I performed the Du'ā and then tied the turbans.

Just as I was preparing to leave, all the students and guests stood up to shake hands with me. I stood up to shake hands and my colleagues were now very upset! Dejectedly, they exclaimed, "Take your time Mufti Sāhib. There is no chance of catching the flight now!" After I had shaken all of their hands, I was offered food. Then I was requested to do Dam (recite Qur'anic verses and then to blow) into some water. I did not expect to see a line of water bottles leading all the way up to our transport! Departing in a most unique manner, I blew into each bottle until I reached the van and then with a farewell bid, we got into the vehicle and rushed to the airport!

We reached the airport at a time when everyone had already finished their customs and were on the plane. An airport officer came up to our group, asking for me, "Where is Mufti Sāhib Hudhoor?" I put myself forward. He took our passports and then ushered us to the waiting room. He comforted us, saying, "Don't worry, everything is ok. Your goods will be put into the plane. I will have all the passports stamped." He then offered us some drinks, requested us for Du'ās and left. As soon as we got onto the plane, it set off! I sat down feeling breathless, after what felt like an adventurous dream. I recapped what had actually happened and was in utter amazement. I was told that it was all a well-planned out strategy, adopted to ensure my attendance at the Jalsa. The people knew I would decline had they invited me outright, due to my travel arrangements. I praised Allāh ﷻ for transforming those few hours which I would have spent waiting in the airport, into the Khidmat (service) of Deen. May Allāh ﷻ make this a means of my salvation in the Hereafter. Āmeen!

# JKN
# History & Projects

## History

Jāmiah Khātamun Nabiyyeen, commonly known as JKN, was established in June 1996, from the residence of Shaykh Mufti Saiful Islām. With the Help of Allāh ﷻ, JKN has accelerated to become a nationally and internationally recognised institute of learning. Some of the projects and activities of JKN, which operate under the guidance and instruction of Shaykh Mufti Saiful Islām, are mentioned below:

## JKN Institute

JKN has over 18 years of experience in teaching classical Islamic Texts to adults from all backgrounds, ranging from the most basic texts in Arabic, up to some of the most advanced classical texts such as Hidāya (Hanafi Fiqh Book) and the six Authentic Hadeeth Books (i.e. Saheeh Al-Bukhāri, Muslim etc).

JKN is one of the first Institutes in the UK that has developed a curriculum, which recognises the needs of and caters for the education of adults with families, those in full-time employment and other commitments. At present, it is one of the few traditional institutes in the UK that teaches classical Arabic texts in Arabic/English, to the most advanced levels. JKN has been continually modifying its course design to suit the needs of its students, such as the academic full-time Ālim course, Hifz course, Tajweed and Nāzirah courses for children and the 'New Modular' Islamic Theology Course in English for male and female adults.

**Schooling Projects**

JKN provides for the secular and Islamic educational needs, from nursery and primary school, up to secondary school, including Hifzul-Qur'ān and the full-time Ālim course.

In 2007, Al-Mu'min Primary School was appraised by a Lead Inspector as, 'a benchmark for all future inspections of Islamic Independent schools, with a good quality of education.' The curriculum framework is based upon seven areas of development; social, physical, spiritual, moral, intellectual, emotional and cultural.

Olive Secondary School for boys opened its doors to the local community in 2005. In 2006 the girls school commenced, opening the doors of opportunity for girls to acquire both Islamic education and secular education through the National Curriculum Syllabus.

Olive Secondary School caters for both boys and girls, in separate facilities and ensures every child reaches their full potential in all aspects of learning and development in a safe, friendly and comfortable environment.

Al-Mumin Nursery was established from September 2011, followed by the establishment of Al-Mumin Secondary School in 2012, catering for the education of both boys and girls with segregation facilities.

## JKN Publications

Over the past 18 years, JKN Publications has produced many books and numerous Islamic literature on various subjects. The most popular of which and also the forefront of JKN is the family magazine, 'Al-Mu'min.'

Al-Mu'min is a widely read magazine with readers worldwide. Currently Al-Mu'min is in its 15th year of publication with subscribers increasing everyday.

## Al-Kawthar Welfare Foundation

Al-Kawthar Welfare Foundation (AKWF) is a UK registered charity project in a joint venture with JKN. AKWF was established in February 2005 by some concerned scholars, in order to help the poorest and needy Muslims around the world. JKN has taken the lead role in maintaining and overlooking the project work and fundraising.

Primarily, JKN and AKWF have jointly set up a number of Makātib (elementary schools) for orphans and poor children. AKWF's major projects include the establishment of Jāmiah Zakariyya and Jāmiah Al-Kawthar in Bangladesh.

## Al-Mu'min Nikāh Service

Considering marriage as an important part of life and with the demand for a match-making service that complies with the Islamic Law, JKN has taken up the responsibility of providing this special Nikāh service.

Many of our Muslim brothers and sisters have taken interest in this service and many are reaping the rewards. Successful cases have lead to Nikāh, performed by Shaykh Mufti Saiful Islām himself.

## JKN Fatāwa Department

One of the busiest projects is JKN's Fatāwa Department which provides answers to religious questions, based on the Islamic Law on a daily basis. JKN Fatāwa Department has successfully dealt with thousands of questions via the telephone, post, e-mail, personal meetings, interviews etc.

## Advice and Counselling

JKN provides a regular advice and counselling service on religious and related social affairs through gatherings, written correspondence and telephone. Enquiries are received from people from all walks of life with a variety of subject matters, such as religious, social, national, international, matrimonial and domestic issues just to name a few.

## Spiritual Guidance

JKN runs programmes that cater for the spiritual upliftment of one's Nafs (inner-self), under the guidance of Shaykh Mufti Saiful Islām. The primary motive of a spiritual traveller is to achieve Divine Pleasure, which is acquired by total obedience to Allāh's ﷻ commands. These are performing Salāh, performing Hajj, giving Zakāt, fasting and Dhikr (remembrance of Allāh ﷻ) and all other obligations.

## Guidance for New Muslims

Through the activities and popularity of JKN, many people have embraced Islām taking the Shahādah at the hands of Shaykh Mufti Saiful Islām. JKN provides free advice, guidance, literature and information to new Muslims as well as non-Muslims.

## Da'wah Activities

JKN reaches out to brothers and sisters all over the UK. Through the JKN books, literature and Al-Mu'min magazine, the true knowledge of Islām is being spread. By the Grace of Allāh ﷻ, many people have come back to practicing Islām.

## Weekly Tafseer Sessions

JKN organises and facilitates a weekly gathering on the commentary of the Holy Qur'ān. These are delivered in English by qualified and authorised scholars and are held at the local Masjid (Tawakkulia Jāmi Masjid).

## Programmes for Brothers & Sisters

JKN has the honour of organising speeches and talks, held at Tawakkulia Jāmi Masjid. Prominent scholars from across the UK are invited to enlighten the gatherings with topics based on Islām.

Weekly and monthly speeches are specially held for women of the local community and beyond. Talks are delivered in English, Urdu and Bangla by qualified female scholars. Scholars from across the UK and abroad offer  advice and guidance on topics relating to women.

**Al-Mu'min Bookshop**

Al-Mu'min bookshop provides a whole range of Islamic books in English, Urdu, Arabic and Bangla. The bookshop also caters for students of knowledge, stocking Dars-e-Kitābs (i.e. classical text books such as al-Hidāya, Saheeh Al-Bukhāri and Tafseer Jalālain etc.)

Al-Mu'min Bookshop is a retailer and wholesaler of Islamic merchandise, with products ranging from audios, CDs, Jilbābs, scarves, Hijābs, Jubbas, Topis, Islamic games, children's books, beautiful fragrances, Islamic frames, gifts and much more.

For more information and latest updates on JKN visit our website:

# www.jkn.org.uk

List of email addresses for further enquiry of our projects;

1. Information regarding JKN institute, Al-Mumin Magazine and bookshop : info@jkn.org.uk
2. Spiritual guidance and Islamic questions, advice and counselling: fatawa@jkn.org.uk
3. Al-Mumin Nikah Service: nikah@jkn.org.uk

# 1. CHAPTER ON IMĀN

# BELIEF

# Definition of Imān

**Q** What does Imān mean?

**A** Imān literally means to believe and to proclaim it verbally. Technically it means to believe in Allāh ﷻ and the teachings of our Holy Prophet ﷺ.

# Definition of Ghaib
# (The Unseen)

**Q** What does Ghaib mean?

**A** Ghaib literally means 'the unseen.' In Islamic terms it refers to all those things that are unseen from mankind such as Jannah, Jahannam, angels etc. However, believing in them is essential, . It is compulsory upon a Muslim to believe that no one has the knowledge of the unseen except Allāh ﷻ.

# Vision of Allāh ﷻ

**Q** Will we be able to see Allāh ﷻ in Jannah? Please can you provide some evidence from the Holy Qur'ān and Ahādeeth.

**A** According to Ahlus-Sunnah Wal-Jamā'at, the people of Jannah will be able to see Allāh ﷻ. In fact, the greatest blessing in Jannah will be the actual vision of Allāh ﷻ by the people of Jannah. Allāh ﷻ states, **"The Day when faces will be radiant looking at their Lord." (75:22-23)** This verse clearly refers to the vision of Allāh ﷻ.

It is narrated by Sayyidunā Suhayb Roomi ৠ that the Holy Prophet
ৠ said, "When the righteous people will enter Jannah, Allāh ৠ will
enquire from them, 'Do you desire that We grant you one
more favour?' (i.e. bestow upon you a blessing in addition to
what you already have received). They will reply, 'You have il-
luminated our faces and saved us from Jahannam and granted us
Jannah. What more can we ask for?' The veil will then be lifted and
they will be able to see Allāh ৠ. This blessing will surpass all other
blessings that had been bestowed upon them."

Thereafter, the Holy Prophet ৠ recited the following verse from
the Holy Qur'ān, **"For those who do good deeds shall be the best
place and even more."** (10:26) In this verse, al-Husnā (best place)
refers to Jannah and Ziyādah (even more) refers to having the
honour of seeing Allāh ৠ Himself.

It is reported in Bukhāri and Muslim that the Holy Prophet ৠ has
said, "You will see your Lord clearly." Sayyidunā Jareer Ibn Abdullāh ৠ narrates, "One night we were sitting with the Holy
Prophet ৠ, when he looked up at the moon. It was the fourteenth
night of the month and the full moon was shining in the sky. The
Holy Prophet ৠ then turned towards us and said, 'Surely you will
see Allāh ৠ as you are seeing the moon. You will not need to make
special efforts to see Him, nor will there be any other difficulty."

(Bukhāri, Muslim)

Allāh ৠ mentions regarding the disbelievers, **"Nay, but surely on
that Day they will be veiled from their Lord (and prevented from
seeing Him)"** (83:15). This verse points towards the fact that the

believers will not be veiled from their Lord but they will be able to see Allāh ﷻ, Inshā-Allāh.

# The Holy Prophet's ﷺ Parents

**Q** When did the Holy Prophet's ﷺ parents pass away?

**A** The Holy Prophet's ﷺ father, Abdullāh passed away before his birth and his mother, Āminah passed away when he was six years old. The Holy Prophet ﷺ received Prophethood at the age of forty. It is evident from this that his parents were not alive during the period of his Prophethood.

# Qiyāmah (Day of Judgement)

**Q** When will Qiyāmah take place?

**A** No one knows the exact day and time of Qiyāmah. However, only this much is known that on one Friday, Sayyidunā Isrāfeel ﷺ will be ordered to blow the Soor (trumpet), which will signify the commencement of Qiyāmah.

# The Holy Qur'ān

**Q** Once, I was talking to an English revert and he asked me a few questions about the Holy Qur'ān. A few days later, I thought about it and tried to answer his questions but have been unsuccessful. Could you please be kind enough to answer my questions? One of the questions he asked was, how do we know that the Holy Qur'ān is in its original format?

A Allāh ﷻ states in the Holy Qur'ān, **"Indeed We have revealed the Reminder (Qur'ān) and We, verily are its Guardians."** **[15:9]**

Thus from this verse, we realise that Allāh ﷻ has taken the responsibility to preserve and safeguard the Holy Qur'ān. It is also clear that no creation can alter or tamper with the authentic book, revealed by Allāh ﷻ, when He has become its absolute Guardian. It is a different matter if a certain sect or person alters or tampers with it. However, the original text and its correct teachings will remain with the righteous Muslims till the Day of Judgement.

The Holy Qur'ān was memorised at the time of the Holy Prophet ﷺ by his Companions ؓ who had extraordinary memories. Whatever portion of the Holy Qur'ān was revealed, it was instantly memorised and also written by his noble Companions ؓ.

The Holy Qur'ān was then compiled during the era of Sayyidunā Abū Bakr ؓ, under strict conditions and close supervision, which are mentioned in detail in the books of Tafseer. Even today, there are millions of Muslim children, young and old who preserve the Holy Qur'ān through memory.

Furthermore, one of the main causes of distortion is human interference, after its revelation. Hypothetically, if the Holy Qur'ān did not maintain its original form because of human tampering, then there would have been many discrepancies and contradictions in the Holy Qur'ān as Allāh ﷻ states, **"Don't they ponder over the Qur'ān? Had it been from anyone besides Allāh, then they would have surely found in it many contradictions."** **[4:82]**

Unfortunately, the distortion of the previous revelations was due to human interferences, after the demise of the Prophets ﷺ. Therefore, the present scriptures do not maintain their original format. Contrary to this, the Holy Qur'ān has been protected from human manipulation and has been preserved through a chain of undisputable transmission, in each era up to today. Hence it contains no discrepancies.

Therefore, there can be no doubt about the authenticity of a book (text), which has been preserved by so many Huffāz (plural of Hāfiz i.e. the one who has memorised the Holy Qur'ān), since the time of its revelation, to the present day.

The Holy Qur'ān challenges the whole of mankind to imitate it or produce a text similar to its own text and style. This claim and challenge of the Holy Qur'ān remains outstanding, even today. The Holy Qur'ān is the only religious book on the face of the earth that gives a falsification test. This means that the Holy Qur'ān is openly challenging mankind to disprove its authenticity, by producing a Sūrah somewhat similar. No one has succeeded in producing anything like the Holy Qur'ān and nor will anyone be able to do so in the future. Hence, it is a clear proof that this Qur'ān is the same original Qur'ān as revealed to the Holy Prophet ﷺ. The authenticity of the Holy Qur'ān has been transmitted to us from the Holy Prophet ﷺ as 'Mutawātir'.

Mutawātir means, anything reported unanimously, by such an overwhelming number of people, that it is impossible to believe that they could either fabricate or collude upon a lie and this condition is found up to the last narrator, who narrated the Hadeeth or fact. To believe in this kind of narration as true, is obligatory upon every Muslim.

# Pillars of Islām

**Q** What are the pillars of Islām?

**A** Islām stands on five pillars which are evident from the Holy Qur'ān and Ahādeeth. The five pillars are as follows:

1. Shahādah (Testimony) - Every Muslim must believe and accept wholeheartedly with sincerity and declare verbally the Kalimah, "There is none worthy of worship but Allāh 🕮 and Muhammad 🕮 is Allāh's 🕮 Messenger."
2. Salāh - Five daily prayers.
3. Zakāh - Charity given at a fixed rate.
4. Sawm - Fasting in the Holy Month of Ramadhān.
5. Hajj - Visiting the House of Allāh 🕮, during the days of Hajj, at least once in a life time.

# Angels

**Q** We are told that many angels exist and they are invisible. Can you mention the reason they are created and the tasks they undertake?

**A** Angels are a special creation of Allāh 🕮, who have been created from light. They have been created to carry out the orders of Allāh 🕮. They have been given various duties to perform but because they are not visible to us, we cannot observe the duties they undertake. From the Holy Qur'ān and Ahādeeth we come to know that various angels are in charge of various duties. Amongst them there are four famous angels that are the most superior from all the others. They are:

1. Sayyidunā Jibreel ﷺ who brought Allāh's ﷻ books, orders and messages to all the Prophets ﷺ. He was also sent to help the Prophets ﷺ at times and fight against their enemies.

2. Sayyidunā Meekāeel ﷺ is in charge of food and rain. Other angels work under him who are in charge of clouds, oceans, seas, rivers and the wind. He receives orders from Allāh ﷻ and thereafter, orders the other angels under his command.

3. Sayyidunā Izrāeel ﷺ takes away life, with the order of Allāh ﷻ. He is in charge of death. Numerous angels work under him. Some take away the lives of good people, whilst others, looking very fearsome in appearance, take away the lives of sinners and disbelievers.

4. Sayyidunā Isrāfeel ﷺ will blow the Soor (trumpet) on the Day of Judgement. The sound will destroy and kill everything that is on earth and in the skies. When he blows for the second time (which will be after 40 years), all will come back to life, with the order of Allāh ﷻ.

Other than the above four famous angels, there are many other angels e.g. the angels constantly with us who record all our deeds called 'Kirāman Kātibeen.' Their duty is to write the good and the bad deeds. The angel on the right side writes the good deeds whilst the angel on the left side writes the bad deeds.

Munkar and Nakeer are the angels who question a person in the grave when he dies. Allāh ﷻ has assigned some angels, who are in charge of Heaven and some of Hell, and some for looking after the children, the old, the weak as well as others, whom Allāh ﷻ wishes to protect.

## Belief in Jinns

Q Can you explain in detail regarding the existence of Jinns? Some people do not believe in Jinns, claiming it to be just a myth. Can you explain the time when Allāh ﷻ created Jinns and from what source are Jinns created? Please can you quote Qur'anic verses as evidence?

A To believe in the existence of Jinns is an integral part of Imān because Allāh ﷻ mentions them in the Holy Qur'ān, in numerous verses. Jinn is an Arabic word, referring to the invisible creatures which were created from fire.

Allāh ﷻ mentions in the Holy Qur'ān, **"And He created Jinns from fire, free of smoke." (55:15)**

In another place Allāh ﷻ says, **"And the Jinn species, We had created them before, from the smokeless fire." (15:27)**

In Sūrah al-A'rāf, it mentions the following, **"He (Allāh) said, 'What prevented you from prostrating when I commanded you?' Iblees said, 'I am better than him. You created me from fire and him from clay'."** (7:12)

Again in Sūrah Sād, after Allāh ﷻ questioned why he refused to prostrate to Sayyidunā Ādam عليه السلام, Iblees answered, **"I am better than him. You created me from fire and You created him from clay."** (38:76)

Regarding the time when Jinns were created, it is mentioned that Allāh ﷻ created them well before the creation of Sayyidunā Ādam عليه السلام. This is mentioned in the verse of Sūrah al-Hijr (26:27). However, nothing is clearly mentioned about the duration of time between the creation of Jinns and mankind.

## Iblees - Jinn or Angel?

**Q** Is Iblees a Jinn or an angel?

**A** The Holy Qur'ān states, **"He was one of the Jinn, so he disobeyed the command of his Lord"** (18:50). Hence, he is a member of the Jinn species and the chief of all the Jinn.

## Previous Divine Books

**Q** How do we know that the Tawrah (Old Testament), Zaboor (Psalms of David) and the Injeel (New Testament) are Divine Books? Is it necessary to have belief in them?

A The Holy Qur'ān affirms the fact that they are Divine Books of Allāh ﷻ.

1. Regarding the Tawrah, Allāh ﷻ says in the Holy Qur'ān, **"Verily, We have revealed the Tawrah and therein is true guidance and light." (5:44)**

2. Allāh ﷻ mentions in the Holy Qur'ān about the Zaboor, **"We bestowed the Psalms (Zaboor) to Dāwood." (4:163)**

3. Regarding the Injeel, Allāh ﷻ says in the Holy Qur'ān, **"We have sent Eesā (Jesus) the son of Maryam (Mary), and bestowed upon him the Injeel (Bible)." (57:27)**

A person who refuses to acknowledge the Tawrah, Zaboor and Injeel as the Books of Allāh ﷻ is a disbeliever because the Holy Qur'ān testifies regarding them, that they are Divine Scriptures. So anyone denying their heavenly descent, disbelieves in the verses of the Holy Qur'ān and thus becomes a disbeliever.

At the same time, we must also remember that these Divine Books have been tampered with by their religious scholars and rulers, throughout history. The Tawrah and the Injeel available nowadays are not in their original form, due to alterations and distortions.

Our belief should be that whatever Allāh ﷻ has revealed in the original format, are the authentic Divine Scriptures of Allāh ﷻ, which were free from any mistakes, alterations and distortions.

# Reincarnation

**Q** Where does the Rooh (soul) go after a person's death? Does Islām accept the belief of reincarnation?

**A** Allāh ﷻ says in the Holy Qur'ān, **"Say the soul is by the command of my Sustainer and you have been given little knowledge pertaining to it." (17:85)**

From this verse, it is clear that a very small amount of knowledge has been given to mankind regarding the soul. The verse mentions that the Rooh is by the direct command of Allāh ﷻ. Unlike matter, the soul does not come into existence through procreation. It comes into existence by the direct command of 'Be' from Allāh ﷻ. Therefore, the soul must not be regarded in the same light as matter.

**Illiyyoon** is the place where the souls of the people of Paradise are kept. It is the record room where the names of the inhabitants of Paradise are recorded and their files kept. It is situated above the seventh Heaven.

**Sijjeen** is the place where the souls of the people of Hell are kept. It is the record room in which the names of the inhabitants of Hell are written. The angels (Kirāman Kātibeen), who are appointed to write the deeds of every soul, deposit the Book in that Record Office (Sijjeen) after their death. After the termination of their lives, on the file of every person, they make a sign whereby it is immediately known that the individual is a dweller of Hell. Sijjeen is situated beneath the seventh earth.

Once the soul leaves the body, it remains there until this world comes to an end. It does not transfer into any other body. Islām does not accept the belief of reincarnation, wherein it is believed that the soul is transferred into the body of some other creature repeatedly, depending on how it spent its life. Islām teaches us that this world is Dārul Amal (the place of deeds) and once a soul has left this abode, it takes its place in another abode, Dārul Jazā (the place of recompense).

For those who believe in the theory of reincarnation, let them answer this question; if a soul is placed in different creatures as a result of its evil or good deeds, then when the soul came into existence, on what basis was it placed in the first creature or being?

# Who are the Ahlus-Sunnah Wal-Jamā'at

Q Who are the real Ahlus-Sunnah Wal-Jamā'at? Nowadays, every sect is claiming to be amongst the Ahlus-Sunnah Wal-Jamā'at. What does the Ahādeeth say regarding this matter? How will I know that I am in the right group? Please explain in detail.

A Ahlus-Sunnah Wal-Jamā'at (the followers of the Sunnah and the group of Sahābah ﷺ) are the Ahle-Haq (the truthful and the authentic people) and the ones who conform to the Sunnah of the Holy Prophet ﷺ and the guided Sahābah ﷺ.

This has been clearly mentioned in one Hadeeth, "My Ummah (nation) will be divided into seventy-three sects. Every sect will be in the Fire of Hell, except one." The Sahābah ﷺ asked, "O,

Rasūlullāh 🌸, which is that sect?" The Holy Prophet 🌸 replied, "That sect which follows the path on which I and my Companions are." (Tirmizi)

The statement, "Every sect will be in the Fire of Hell except one", implies that they will be thrown into Hell on account of their evil beliefs. Subsequently, those whose beliefs did not transgress to Kufr (disbelief), will after serving the punishment on the account of their sins, come out of Hell and be admitted into Paradise.

Sayyidunā Abdullāh Ibn Umar 🌸, in a long Hadeeth, mentions ten signs of Ahlus-Sunnah Wal-Jamā'at. He says, "Anyone who has in him the following ten signs, is of the Ahlus-Sunnah Wal-Jamā'at."

1.   He performs the five times Salāh with the congregation.
2.   He does not speak ill of any of the Sahābah 🌸.
3.   He does not draw his sword against a (upright) Muslim ruler.
4.   He does not doubt in his own Imān (belief) and he calls himself a believer and a Muslim.
5.   He has belief in fate, that good and bad is from Allāh 🌸.
6.   He does not dispute about the religion of Allāh 🌸 (i.e. he does not argue nor object against it).
7.   He does not accuse anyone of Kufr (disbelief) on the account of sin.
8.   He does not omit the funeral prayer of anyone who is a Muslim.
9.   He accepts the permissibility of wiping over leather socks whilst on a journey and at home.
10.  He considers it proper to perform Salāh behind an Imām, pious or sinful. (Bahrur-Rāiq)

Hence, those people who conform to the ten signs, will Inshā-Allāh be classified as Ahlus-Sunnah Wal-Jamā'at. May Allāh ﷻ bestow the correct guidance and understanding upon everyone. May He make us all true Ahlus-Sunnah Wal-Jamā'at. Āmeen!

# Seventy-Two Sects

**Q** Seventy-two groups will appear, so do we know their names and where they originated? Is Tableegh Jamā'at amongst them?

**A** The Hadeeth which you are referring to, is mentioned in Tirmizi, related by Sayyidunā Abdullāh Ibn Amr Ibnul-Ās ؓ, that the Holy Prophet ﷺ said, "Verily the Banoo Isrāeel were divided into seventy two different sects, whereas, my Ummah will divide into seventy three different sects. All of them will be in Hell-Fire except for one group." The Sahābah ؓ inquired, "Which group will that be, O Messenger of Allāh ﷺ?" The Holy Prophet ﷺ replied, "The path that I am on and the path of my Companions."

The division of the groups that the Holy Prophet ﷺ indicated to, is based upon the differences in the fundamental articles of faith. In other words, the remaining seventy two sects, will possess such beliefs that will be contrary to the fundamental beliefs of Islām. This Hadeeth is not referring to the differences in the branches of faith (Jurisprudential issues), as this also existed amongst the Sa-hābah ؓ. The Sahābah ؓ had some degrees of differences amongst themselves in actions and the branches of faith. However, in the articles of faith they had no differences whatsoever. For instance, all of the Sahābah ؓ unanimously agree that Salāh is Fardh (which is an article of faith), but there are different opinions in the method of performing Salāh. These dissimilarities were due to the different degree and level of understanding, application, deduction and critical analysis. It is also the case with the four Imāms that in the articles of faith they were all united. Their differences only existed in the branches of faith.

Before I commence to explain the different groups, I feel that it is incumbent to primarily elaborate on the meaning of the 'saved group' that the Holy Prophet ﷺ was referring to.

Shaykh Idrees Khandelwi ﷺ, in his book "Islamic Fundamental Beliefs", has explained the aforementioned Hadeeth in great detail. In summary, the words used in the text of the Hadeeth "the path that I am on and the path of my Companions", means to adopt the traditions and the articles of faith similar to that of the Holy Prophet ﷺ and the Sahābah ﷺ. If an individual or a group was to possess such beliefs that conflict with the beliefs of the Holy Prophet ﷺ and the Sahābah ﷺ, then that is a deviant sect and will come into the category of the seventy two doomed sects. Thus, those people that followed the path of the Holy Prophet ﷺ and the Sahābah ﷺ were later referred to as Ahlus-Sunnah wal-Jamā'at. This will be the saved sect which the Holy Prophet ﷺ referred to. Some scholars have stated, that these different groups have already emerged. There are six major sects; each sect is further divided into different groups, which total to seventy-two groups.

Some scholars, like Shaykh Idrees Khandelwi ﷺ, are of the opinion that as a precaution, since the Holy Prophet ﷺ did not specify the time and place of the emergence of these deviant groups, there is a possibility that these groups may not have emerged yet. Thus, in the future they will emerge, or some may have emerged, but they have not accumulated to seventy-two as of yet.

With regard to the Tableegh Jamā'at, I will stress that it is not a particular sect in Islām and neither a deviant one. Rather, it is a branch of Da'wah. There are many forms of doing Da'wah and re-forming the society to elevate the word of Allāh ﷻ. For instance, learning, teaching, establishing Madrasahs (Islamic institutes) etc, similarly, Tableegh is one amongst them. Those people involved in Tableegh work, have the fundamental beliefs similar to that of the Holy Prophet ﷺ and the Sahābah ﵃. For more details about the work of Tableegh Jamā'at, refer to the book, "Fazāil-e-A'māl", written by Shaykhul-Hadeeth Maulāna Muhammad Zakariyya ﵁, in which he has written a chapter on 'The Virtues of Tableegh'.

# Sūfism

**Q** What is Sūfism? Are Sūfis part of the Ahlus Sunnah Wal Jamā'at?

**A** The most appropriate word to be used for this is 'Tasawwuf' or 'Tazkiyah.' Tasawwuf or Tazkiyah both terms imply to self refor-mation, reviving the teachings and spirit of Islām within oneself and restraining oneself from sins. This was amongst the funda-mental and important missions of the Holy Prophet ﷺ to fulfil, as Almighty Allāh ﷻ states in the Holy Qur'ān, **"As We have sent within yourselves a Messenger from amongst you to recite upon you Our signs and to purify you....."** (2:151).

The Scholars of the past adopted the term Tasawwuf to imply self reformation. Irrespective of whether one calls it Tasawwuf, Tazkiyah or Sūfism they all denote to the same concept. However, it is imperative that the method of Tazkiyah is in accordance to the Qur'ān and Sunnah. If its method is contrary to the fundamental teachings of the Holy Qur'ān and Sunnah, then this will become a means of deviance rather than guidance.

# To Dislike and Mock the Beard

Q Many people nowadays, dislike the keeping of the beard and look down upon it. Some people even go to the extent of mocking at the person who keeps a beard. What does the Shari'ah say about such people?

A To understand the answer to this question, one should bear in mind the basic principle that, to mock or jeer at any of the distinguishing features of Islām and to degrade or disgrace any Sunnah of the Holy Prophet 🌸, is equal to Kufr (disbelief), whereby a person leaves the fold of Islām. The Holy Prophet 🌸 has affirmed in many Ahādeeth, that the beard is a distinguishing sign of Islām and the unanimous practice of all Prophets 🌿.

Therefore, those people who consider the beard as disgusting and detestable and prevent those who aspire to keep a beard from amongst their friends or mock and jeer them, should seriously ponder over the condition of their Imān. It is incumbent upon them to sincerely repent.

Shaykh Ashraf Ali Thānwi ﷲ writes in his book, Islāhur-Rusoom, "Amongst these customs, the shaving of the beard, trimming it in such a way that it remains less than one fist in length and the lengthening of the moustache, is considered in today's time as stylish by most youth."

In a Hadeeth it is stated that the Holy Prophet ﷺ said, "Lengthen the beard and trim the moustache." (Bukhāri, Muslim)

It should be noted that the Holy Prophet ﷺ has used the commanding tense in imploring both these actions and the commanding tense in the Arabic language signifies obligation and incumbency of an action. Hence, we conclude that these two actions are Wājib and to disregard them is Harām (forbidden). Therefore, both the shaving and the trimming of the beard is Harām.

Furthermore, it has been mentioned in another Hadeeth that the Holy Prophet ﷺ said, "The person who does not trim his moustache is not from amongst our group." (Tirmizi, Ahmad and Nasai)

When we have now established it to be a sinful act, then those people who persist in doing it, consider the lengthening of the beard as a defect and jeer and ridicule those who keep a beard, should know that it could threaten their Imān. It is necessary on such people to sincerely repent, renew their marriages and formulate their lifestyle in accordance to the order of Allāh ﷻ and His beloved Prophet ﷺ.

# The Holy Prophet ﷺ: Light or Human?

**Q** Is the Holy Prophet ﷺ 'Noor' (light) or 'Bashar' (human)?

**A** Allāh ﷻ has informed us through the Holy Qur'ān, that the Holy Prophet ﷺ is from amongst the human beings. Allāh ﷻ states, **"Say, (O Muhammad), 'I am only a human like you. It has been inspired to me that your God is One God (Allāh)'."** (18:110)

In another verse, Allāh ﷻ says, **"Say, (O Muhammad), 'Glorified (and Exalted) be my Lord (Allāh) (above the evil they [the polytheists] associate with Him), I am but a human (sent as a) Messenger'."** (17:93)

Shaykh Yūsuf Ludhyānwi ﷫ states in his book, 'Differences in the Ummah and the Straight Path', "My belief regarding the Holy Prophet ﷺ is that, not only is he amongst the human kind, but he is the highest and the most noble of all humans."

Not only is he the son of Sayyidunā Ādam عليه السلام, but he is also the chief and leader of all the children of Sayyidunā Ādam عليه السلام. The Holy Prophet ﷺ, is reported to have said the following regarding himself, "I will be the leader of Ādam's عليه السلام progeny on the Day of Judgement."

Therefore, it is not only the Holy Prophet's ﷺ honour to be a human, but him being from mankind is a fact that inspires envy even amongst the angels. Since the Holy Prophet ﷺ is the noblest of man 'Bashar', in the field of Divine Guidance, his teachings are a luminous light 'Noor'. This is the 'Noor' that makes man recognise his Creator and it is a 'Noor' that will illuminate and remain until the Day of Judgement. Thus my belief regarding the Holy Prophet 🕊 is that he is 'Bashar' as well as a source of 'Noor'.

To accept one point and reject the other is a grave error. 'Bashar' and 'man' mean the same thing. By rejecting the quality of Bashar from the Holy Prophet 🕊, one expels the Holy Prophet 🕊 from being amongst mankind. On many occasions, Allāh ﷻ in the Holy Qur'ān, clearly proclaims the Prophets as having come from amongst the species of man. Although the Holy Qur'ān has referred to the Holy Prophet 🕊 as Noor and Bashar, he has been referred to as Bashar more often than Noor. It is the unanimous belief of the Ahlus-Sunnah Wal-Jamā'at that Allāh ﷻ has only chosen Prophets from amongst mankind.

The famous book on the beliefs of the Ahlus-Sunnah Wal-Jamā'at, 'Sharah Aqā'id Nasafi', defines a Rasool (Messenger) in the following words, "A Prophet is a man, whom Allāh ﷻ has chosen to propagate His message and laws."

In another famous Hanafi Fiqh book, 'Fatāwa Ālamgeeri', it mentions, "The one who says, 'I do not know whether the Holy Prophet 🕊 is a man or Jinn', is not a Muslim."
Hence, we learn that no person of sound reason, can reject or negate the fact that the Holy Prophet 🕊 was 'Bashar' (human).

How absurd can we be to put Allāh ﷻ and His creation on one and the same level? People of earlier generations corrupted their religion with such excesses and exaggeration. The Holy Prophet 🕌 also feared the inevitable occurrence of such excesses and exaggeration in his Ummah. He therefore, forewarned us against such exaggeration in the following words, "Do not praise me excessively as the People of the Book have praised Sayyiduna Eesā ﷽. They have made him god and the son of god. I am Allāh's 🕌 servant and His Messenger. Regard me only as the servant of Allāh 🕌 and the Messenger of Allāh 🕌." (Bukhāri)

In the light of the above Ahādeeth, it can be quite clearly concluded that the Holy Prophet 🕌 is the best of all creation. No creation can surpass his high and noble qualities and character. However, he is human, not Allāh 🕌 and nor a part of Allāh 🕌. These are the teachings of Islām and upon them are our beliefs.

## Q Was the Holy Prophet 🕌 'Noor' or 'Bashar' (Light or Human Being)?

A The correct belief of the Ahlus-Sunnah wal-Jamā'at is that the Holy Prophet 🕌 was 'Noor' and 'Bashar' simultaneously. 'Bashar' denoting that the Holy Prophet's 🕌 physical creation was 'Bashar' as the Holy Qur'ān states, **"Say (O Muhammad), 'I am a Bashar (human being) like you. It has been inspired to me that your Lord is only One Lord'."** (18:110) **"Say (O Muhammad), 'Glory be to my Lord. I am not but a Bashar (human) Messenger'."** (17:93)

There are many Ahādeeth that categorically prove that the Holy Prophet 🕌 was a Bashar (human being), amongst which a few are mentioned below:

Sayyidunā Abdullāh Ibn Mas'ood ﷺ relates, that on one occasion the Holy Prophet ﷺ led the congregation in Zuhr Salāh of five Rak'ats (by mistake instead of four). Thereafter, he was asked, "Has the Salāh increased?" The Holy Prophet ﷺ responded, "What happened?" They remarked, "You read five Rak'ats." The Holy Prophet ﷺ then performed Sajdah Sahwa after Salām. In one narration of another Hadeeth, the Holy Prophet ﷺ remarked (thereafter), "For I am a Bashar (human) like you. I forget as you forget so if I forget then remind me." (Bukhāri, Muslim)

Sayyidah Ā'ishah ﷺ, on one occasion was questioned regarding the Holy Prophet's ﷺ domestic affairs (at home). She replied, "He was a human amongst other humans; he would remove lice from his clothes (if by chance they appeared), milked the goats and did all his work himself." (Tirmizi)

The aforementioned verses and Ahādeeth are but a few, amongst an immense collection of those verses and Ahādeeth that are clear evidence that the Holy Prophet's ﷺ physical creation was a human. Our belief is also that as well as being Bashar, the Holy Prophet ﷺ is also Noor, as the Holy Qur'ān states, **"O' the people of the Book! Verily Our Messenger has come to you, clarifying many of those matters to you, which you conceal from the Book, while he overlooks many. Verily a Light and a clear Book has come to you from Allāh." (5:15)**

Undisputedly, the 'Light' mentioned in the above verse is referring to the Holy Prophet ﷺ. Having said this, there are two crucial points worth noting, which will Inshā-Allāh dispel all confusion regarding this matter:

1) To implicate the Holy Prophet ﷺ to be a Bashar i.e. a human being, in his physical creation is not an act of blasphemy. It is a privilege and an honour to be a Bashar because Allāh ﷻ has revered the sons of Ādam ﷺ in the Holy Qur'ān, as He states, **"And verily We have honoured the sons of Ādam and We have placed them within the earth and sea and We have provided them with a variety of pure sustenance and We have conferred favours upon them above many of Our creations."** (17:70)

Similarly, when Allāh ﷻ created Sayyidunā Ādam ﷺ, He instructed all the angels in the Heavens to prostrate before him. This prostration was to revere and honour Sayyidunā Ādam ﷺ (not for worship). Sayyidunā Ādam ﷺ was also a Bashar Prophet (15:28). So this demonstrates, that to be a Bashar is an honourable matter. There is no doubt that the Holy Prophet ﷺ was a physical descendant of Sayyidunā Ādam ﷺ.

Some people unfortunately, have succumbed to the misunderstanding that, due to the Holy Prophet ﷺ being the best of all Allāh's ﷻ creation, it would be highly disrespectful to ascribe the word Bashar to him as he is far superior than this. Furthermore, such a person would become (Allāh ﷻ forbid) an enemy of the Holy Prophet ﷺ. If this was the case, then why would the Holy Prophet ﷺ refer to himself as Bashar and why would Allāh ﷻ refer to him as Bashar? Why would Allāh ﷻ command the angels (who are created from Noor) to bow before Sayyidunā Ādam ﷺ who was created from clay? Allāh ﷻ, being the most Wise and the Knower of all the unseen affairs, knows best regarding what qualities He should attribute to the Holy Prophet ﷺ.

Furthermore, if it is an act of dishonour to the Holy Prophet ﷺ, then why would Sayyidah Ā'ishah ﷺ refer to him as Bashar? In the above Hadeeth, she categorically states, "He was a human amongst other humans," and the Arabic term she uses is Bashar. Of course, no true Muslim will be absurd enough to accuse Sayyidah Ā'ishah ﷺ of dishonouring the Holy Prophet ﷺ (Allāh ﷻ forbid), as her love for the Holy Prophet ﷺ compared to our love for him, is unimaginable. Hence, it is a privilege for the Holy Prophet ﷺ to be a Bashar Messenger.

2) The second point is that in the Holy Qur'ān, the word Noor implies two meanings; the literal or common implication (Haqeeqat) and the metaphorical implication (Majāz). When applying the literal meaning, then it would refer to the physical creation of a particular thing and this has been referred to, regarding the creation of the angels. When the metaphorical meaning is adopted then it will refer to spiritual guidance. In this context, the term Noor that the Holy Prophet ﷺ is being referred to in the Holy Qur'ān denotes to him being a spiritual guide for the whole of mankind. Just as in the midst of darkness when one kindles a light in order to acquire guidance, similarly, when the world was in total darkness, Allāh ﷻ sent the Holy Prophet ﷺ to bring mankind towards the light of Islām. Moreover, in the Holy Qur'ān, Allāh ﷻ has not only attributed the quality of Noor to the Holy Prophet ﷺ, but He has

also attributed it to the Holy Qur'ān (in Sūrah an-Nisā, verse 174), to the believers (in Sūrah Hadeed, verse 12) and to Islām (in Sūrah Tawbah, verse 32). The Noor referred to, in all these instances is the light of guidance.

If hypothetically, the term Noor was to be taken literally in every place of the Holy Qur'ān, referring it to physical creation then:

a) The Holy Qur'ān should also be considered a physical Noor i.e. when turning out the lights, the Holy Qur'ān will glow in the dark. It would be absurd and wrong for one to believe in this concept as this does not happen.

b) The true believers would be physically created out of Noor. Again, this notion is completely wrong and folly.

c) The Holy Prophet ﷺ would be physically Noor and this would contradict with those verses that mention that he was Bashar. The physical creation of Noor and Bashar cannot co-exist simultaneously in one person unless the term Noor means spiritual guidance.

In summary, the correct belief of the Ahlus-Sunnah wal-Jamā'at is that the Holy Prophet ﷺ was Bashar in his physical creation and also Noor in terms of spiritual guidance.

# The Blessed Shadow of the Holy Prophet ﷺ

**Q** Did the Holy Prophet ﷺ have a shadow?

**A** Before answering this question, one must firmly understand that all the miracles the Holy Prophet ﷺ showed throughout his noble life, have all been preserved and established through authentic narrations. In order to assert that the Holy Prophet ﷺ did such and such a miracle, one must primarily present an established and authentic proof, which will only then be accepted otherwise it is rejected. As far as this question is concerned, there are authentic narrations suggesting that the Holy Prophet ﷺ did have a shadow. Sayyidah Ā'ishah ﷺ narrates, "Once while the Messenger of Allāh ﷺ was on a journey, the camel of his wife Sayyidah Safiyyah ﷺ fell ill. However, his other wife Sayyidah Zaynab ﷺ had an extra camel. The Holy Prophet ﷺ said to Sayyidah Zaynab ﷺ, "The camel of Safiyyah ﷺ has become ill, can you lend her your extra camel?" She replied, "Should I give one to that Jew?" (Sayyidah Safiyyah ﷺ was originally a Jewess). So (upon hearing this, the Holy Prophet ﷺ became upset and) he separated from her for two or three months and he would not come to her. She says: "Until one day, at midday, I could see the shadow of the Messenger of Allāh ﷺ approaching….." (Musnad Ahmad)

However, there is a Hadeeth that Imām Jalāludeen Suyooti ﷺ relates, in his work, on the authority of Sayyidunā Zakwān ﷺ, that the Holy Prophet's ﷺ shadow was not seen in the sun (during the day) and neither in the moon (during the night). This indicates that he did not have a shadow. Nevertheless, Mufti Muhammad Shafee

Sāhib 🌸 states, that this Hadeeth is not acceptable due to the following reasons:

a)   The narrator Abdur Rahmān Ibn Qais Zafrāni mentioned in the chain of narration has been criticized to be an imposter and highly unreliable.

b)   This Hadeeth is Mursal (the student of the Sahābi states the Holy Prophet 🌸 said, exempting the Sahābi) which many great scholars of Hadeeth do not accept.

c)   Whenever the Holy Prophet 🌸 travelled during the day on an expedition, a huge gathering of the Sahābah 🌸 would also accompany him. If the Holy Prophet 🌸 was devoid from having a shadow miraculously then a huge number of the Sahābah 🌸 would surely have narrated this because they witnessed before their eyes and recorded every minute Sunnah and miracle of the Holy Prophet 🌸 (and this was the case with the other miracles). This would then attain the level of Tawātur (undisputable fact). (Jawāhirul Fiqh vol. 3 pg. 20)

Due to the abovementioned reasons, the Hadeeth (mentioned by Imām Jalāludeen Suyooti 🌸) cannot be accepted. Therefore, we conclude that the Holy Prophet 🌸 did have a shadow because there is no Hadeeth which authentically reports that the Holy Prophet 🌸 did not have a shadow.

## Mukhtār-e-Kul (Omnipotent)

**Q** Has the Holy Prophet ﷺ got overall power over the creation?

**A** Shaykh Yūsuf Ludhyānwi ﷺ writes in his famous book, 'The Differences in the Ummah and the Straight Path', "The fatal consequences of ascribing the exclusive qualities of Allāh ﷻ unto the Holy Prophet ﷺ, is the belief that the Holy Prophet ﷺ shares certain powers with Allāh ﷻ. Hence, we have people holding the erroneous view that Allāh ﷻ has granted the Holy Prophet ﷺ, complete power over His creation."

They believe that the Holy Prophet ﷺ is Mukhtār-e-Kul. However, according to the Holy Qur'ān, Hadeeth and the belief of the Ahlus-Sunnah Wal-Jamā'at, there is no room for such beliefs in Islām. Allāh ﷻ has not given any such overall control or power to any of His creation.

Islām teaches us that only Allāh ﷻ has full control and power over everything and nobody shares this attribute with Him.

Life, death, health and illness are all in Allāh's ﷻ power. Therefore, from Sayyidunā Ādam ﷺ to our beloved Prophet ﷺ, all the Prophets used to supplicate to Allāh ﷻ alone. They regarded only Allāh ﷻ as the Provider of good and bad, profit and loss, life and death, health and sickness. This was also the case with all the pious servants of Allāh ﷻ.

No Prophet or saint has even claimed to possess power or control over any portion of Allāh's 🕮 creation. The Holy Prophet's 🕮 belief in regard to this attribute of Allāh 🕮, can be judged by the following Hadeeth: Sayyidunā Abdullāh Ibn Abbās 🕮 reports that he was once riding behind the Holy Prophet 🕮. The Holy Prophet 🕮 told him, "O' Child! Protect the rights of Allāh 🕮 and Allāh 🕮 will protect you. Protect Allāh's 🕮 rights and you will find Allāh 🕮 with you. Whenever you ask for anything, ask from Allāh 🕮. When you are in need of help, turn towards Allāh 🕮 and be assured that if everybody gets together to do any good to you, they would not be able to benefit you, but to that extent which Allāh 🕮 has ordained for you and if everybody gets together to harm you, they will be unable to inflict harm, but that which Allāh 🕮 has ordained for you." (Mishkāt)

In explaining this Hadeeth, Mulla Ali Qāri 🕮 writes, "'Ask Allāh 🕮' means ask Allāh 🕮 alone, for only He owns everything, whatever we have is all from Allāh 🕮."

He is most Generous and He is Independent. We should therefore only hope for His blessings and only ask Him.

We should rely on Him alone and we should not ask from anybody but Allāh 🕮, for none but He has the power to give.

He has power over everything. In the explanation of the word 'everybody' used in the Hadeeth, he writes, "Without doubt the whole Ummah, meaning, all the creation, Prophet or non-Prophet, pious or non-pious, if the whole creation gets together to harm you they will not be able to harm you."

Shaykh Abdul Qādir Jīlāni ﷺ says, "Most certainly the entire creation is powerless and incapable. They do not have the power to destroy, nor do they have any ownership. They do not have wealth, nor do they possess property. Besides Allāh ﷻ, they have no Deity, no Giver, no Protector, and no Giver of life or death." This is the belief of the pious people and the Ahlus-Sunnah Wal-Jamā'at.

Whatever miracles were experienced by the Prophets ﷺ, or whatever supernatural act is experienced by any pious person, is a direct blessing of Allāh ﷻ, conferred on them, and it is only the Power of Allāh ﷻ i.e. a manifestation thereof. It is called a 'Mu'jiza' or 'Karāmat'. Allāh ﷻ states, **"And no Prophet is able to bring forth any sign except with the permission of Allāh." (40:78)**

To attribute the quality of control over the universe to a person, merely because he carried out a few miracles is most surprising. The People of the Book fell prey to this same concept, when certain miracles were performed through the hands of Sayyidunā Eesā ﷺ. They fell prey to the belief of trinity and attributed Sayyidunā Eesā ﷺ with qualities of divinity. The Holy Qur'ān invites man to the Oneness of Allāh ﷻ. The main task of the Prophets was to invite man to the realisation of the Divine Oneness of Allāh ﷻ.

The Oneness of Allāh ﷻ has been explained very clearly in the Holy Qur'ān, with substantiated proofs. The Holy Qur'ān questions man, "Who is the controller of the universe? Who gives sustenance? Who has the power over life, death, illness and health?"

Ascribing partners to Allāh ﷻ in His attributes, would in fact be a negation, and an attempt to render void almost one third of the Holy Qur'ān. Surely if others are made partners with Allāh 🕮 in these attributes, a third of the Holy Qur'ān will be left void.

All the Prophets and pious saints have regarded themselves completely under the control of Allāh's 🕮 Will. Thus, attributing the qualities of Mukhtār-e-Kul to anybody is also against the teachings of the Prophets and the pious servants of Allāh 🕮.

# Hāzir Nāzir (Omnipresent)

**Q** Is the Holy Prophet 🕮 'Hāzir Nāzir' (Omnipresent)?

**A** Shaykh Yūsuf Ludhyānwi 🕮 writes, "It is necessary to primarily understand what is 'Hāzir Nāzir'. This is an Arabic term which means 'present and seeing'. When used together it qualifies a being whose presence encompasses the entire universe and he sees and has complete knowledge of everything in the universe. Our belief is that only Allāh 🕮 is 'Hāzir Nāzir' and this is an exclusive attribute of Allāh 🕮.

We are all aware that the Holy Prophet 🕮 is resting in his Holy Grave in Madeenah Munawwarah and all the Muslims travel to Madeenah for the 'Ziyārat' (visitation) of the Holy Prophet's 🕮 grave. Thus, to believe that the Holy Prophet 🕮 is present at all places and is seeing everything is contrary to sound reason as well as contrary to the Islamic beliefs.

'Hāzir Nāzir' is the attribute of Allāh 🕮 only and no creation shares this attribute with Him. It is also a false belief to say that after the departure of the Holy Prophet 鸞, his soul has been given the power to present itself whenever it wishes. Even if this false belief was true hypothetically, it would still not qualify the Holy Prophet 鸞 as being 'Hāzir Nāzir'.

Even a citizen of a country has the right to go to any part of his country; this does not make him 'Hāzir Nāzir'. To be given the right to go wherever one wishes, does not make one present every-where. On the other hand to say the Holy Prophet 鸞 is present at a certain place, is an independent claim, for which requires substantial evidence.

Since there is no substantial proof from the Holy Qur'ān and Ahādeeth, to hold such a belief is not permissible. Some people go to the extent of attributing the qualities of 'Hāzir Nāzir' to the saints. I am surprised at the claim of these people. How casually they associate the exclusive attributes of Allāh 鸞 to His creation. The scholars of the Ahlus-Sunnah Wal-Jamā'at do not tolerate these false beliefs. Thus it is stated in Fatāwa Bazāzia, "Our schol-ars have stated that whomsoever says, 'The souls of the pious are present and that they know everything', is a disbeliever."

# Splitting of the Chest of the Holy Prophet 鸞

**Q** **I have read that the Holy Prophet's** 鸞 **chest was split open and washed by Sayyidunā Jibreel** 🕮 **with Zam Zam water when he was young, is this authentic?**

**A** What you have read is completely true and authentic. One of the specialities of the Holy Prophet ﷺ, is that on various occasions, the Holy Prophet's ﷺ blessed chest was split open and his heart was washed and filled with faith and wisdom. Hence, it was 'immunised' against devilish influences and evil whispers.

This phenomenon is referred to as 'Shaqqus-Sadr'. Shaqqus-Sadr, as the narrations indicate, occurred four times during the Holy Prophet's ﷺ lifetime.

**The First Occasion**
The first occasion was during early childhood, when the Holy Prophet ﷺ was living at the home of his foster mother Haleemah Sa'diyah ﵂. One day whilst the Holy Prophet ﷺ was playing outside, Sayyidunā Jibreel ﵇ appeared and after making the Holy Prophet ﷺ lie down, he split open his blessed chest and removed the heart. He split open the heart and removed a blood clot from it. He then washed the Holy Prophet's ﷺ heart in Zam Zam water, which he had brought with him in a gold utensil. Thereafter, he replaced the heart and stitched up the Holy Prophet's ﷺ blessed chest.

The other children who were with the Holy Prophet ﷺ at the time, rushed to his foster mother Haleemah Sa'diyah ﵂ and informed her that somebody was killing the Holy Prophet ﷺ.

She immediately hurried out, and when she saw the Holy Prophet ﷺ, he looked frightened and pale. After narrating this story, Sayyidunā Anas ﷺ stated, that the stitches of that 'operation' were clearly seen.

### The Second Occasion
Shaqqus-Sadr occurred for the second time when the Holy Prophet ﷺ was approximately ten years old. This Hadeeth has been reported by Sayyidunā Abū Hurairah ﷺ, and it is recorded in Saheeh Ibn Hibbān.

### The Third Occasion
The third occasion of Shaqqus-Sadr was at the time when the Holy Prophet ﷺ received Prophethood. The incident is recorded in the Musnad of Abū Dāwood at-Tayālisi.

### The Fourth Occasion
This occurred prior to the miraculous journey of Mi'rāj. According to the Hadeeth reported by Sayyidunā Mālik Ibn Sa'sa'ah ﷺ, the Holy Prophet ﷺ narrated that one night, whilst he was resting in the Hateem area of the sacred Ka'bah, two angels appeared.

The procedure of this incident is almost identical to the procedure mentioned under the first occasion of Shaqqus-Sadr. (Mishkāt)

**Note:** The phenomenon of Shaqqus-Sadr surely defies all reason and logic. However, it has been reported through numerous chains which makes it compulsory to have faith upon it.

### The Purpose of Shaqqus-Sadr
On the first occasion, a blood clot was removed from the Holy Prophet's ﷺ heart. This in actual fact, was symbolic as being the

source of sin and vice, from which the Holy Prophet 🌟 was divinely purified. The heart was washed as well so as to remove any traces of the blood clot.

The second time this occurred was for the sake of purifying the Holy Prophet's 🌟 heart from the natural tendencies of getting involved in play and amusements, which usually begin at around that age. The third time this phenomenon occurred was to prepare the Holy Prophet 🌟 to receive the pure speech of Allāh 🌟, and to contain the vast knowledge of the recognition of Allāh 🌟.

The fourth occasion was for the sake of preparing the Holy Prophet 🌟 for his journey into the unseen and for the direct communion with Allāh 🌟.

**Note:** Shaqqus-Sadr was an occurrence that was the speciality of the Holy Prophet 🌟. Other Prophets 🌟 did not share this privilege. The Muhaddithoon (scholars of Hadeeth) and historians differ regarding the number of times this phenomenon occurred. Suhayli 🌟 for instance views that it occurred twice, whilst Hāfiz Ibn Hajar 🌟 says that it occurred thrice.

# Imām Mahdi

**Q Is Imām Mahdi already born?**

**A** I do not know; only Allāh 🌟 knows.

# The Use of Words 'We' and 'He' by Allāh ﷻ

**Q** In Sūrah Yāseen it says the following, "We have not taught the Prophet poetry, nor is it suitable for him."...."Does not man see that We have created him from Nutfah (semen). Yet behold he stands forth as an open opponent. And he puts forth for Us a parable and forgets his own creation. He says, 'Who will give life to these bones after they are rotten and have become dust?' Say, 'He will give life to them Who created them for the first time! And He is the All Knower of every creation"..."Verily, His Command, when He intends a thing, is only that He says to it, 'Be!' and it is!" (36:69, 77-79, 82)

I believe in Allāh's ﷻ words but why does He refer to 'We', 'Us', 'He' when it is Allāh ﷻ Himself speaking to the whole of mankind via Sayyidunā Jibreel عليه السلام and the Holy Prophet ﷺ. Could you please answer my question as soon as possible as I would like to tell another brother the answer to this puzzle?

**A** In the Arabic language, plural is used for two purposes:

1. For its original use, i.e. the multiple of singular.
2. To express respect (royal plural).

It is only natural and customary, for Allāh ﷻ to use the pronouns of the plural terms in many verses of the Holy Qur'ān. We believe He is the One and Only God and He has no partners nor children. However, He uses the plural term to express His honour, dignity and pride. Without any doubt, He alone is worthy of all honour, dignity and pride.

The Holy Prophet ﷺ narrates a Hadeeth Qudsi, that Allāh ﷻ states, "Pride is my upper garment and dignity is my lower garment. Whoever attempts to snatch them from Me, I shall throw him in the Fire of Hell." The Holy Prophet ﷺ also said, "In comparison to Allāh ﷻ, there is none who loves being praised so much."

We understand, from the two narrations, that only Allāh ﷻ is worthy of worship. He is our Lord, the Glorious, the Creator, the Sustainer and only He is worthy of all praises. This is why He uses the pronoun 'We' for respect.

It is necessary to be aware that we should not be confused, nor should we create questions in our mind that if Allāh ﷻ is One, then why does He say, "We have done this, We have created this etc." Thus, come to the conclusion that the word 'We' points towards the belief of the Trinity.

The answer is very clear from what I have mentioned that He uses the plural pronoun solely to express respect, highness and dignity.

Also the same Holy Qur'ān which uses 'We' rejects any partnership to Allāh ﷻ, by saying, **"Surely those disbelieve who say Allāh is the third of three."** The Holy Qur'ān declares the Oneness of Allah ﷻ by proclaiming, **"Say! He is Allāh, the One. Allāh the Eternally Independent. He begets not, nor was He begotten and there is none equal unto Him." (112:1-4)**

The Holy Qur'ān has the finest articulate and eloquent Arabic. Thus Allāh ﷻ also uses We, Us, and He to enhance the eloquence and the beauty of the Arabic language. (Mukhtasarul-Ma'āni)

# Existence of Planets

Q Do planets exist according to Islamic belief? If so could you please give some Islamic proof regarding this statement?

A To believe in the existence of other planets is not a fundamental part of Islamic belief. However, Allāh ﷻ has created the universe and many things therein. Although the existence of the other planets in the Solar System is not clearly mentioned in the Holy Qur'ān, we know that there are so many other things in the universe that exist other than our Earth.

# Evolution Theory & the Existence of Dinosaurs

Q What is the Islamic view point of the Evolution Theory and the existence of dinosaurs?

A The Holy Qur'ān and the Ahādeeth do not mention anything regarding the existence of dinosaurs. However, it is an established fact that fossil scientists have excavated the remains of dinosaurs and proved that they once existed. This does not contradict the fundamental articles of Islām because although the Holy Qur'ān has not mentioned them, this does not necessarily mean that it denies their existence in the past.

As far as the Evolution Theory of man evolving from apes is concerned, Islām rejects it. Even to this day, not all scientists unanimously agree upon the established fact of the Evolution Theory. The more the advocates attempt to justify it, the more the anti-evolution scientists refute it. The founder of this ideology was

Charles Darwin. It is mentioned in his work "The Origin of Species" that once Darwin travelled on a boat to an island where he saw a bird (more of a wood pecker) pecking on a tree. On observing this, Darwin concluded that this bird's continuous pecking on the tree resulted in the evolvement of the shortening of it's beak through a period of time. It was incidents like this that convinced Darwin to propound the Theory of Evolution.

As Muslims, we believe that it is Allāh ﷻ Who is the Creator of everything that is in the heavens and the earth. The Evolution Theory is based on the fact that the Universe along with all of the living species on it emerged spontaneously (all of a sudden) and that there is no God. All living things including dinosaurs evolved from non-living matters i.e. from rocks millions of years ago. Evolutionists also assert that animals evolved from one another, for instance, birds were developed from lizards. However, contemporary renowned scientists like Louis Paster (France) and Jeffery Bade, researched and conducted experiments on this issue. These anti-evolutionists concluded that it is impossible for animals to have evolved from non-living matter or from one another through transition. The reason being is that to prove of their occurrence, the animal which evolved, must still contain some traits of its original species. For instance, with regard to the theory that birds evolved from lizards, can only be proved by traits of the lizard in the birds. However, if we analyze both of them, their physical appearance and their genetic information are completely different from one another. Lizards are covered with scales, whereas birds are covered with feathers. Furthermore, birds have no traits of scales. Similarly, dinosaurs are a completely different species from human beings; dinosaurs are reptiles whereas humans are mammals. Allāh ﷻ has created every living thing in a unique form, different from one another.

Allāh ﷻ has created everything right down to the structure of a DNA in such a perfect balance that it is impossible for all this to occur coincidently. For someone to claim that everything emerged in a perfect equilibrium spontaneously, is like someone claiming that an aero-plane emerged coincidently from birds. If we look at the engineering mechanical design of an aero-plane, we instantly come to know that this is the design of an expert engineer. It is absolutely folly to believe that it appeared all of a sudden: Similarly, the perfect design of the whole universe is far superior than an aero-plane. If one cannot comprehend that an aero-plane emerged suddenly, then how can someone believe that the universe emerged suddenly in a perfect balance? The universe has existed for many years, yet it has still maintained its perfect balance and is free from any defects. Allāh ﷻ states in the Holy Qur'ān, **"It is He Who has created the seven heavens one above the other, you can see no faults in the creation of the most Merciful, then look again do you see any rifts?" (67:3)** Put this challenge before the non-Muslim to explain this.

Moreover, if we look at the complex structure of the DNA, scientists have said that the DNA withholds so much genetic information about an individual, that a tea spoon quantity of a DNA is sufficient to store the capacity of all of the information contained in all the books in the world. The question is, can this DNA structure emerge coincidently? If animals evolved from one another or from non-living substances, then how did its origin come into being? Many more examples can be given but for simplicity I have sufficed with this.

We believe that there is a Magnificent Designer, Who created and designed all this in a perfect balance. He is the One and only Allāh 🕮, Who is the Creator of everything. Allāh 🕮 states in the Holy Qur'ān, **"He is Allāh the Creator, the Inventor, the Designer; to Him belongs the beautiful names."** (59:24)

Evolutionists claim that life was generated from non-living matter. As a result cells emerged and later on, became the ancestors. Maulāna Dr. Rafāqat Rashid Sāhib has refuted the evolution theory in great detail in his book "What's with the Monkey Business?" For simplicity I shall highlight the main points. The Evolution Theory is based upon three foundations: 1) Natural selection 2) Mutation 3)Fossils remaining.

1) 'Natural selection' means that in a particular region, the strongest who are well adapted will survive against the weak. In brief to this reply, natural selection at the most, eliminates the weak in that region but does not involve any evolutionary power. No animals can evolve from one another on the basis of this.

2) 'Mutation' means the alteration and distortion of a genetic code. Scientists have refuted this claim, stating that mutation can only damage the cells but cannot benefit nor increase genetic information. A renowned evolutionist and atheist, Richard Dawkins, was once interviewed and asked to explain the increase of genetic

information through mutation. Even he could not explain this because he knew that it was not a practical possibility.

3) 'Fossils remaining' is where fossil scientists excavate the remaining fossils of dead animals many years ago. Fossil scientists concluded that there are no signs of any transition forms from one animal to the other. The fossils found are similar to the animals today; in other words, present animals existed from a long time ago. Furthermore, evolutionists prove their theory, by asserting that they have excavated skulls which have different shapes, so there is a possibility of evolvement. Scientists have again refuted this, stating that, even in the present time, we have people who have different skull structures. This difference is because of different racial backgrounds. For a more detailed explanation you can refer to Dr. Rafāqat Rashid's book, "What's with the Monkey Business?"

**Q** Can you explain what Evolution is and how wrong Charles Darwin's theory is regarding man? What does the Holy Qur'ān say about the beginning of life?

**A** The Evolution theory discusses the origin of life on Earth, based on a doctrine that all living species evolved from one another i.e. man evolved from apes etc. This theory has been attributed to a well known Evolutionist, Charles Darwin. To commemorate this great discovery for the Materialists, you can now find him on a £10 note. When this theory was propounded to many scientists, they refuted it. Here is a brief explanation of his theory. He proposed that, at the beginning there was no life, and suddenly due to great lengths of time and chance, the correct conditions were found for life to initiate by itself.

He further theorised that once life had started, through mutation and natural selection, the simple one-celled creature (amoeba) evolved, over a long period of time (millions of years), into all the creatures around us. The theory has been refuted scientifically and by the only true religion, Islām. I will begin by primarily explaining ,through logic and science. Thereafter, I will conclude with the highest knowledge (Allāh's ﷻ Word).

To this day, no scientist anywhere in the world has been able to start life in a laboratory, although they have access to the technology, chemicals and knowledge of all mankind from now back to the dawn of science. In fact, the starting blocks of life, amino acids, cannot be produced in the laboratory without isolating them and putting them under very specific conditions. If left "cooking" with everything else, they return to the base elements. To elaborate further, the chances of an average protein molecule being arranged in the correct quantity and sequence, in addition to the chance of all the amino acids it contains to be left-handed and being combined with only peptide bonds, is one in $10^{950}$. That means one chance in a number one with 950 zeros after it. This is mathematically proved to be impossible. Let us give the believers in evolution the benefit of doubt and say that life came into existence spontaneously.

The next phase of the theory is that one species evolved into another species by mutation. This means that for some reason, one creature mutated and that this mutation was beneficial. This mutation was such, that the original species had now become a different species altogether.

Let me explain by example. Imagine a fish-type species living in the water which swims about looking for food. Then, a normal pair of male and female fish have a baby fish. However, this baby fish is a mutant and has long legs!

This proves to be an advantage because when food is scarce in the water, the baby fish would walk on to the beach and look for food. It survives, meets another mutant, gives birth to more fish-leg creatures and gradually they evolve to become land creatures, distinctively different from their forefathers i.e. a new species.

Their is also a problem with this part of the theory. All the mutations observed in the world have proved to be detrimental and no advantage has been observed. In fact it has been quite the opposite. Research carried out on the fruit fly has produced all sorts of mutants. Legs growing out of the head, eyes on the abdomen, two pairs of wings and the list is endless. No mutant gave an advantage over its normal parent. Few lived as long as their normal relatives. They had problems moving, eating and in all other activities. When the mutant fruit fly had offspring, then not surprisingly they were normal fruit flies, not mutants.

Let us look back at our land fish. Our land fish needs to mutate several times in order to survive on land because it isn't possible with only legs. It must develop balance and a sense of awareness;

its body must be able to cope with the pressure or lack of pressure on the land; it must develop a means of breathing and all the required anatomy; it must have something to protect its eyes; its skin will need to be able to adapt to a dry environment; its digestion system will need to develop as its food has changed and there are many more. All of these mutations have to occur at the same time.

If any one of them is missing, the land fish will not survive. It seems contrary to common sense that, all of these mutations occurred after such a long time when, for a period nothing happened and then all of them happened after that, at the same time! There are many other reasons why the evolution theory is flawed, e.g. lack of intermediate species, anomalies (irregularities) and lack of knowledge (which is available now) at the time when the theory was put forward, are to name a few; however, that would require a book.

So after all of this, why do the Materialists still believe in evolution if it has so many flaws? I will answer that by posing a question. What would they believe in instead? Now, presenting it in another perspective, if life did not start by itself then it must have been created. They would then have to acknowledge and accept a Greater Being and a Creator. However, the Materialists have everything to lose if they accept that fact.

If evolution is not the means by which we have come about, then how did humans inhabit the world? What was our beginning? Where have we come from? Are we a product of chance or have we a purpose? Did a one-celled being evolve into an ape-like creature? Did man evolve from him or was man as he is now, from the beginning?

Let us look at the Holy Qur'ān. There are many verses in the Holy Qur'ān which give answers to all these questions. However, as before, it would require a book to include them all. Nevertheless, one particular verse, which is quoted below, summarises the origin of man and his potential state.

Allāh ﷻ is the Creator of the Universe and everything it contains, and He is One Who possesses Infinite Knowledge. In fact, who else would know about the origin of man, if not the Creator Who was there at the time and created man with His Hands? Allāh ﷻ, says, **"Indeed, We created mankind from dried (sounding) clay of altered mud. The Jinn, We created before, from a smokeless flame of fire. (Remember) When Your Lord said to the angels, 'I am going to create a man (Ādam) from dried (sounding) clay of altered mud. So when I have fashioned him completely and breathed into him the soul that I have created for him, then fall down prostrating yourselves to him'." (15:26-29)**

# Bai'ah (Oath of Allegiance) in Islām?

Q What is the reality of Bai'ah? Please explain in detail regarding this controversial issue.

A It is unfortunate to say that the topic of Bai'ah has become a great controversial issue. People have become so neglectful of it, to the extent that, some individuals have even gone as far as condemning it as an act of innovation (Bid'ah). This is due to a lack of understanding of its concepts. Furthermore, incorrect conclusions are made by looking at it partially rather than fully understanding it. In fact, there are many verses of the Holy Qur'ān and Ahādeeth of the Holy Prophet ﷺ, that mention and explain the practice of Bai'ah. Many books and articles have been written on this topic. However, at this point, I feel it necessary to elaborate on the most relevant points which will be, by the Will of Allāh ﷻ, sufficient for anyone who is confused regarding this topic. The following points that will be discussed are;

- Bai'ah in Islām (evidence, definition and its classification)
- The need for Bai'ah (Rectification of the soul)
- Finding the right Shaykh (Spiritual Guide)

The literal meaning of Bai'ah is to "sell". In the old Arab culture, whenever two parties would pledge an agreement with one another, they would hold hands to promise to fulfil the agreement. Mufti Shafee Sāhib ﷫ defines Bai'ah in the terminology of Shari'ah in the following manner: "The word Bai'ah means to take a promise for performing a special deed. It was the Sunnah of the Holy Prophet ﷺ that both parties would hold each other's hands in order to pledge an allegiance. Once they pledged, it was imperative to fulfil the obligation and breaking it would not be permissible." (Ma'āriful Qur'ān)

This pledge of allegiance would be taken on many occasions such as, participation in Jihād, performance of good deeds and abstinence from all forms of sins or at times upon entering Islām. The evidences of Bai'ah are to be found in the Holy Qu'rān and in many Ahādeeth, some of which are as follows: Allāh ﷻ states,

"Verily those people who pledge their allegiance to you then they are pledging their allegiance to Allāh, the hand of Allāh is above their hands." (48:10)

"O' Prophet when the believing women approach you to pledge their allegiance that they will not associate any partners with Allāh, nor will they steal, nor fornicate, nor kill their own children, nor bring forth any form of slandering that they have devised between their hands and feet, nor would they disobey you in any good (affairs), then accept their pledge and seek forgiveness from Allāh for them, verily Allāh is Forgiving and Merciful." (60:12)

Sayyidunā Ubādah Ibn Sāmit ﷺ relates, that the Holy Prophet ﷺ was once seated whilst his Companions were seated around him. He said, "Pledge your allegiance to me that you will not associate any partners with Allāh ﷻ, nor will you commit theft, nor will you fornicate, nor will you kill your own children, nor will you bring forth any form of slandering that you produce between your hands and feet, nor will you disobey in any good (affairs)." (Bukhāri)

Sayyidunā Auf Ibn Mālik al-Ashja'ee ﷺ relates that, once there were nine, eight or seven of us with the Holy Prophet ﷺ. The Holy Prophet ﷺ said, "Will you not pledge your oath with the Prophet of Allāh ﷺ?" We extended our hands and said, "Upon what shall we pledge, O' Messenger of Allāh ﷺ?" He replied "That you worship Allāh ﷻ and associate no partners with Him, and you perform your five daily prayers, and you listen and obey." Then he lowered his voice saying, "And you do not ask anything from others." The (narrator says), "I saw some of these people (who pledged); whenever they dropped their whip (while riding) they would not ask anyone to pick it up for them." (Muslim, Abū Dāwood)

There are many more verses from the Holy Qur'ān and the Ahādeeth of the Holy Prophet ﷺ regarding Bai'ah but I have sufficed upon the aforementioned ones for simplicity. From the above mentioned Ahādeeth, many of the prominent scholars, like Shaykh Ashraf Ali Thānwi ﷭ and Shaykh Muhammad Zakariyyah ﷭, have deduced the establishment of Bai'ah in Islām. Moreover, they have stated that it is necessary upon a person to be aware and mindful of ones inner and outer behaviour. This is what Sūfism or Tasawwuf is based upon i.e. the rectification of the soul by pledging one's oath to a pious Shaykh. This is also termed as Bai'ah of Tareeqah.

The Holy Prophet ﷺ would pledge allegiance on different occasions from his Companions ﷢. It was not merely restricted to Jihād or accepting Islām' as it is commonly understood by many people today due to ignorance. The different categories of Bai'ah that the Holy Prophet ﷺ had pledged from his Companions ﷢ are as follows:

**Bai'ah Upon Islām:** When an individual or a group of people or even a delegation approached the Holy Prophet ﷺ to embrace Islām, then the Holy Prophet ﷺ used to take a covenant or an oath from them.

**Bai'ah Upon Jihād:** This form of Bai'ah was taken on the occasion of Jihād, for instance, at Hudaibiyah when upon receiving the news of Sayyidunā Uthmān's ◈ death, the Sahābah ◈ pledged their allegiance with the Holy Prophet ◈ to fight against their enemies and avenge the death of Sayyidunā Uthmān ◈. Subsequently, the Holy Prophet ◈ and the Sahābah ◈ came to know that it was a false rumour. However, Allāh ◈ revealed some verses in the Holy Qur'ān, expressing His Divine Pleasure in regards to this particular allegiance.

**Bai'ah for Caliphate:** This type of oath of allegiance was taken upon accepting a new leader for the Muslims in order to pledge obedience to every command of this ruler. This type of Bai'ah occurred after the demise of the Holy Prophet ◈, when the Sahābah ◈ unanimously agreed to elect Sayyidunā Abū Bakr ◈ to rule over the Muslims. The Muslims pledged their allegiance to Sayyidunā Abū Bakr ◈ that they would obey him in all matters.

**Bai'ah Upon Performing Good Deeds:** There were some occasions, when the Holy Prophet ◈ would take an oath from the Sahābah ◈ to perform good deeds, like the Hadeeth of Sayyidunā Auf Ibn Mālik ◈ mentioned above. There is another Hadeeth narrated by Sayyidunā Jareer ◈ stating, "I pledged to the Holy Prophet ◈, upon establishing prayers, giving Zakāt and desiring good for all Muslims." (Bukhāri, Muslim, Ahmad)

**Bai'ah to Abstain and Repent from Committing Major Sins (Bai'ah Tawbah):** Likewise, there were instances when the Holy Prophet ◈ took an oath from the Sahābah ◈ to refrain from major sins. The evidences for this category are mentioned above. Bai'ah of Tareeqah is based upon the last two categories. From this, we come to realize that Bai'ah and Tasawwuf (purification of the soul), were both practiced during the era of the Holy Prophet ﷺ.

Although the term Tasawwuf was not used at that time, it was after a few centuries that the later scholars adopted it.

## The Need for Bai'ah
Every human being's body constitutes two things; the physical body and the soul. Many other ideologies, like materialism, are based upon a doctrine that denies the very existence of the soul. On the contrary, Islām teaches us that there is another thing which Islām caters for and it is attached to the physical body which is the soul. Every human being requires food and nutrition in order to sustain life. Allāh ﷻ has endowed us with this gift and it is our responsibility to maintain it. Similarly, the spiritual aspect also requires certain nutrition in order to maintain a healthy state. Allāh ﷻ is the ultimate Benefactor and our Creator and He knows what our soul requires to be healthy, for instance, establishing our prayers, Dhikr, abstaining from sins etc. It is through the Holy Prophet ﷺ, that Allāh ﷻ has taught us how to maintain it. If the body is not maintained well, then it will not function well; likewise, with the soul.

Tazkiyah (rectification of the soul) was one of the major missions and responsibilities of the Holy Prophet ﷺ, as Allāh ﷻ confirms, **"It is He Who has sent amongst the unlettered ones, a Messenger amongst them to recite unto them His (Allāh's) verses, to purify them and teach them the book and wisdom." (62:2)**

Furthermore, Allāh ﷻ has guaranteed success, for those who have strived to rectify and control their evil desires to obey Allāh ﷻ, **"Indeed he has succeeded, who has purified his own soul."** (91:9)

The Holy Prophet ﷺ has said, regarding the importance of rectifying the soul, "Truly in the body there is a piece of flesh; if it is upright then the whole body will be upright and if it is corrupt then the whole body is corrupt; truly it is the heart." (Bukhāri, Muslim)

This Hadeeth is sufficient to show how important it is to rectify the soul. However, it is not a simple or a straightforward task, whereby a layman can pick up books on spiritual discourses and strive to rectify his soul by himself, through studying, without requiring an expert. Relatively, there are procedures and methods that one must follow in order to achieve that status and that is to refer to a Shaykh. If a layman is diagnosed with a severe illness or disease, then inspite of having books and encyclopedias on medicine, this layman would still refer to a doctor. This is because, it is a known fact that, if this individual attempts to search for medical treatment, without any sound knowledge, then such a person will jeopardise his/her own life. In a similar context, there would be a higher possibility for a person to endanger his/her soul, without referring to an expert who can detect the spiritual disease. Giving Bai'ah to a Shaykh is like registering to a doctor to whom a person refers to at times of illness.

A Shaykh is specialized in this field and it is his profession to deal with the illnesses of the soul, through the knowledge that Allāh ﷻ has endowed him with. Therefore, it would be appropriate and wise if a person would take Bai'ah from a Shaykh for the benefit of his/her soul.

## Finding the Right Shaykh

Having said this, a question may arise in the mind of the inquisitive reader that, how can you judge the credibility of a particular Shaykh? How will a person know whether such a person is capable to become a spiritual doctor?

Shaykh (Dr.) Muhammad Ismāil Memon has listed in his book, 'The Truth about Bai'ah', the following major requirements, for the reliability of a Shaykh:

* He must be very knowledgeable, or at least, have the necessary knowledge of Shari'ah, either through academic education, or through the company of the pious and prominent scholars. This is so that he is able to safeguard his Imān, as well as the Imān of his disciples, from false beliefs and from different trials that emerge.

* His beliefs, character, conduct and actions are in accordance with the Holy Qur'ān and the Sunnah.

* He prefers the life of the Hereafter over the life of this world. He continuously discharges his personal and social religious obligations.

* He has acquired blessings and benefits from the pious scholars through their continuous company.

* What he does is solely for the pleasure of Allāh 🕮 and not for worldly gain.

* He is kind, compassionate, considerate and graceful to-

wards his disciples. He admonishes them in the best manner possible and if he perceives any faults or mistakes in his disciples, he instantly rectifies their mistakes rather than letting them loose.

- Looking at the overall condition of his followers, to see whether they are practicing according to the Holy Qur'ān and Sunnah or not, or if they prefer the life of this world or the Hereafter.

- The Shaykh is well respected and esteemed by other pious scholars.

- More pious and distinguished people are inclined towards him than the general public.

- By accompanying the Shaykh, it will result in one to remember Allāh ﷻ abundantly within himself and will prefer the love of the Hereafter over the worldly life.

- He himself constantly remembers Allāh ﷻ, as well as encouraging others.

- He is not only pious himself, but also competent to attract others towards piety.

- He is proficient in diagnosing the spiritual illnesses and able to prescribe the correct remedies for it in accordance with the Shari'ah.

# Meaning of the word "Tableegh"

**Q** I have observed people who criticize the word "Tableegh". Why is this?

**A** Regarding what you have stated about the word "Tableegh" and why people criticize it, it is just a misunderstanding that people have. Rather than referring to the scholars for its purpose, they just draw their own conclusions by judging the followers. Firstly, I would like to mention that not every human being is perfect. Everybody makes mistakes; there is a famous saying, "There are black sheep in every community." In other words, you will always find someone in a community or in some line of work who may not adhere to the correct teachings or methods. In spite of this, no one has the right to depict the black sheep as exemplary people. In order to judge whether any line of religious work is genuine or not, one must judge through authentic sources by going to the roots to discover the purpose of a particular work. This rule does not only apply to Tableegh work but it applies to all lines of work in Islām, i.e. teaching, learning, opening Madāris, Jihād etc.

As far as Tableegh is concerned, we firmly believe that it is genuine and one of the great lines of religious work, which is set up solely for the purpose to strive for the service of the Muslim Ummah. Many books have been written on this subject. Shaykhul-Hadeeth Maulāna Muhammad Zakariyyah ﷺ has composed a chapter on the virtues of Tableegh in Fazāil-e-A'māl, which is worth reading. Hence, I would strongly suggest that for more details on the topic of Tableegh, refer to Fazāil-e-A'māl and other books written by the scholars, rather than listening to people with no knowledge.

## The Work of Tableegh

**Q** Please explain the Tableegh work of Shaykh Muhammad Ilyās ﷺ, in regards to the revival of Deen? Some people think that the work is wrong (I totally agree with this work of Da'wah).

**A** The work of Tableegh Jamā'at is, Māshā-Allāh, an excellent work of Da'wah and Islāh (self reformation). I do not know any of its fundamentals to be contrary to the Holy Qur'ān and Sunnah. Shaykh Muhammad Ilyās ﷺ undertook enormous sacrifices to revive the work of Da'wah. Some people often criticize this noble work, either out of hatred, arrogance, ignorance and lack of understanding or obtaining information from the wrong people. Many great scholars have approved of this work as not only being beneficial, but also imperative, in this day and age for the Ummah.

## Fazāil-e-A'māl

**Q** What is your opinion regarding Fazāil-e-A'māl?

**A** We firmly believe that the book Fazāil-e-A'māl is a very useful book and the author , Shaykhul-Hadeeth Maulāna Muhammad Zakariyyah (may Allāh ﷺ shower His mercy upon him and enlighten his grave), was a great scholar of his time and contributed immense efforts towards Deen. One of his famous works was Fazāil-e-A'māl in which he has compiled the lives of the Companions of the Holy Prophet ﷺ and Ahādeeth pertaining to the virtues of different worship; like the virtues of Salāh, fasting, giving charity, recitation of the Holy Qur'ān etc. Therefore, we accept Fazāil-e-A'māl to be a very beneficial book and highly recommended.

## Allāh ﷺ Knows Best

# 2. CHAPTER ON ILM
# KNOWLEDGE

# Evil Dreams

Q Sometimes I see such evil dreams which cause me extreme anxiety, e.g. having sexual relations with a Mahram relative. Please advise me.

A A person is not accounted for dreams no matter how bad and evil a dream may appear. One will not be questioned by Allāh ﷻ because nobody has any control over them. Sometimes an extremely bad dream can have a beautiful interpretation. A person should therefore, not become unduly disturbed if one sees such dreams. However, if one ponders over such matters during one's time of wakefulness, then it is quite possible that the bad dream could be the result of such thoughts, which then reflect in the dreams. If one is in the habit of such thoughts, one should repent and refrain from them.

# Types of Dreams

Q I saw an evil dream, after which I suddenly woke up feeling very frightened. What should I do to calm myself?

A Sayyidunā Abū Hurairah ؓ narrates that the Holy Prophet ﷺ said, "If a person sees an evil dream then he should change sides, spit thrice to his left, seek Allāh's ﷻ protection from the evil of it, and ask for the good of it." (Ibn Mājah)

In a narration of Imām Muhammad Ibn Sīreen ﷭, reported by Imām Bukhāri ﷭, it is mentioned that one should perform Salāh immediately after seeing such a dream and one should not narrate it to anyone. (Bukhāri)

Hāfiz Ibn Hajar Al-Asqalāni ﷺ (a renowned commentator of Saheeh-Bukhāri) writes in his works, that the following etiquettes should be adhered to after seeing a bad dream:

1.    One should seek Allāh's ﷻ protection by reciting Ta'awwudh etc.
2.    One should spit to the left side.
3.    One should refrain from discussing it with anyone.
4.    One should change sides.
5.    One should stand up to perform Salāh.
6.    Some scholars have suggested the recital of Āyatul-Kursi on this occasion. Imām Qurtubi ﷺ writes that performing Salāh encapsulates all the above etiquettes. (Fathul-Bāri)

Sayyidunā Abū Qatādah ﷺ relates that he heard the Holy Prophet ﷺ saying, that there are three types of dreams:

1.    Dreams that are made up of one's thoughts and imagination. There are no interpretations for such dreams.
2.    Dreams from Shaytān. If one sees an unpleasant dream of this nature, he should seek protection with Allāh ﷻ against the accursed Shaytān and spit to his left side thrice. Inshā-Allāh, he will be saved from harm.
3.    Dreams from Allāh ﷻ which signify glad tidings for a believer. It is related in one Hadeeth, that the dream of a believer is a forty-sixth portion of prophethood.

After seeing a dream of the third category, one should narrate it to a person who is an expert in dream interpretation. (Seerah)

Hāfiz Ibn Hajar Al-Asqalāni ﷺ further writes that dreams are not only confined to the above three types. Sometimes a person sees a dream, wherein he is doing something that he normally does. For example, he sees himself having a meal etc. (Fathul-Bāri)

It is important to remember that many times, thoughts and imaginations can lead to visual forms in a person's dream. Such dreams have no interpretation. Only those dreams have an interpretation which are a source of glad tidings for the believer. This has been termed as Mubash-shirāt (The bearers of glad tidings).

# Khātamun Nabiyyeen

**Q** What is the meaning of Khātamun Nabiyyeen?

**A** In the Holy Qur'ān, Allāh ﷻ has referred to our Holy Prophet ﷺ as Khātamun Nabiyyeen in Sūrah Al-Ahzāb (33:40). This refers to 'the seal of the Prophets' i.e. no Prophet is to come after him. If anyone claims Prophethood after the Holy Prophet ﷺ, then such a person is an imposter and a disbeliever.

# Definition of Taqleed

**Q** What is the definition of Taqleed? Will a person still remain a Hanafi if he acts upon Imām Abū Yūsuf's ﷺ or Imām Zufar's ﷺ view? Also will he still remain a Hanafi if he acts upon the opinion of Imām Shāfi'ee ﷺ or Imām Mālik ﷺ at the time of need?

A **Definition**: Taqleed means, to follow and accept the opinion or a legal verdict of a particular Mujtahid, without demanding evidence from him. The Mujtahid must have attained the highest calibre and proficiency in the four sources of Islamic Law i.e. the Holy Qur'ān, Hadeeth, Ijmā and Qiyās, and mastered all of the necessary requirements, in order to achieve that status of proficiency, along with meeting the spiritual requirements. This is known as Taqleed.

The statement 'without demanding proof', does not imply that it is impermissible to demand proof, nor does it imply that the Imām will have no evidence at all. Rather, it suggests accepting the Imām's statement, with the conviction that his legal opinion has been derived from the four sources of Shari'ah i.e. the Holy Qur'ān, Hadeeth, Ijmā and Qiyās. Therefore, there is no need to ask for any proof, due to his expertise. For a non-Mujtahid to follow a Mujtahid, trusting that he has the proof and evidence, without asking him for the evidence, is also known as Taqleed.

It is the jurisprudential principles set by Imām Abū Haneefah ☙, that his students, such as Imām Abū Yūsuf ☙ and others, have used and developed through the course of time, in order to derive further Masā'il related to Shari'ah. Whether these Masā'il are directly from Imām Sāhib ☙ or not, a person who follows them will still remain a 'Hanafi'.

The views of Imām Sāhib's ☙ students are in actual fact, Imām Sahib's ☙ views. Therefore, not acting upon Imām Sāhib's ☙ opinion and preferring his student's opinion, on specific occasions, does not expel an individual from the Hanafi Madhab. Rather, he will remain a Hanafi. (Rasmul Mufti by Allāmah Shāmi ﷺ).

Furthermore, due to the change of time, customs and occurrences, a ruling of one issue can vary. However, the scholars of the latter era understood that if Imām Sāhib ﷺ was alive today, he would have also issued a similar verdict. Therefore, they would issue a different ruling, regardless of whether that was the same view of Imām Shāfi'ee ﷺ or of any other Imām.

# Taqleed - Following a Madhab of an Imām in the Matters of Shari'ah

Q Some people assert that Taqleed (following the school of an Imām) is unlawful in Shari'ah. They insist that a true Muslim should directly follow the Holy Qur'ān and Sunnah and following a Madhab of an Imām, in the matters of Shari'ah, is equivalent to Shirk (polytheism). They also claim that the Hanafi, Shāfi'ee, Māliki and Hanbali schools were formed some two hundred years after the departure of the Holy Prophet ﷺ from this world; therefore, these schools are an innovation (Bid'ah). Some also stress, that a Muslim should seek guidance directly from the Holy Qur'ān and Sunnah and no intervention of an Imām is needed to practice upon the Shari'ah. Please explain how far this view is correct.

A Shaykh Mufti Taqi Uthmāni Sāhib has given the following response in regards to this assertion: This view is based on certain misunderstandings arising from unnecessary treatment of the complicated issues involved. The full clarification of this mistaken view requires a detailed article. However, I will try to explain the basic points as briefly as possible.

It is true that obedience, in its true sense, belongs to Allāh ﷻ alone. The obedience of the Holy Prophet ﷺ, has also been ordained upon us, because he conveyed to us the divine commandments of Allāh ﷻ; otherwise he has no status deserving our obedience. By obeying and acting according to the teachings of the Holy Prophet ﷺ, we obtain the pleasure of Allāh ﷻ.

However, the root of the matter is, that the interpretation of the Holy Qur'ān and the Sunnah is not a simple one. It requires an intensive and extensive study of the sacred sources of Shari'ah, which cannot be undertaken by a person unqualified in the field. If every Muslim was obliged to directly resort to the Holy Qur'ān and Sunnah on each and every problem arising before him, it would burden him with a responsibility that would be almost impossible to fulfil. This is because the derivation of the rules of Shari'ah from the Holy Qur'ān and Sunnah, requires a thorough knowledge of the Arabic language and all the relevant sciences - a combination which every person is not known to have. The only solution to this problem is that, a few individuals from each locality should undertake the responsibility of acquiring an in-depth knowledge of the Islamic Law, so that other members in that locality could enquire from them, the ruling of an issue occurring in their day-to-day affairs. This is exactly what Allāh ﷻ has ordained for the Muslims in the following words:

"And not (all of) the Believers should advance altogether, so from every group why shouldn't there be a party that would go forth, that they (who are left behind) may attain (a deep) understanding in religion, so that they may warn their people when they return to them, so that they may beware (of evil)?" (9:122).

This verse of the Holy Qur'ān indicates in clear terms, that a group of Muslims should devote themselves to acquiring the knowledge of Shari'ah and all others should consult them for their rulings. Now, if a person asks a reliable scholar about the juridical (Shari'ah) ruling regarding a specific matter and acts upon his advice, can any reasonable person accuse him of committing Shirk on the ground that he has followed the advice of a human being, instead of the Holy Qur'ān and Sunnah? Certainly not.

The reason is obvious, because he has not abandoned obedience to Allāh ﷻ and His Messenger ﷺ. Rather, he is in search of a way to obey them. Being unaware of the Shari'ah commands, he has consulted a scholar, in order to know what he is required to do by Allāh ﷻ. He has not taken that scholar as the subject of his obedience, but rather, as an interpreter of the divine commands. Nobody can accuse him of committing Shirk.

This is the essence of Taqleed; whereby a person who does not have an in depth understanding of the legal applications of the Holy Qur'ān and Sunnah, resorts to the interpretation of a Muslim jurist, often termed an Imām, and acts according to his interpretation of the Shari'ah. The person never considers the Imām worthy of obedience, nor binding upon him, but seeks his guidance, in order to know the requirements of the Shari'ah.

**Fiqh-ul-Imām -** This is due to not having direct access to the Holy Qur'ān and Sunnah or not having adequate knowledge for deriving the rules of Shari'ah from these sources. This behaviour is called Taqleed of that jurist or Imām. Thus, how can it be said that Taqleed is equivalent to Shirk?

The qualified Muslim jurists or Imāms, who have devoted their lives to Ijtihād, have collected the rules of Shari'ah, according to their respective interpretations of its sources, in an almost codified form. This collection of the rules of Shari'ah, according to the interpretation of a particular jurist, is called the Madhab or "school" of that jurist.

Thus, the school of an Imām is not something parallel to the Shari'ah, nor something alien to it. In fact, it is a particular interpretation of the Shari'ah and a collection of the major Shari'ah rules, derived from the Holy Qur'ān and Sunnah by a reliable jurist and arranged subject-wise, for the convenience of the followers of the Shari'ah. So, the one who follows a particular school, actually follows the Holy Qur'ān and Sunnah, according to the interpretation of a reliable jurist, whom he or she believes to be the most trustworthy and most well-versed in the matters of Shari'ah.

As for the differences in the schools, they have emerged through the different possible interpretations of the rules, mentioned in or derived from the Holy Qur'ān and Sunnah. In order to understand this point properly, it is necessary to know that the rules mentioned in the Holy Qur'ān and Sunnah are of two different categories.

The first category of rules are those which arc stated in these sacred sources in such clear words that they allow only one interpretation. No other interpretation is possible thereof, such as the obligation of Salāh, Zakāt, fasting and pilgrimage and the prohibition of pork and adultery. With regard to this set of rules, no difference of opinion has ever occurred. All the schools of jurists are unanimous in their interpretation. Hence, there is no room for Ijtihād or Taqleed in these matters. Also, since everyone can easily understand them from the Holy Qur'ān and Sunnah, there is no need for consulting an Imām or jurist.

On the other hand, there are some rules of Shari'ah derived from the Holy Qur'ān and Sunnah, where any of the following situations may arise:

**1)** The wording used in the sacred sources may allow more than one interpretation. For example, while mentioning the duration of the waiting period (Iddah) for a divorced woman, the Holy Qur'ān has used the following expression, **"And divorced women shall wait (as regards to their marriage) for three periods of Qurū." (2:228)**

The word 'Qurū' used in the above verse has two meanings. It stands both for the 'period of menstruation' and the 'period of cleanliness' (i.e. Tuhr). Both meanings are possible in the verse and each of them results in different legal consequences.

The question that requires scholarly efforts here is: Which of the two meanings is intended? Whilst answering the question, the juridical opinions may naturally differ, as is the case. Imām Shāfi'ee ﷺ interprets the word Qurū as the 'period of cleanliness,' while Imām Abū Haneefah ﷺ interprets it as the 'period of menstruation'. Both of them have a number of reasons in support of their respective views and neither can be completely rejected. This example highlights one of the causes for differences of opinion amongst different schools.

**2)** Sometimes disparity appears between two Ahādeeth of the Holy Prophet ﷺ and a jurist has to reconcile between them or prefer one of them over the other. In this case also, the view points of the jurists may differ from one another. For example, there are two sets of traditions found in the books of Ahādeeth, narrating different behaviours of the Holy Prophet ﷺ while bowing (Rukū) in prayer. The first set of Ahādeeth mention that he used to raise his hands before bowing, while the other Ahādeeth mention that he did not raise his hands except at the beginning of Salāh. The jurists, whilst accepting that both ways are correct, have expressed different views regarding the question: Which of the two ways is more preferable? Thus, situations like these also cause differences of opinion between various schools.

**3)** There are many issues which are not specifically addressed in the Holy Qur'ān and Sunnah. The solution to these issues is sought either through analogy or through examples, found in the sacred sources, that have an indirect bearing on the subject. Here again, the jurists may have different approaches to extracting the required solution from the Holy Qur'ān and Sunnah.

Such are the basic causes of differences of opinion between the schools. These differences are in no way a defect in Shari'ah; rather, they are a source of flexibility, composing a vast field of academic research, governed by the principles of Shari'ah and settled by means of the Holy Qur'ān and Sunnah, for all time to come.

A Muslim jurist, who has all the necessary qualifications for Ijti-hād, is supposed to attempt his utmost to extract the actual meaning of the Qur'ān and Sunnah. If he does this to the best of his ability and with sincerity, he will be rewarded for accomplishing his duty and nobody can accuse him of disregarding the Shari'ah, even though his view may seem to be weaker when compared to others. This is a natural and logical circumstance, certain to be found in every legal system.

The established laws in every legal framework do not cover every minute detail and possible situation. Also, these laws are often open to more than one interpretation. Different courts of law, while attempting to understand them, often disagree about their meanings. One court may interpret the law in a particular way, while another court may understand it in quite a different sense. Thus, nobody can say that the jurists have disrespected the laws of Islām by arriving at different opinions. And since every court of law intends to apply the established law to the best of its ability, its duty towards the Lawmaker (Allāh ﷻ) will be discharged and its jurists will be rewarded for it.

For example, if one of the courts mentioned earlier was a high court, all the lower courts and the people living under its authority would be bound to follow judgements made by the high court, even though their personal opinion might not conform to the opinion of the high court. In such a case, if the lower courts follow the decision of the high court, nobody can say that they are not following the law or that they take the high court to be a legislator of the law. This is because, in actual fact, the lower courts are following the decision of the high court as a trustworthy interpreter of the law and not as a legislator.

In exactly the same way, the school of a Muslim jurist provides nothing more than a reliable interpretation of the Shari'ah. Another qualified jurist may disagree, regarding the interpretation of that jurist. However, neither can he be accused of disregarding the laws of Shari'ah, nor can anyone accuse the followers of a particular school of following something other than the Shari'ah or committing Shirk. The reason for this is that these Muslims are following the school as a trustworthy interpretation of Shari'ah.

The next question which may arise here is: What should a person do with regard to these different schools and which one of them should he follow? The answer to this question is very simple. All of these schools have been sincere in their efforts to infer the true meaning of the Shari'ah; therefore, they are all equally valid. A person should follow the school of any of the recognised Imāms, whom he believes to be most knowledgeable and most pious.

Although the Muslim jurists who have undertaken the exercise of Ijtihād have been many in number, the schools of the four Imāms -

Imām Abū Haneefah ﷺ, Imām Mālik ﷺ, Imām Shāfi'ee ﷺ and Imām Ahmad ﷺ, are found to be more comprehensive, well-arranged and well-preserved up to the present day. The Muslim Ummah as a whole have regarded these four Imāms as having the most reliable interpretations of Shari'ah. The four schools are known as the Hanafi, Māliki, Shāfi'ee and Hanbali schools. The rest of the schools (Madhabs) are either not comprehensive enough, in the sense that they do not contain all aspects of Shari'ah, or have not been preserved in a reliable form. For this reason, the majority of the Muslim Ummah belong to one of these four schools. If a person adopts a school of Islamic law as an interpretation of the Shari'ah, his obligation to follow the Shari'ah stands fulfilled.

This is the true picture of the term Taqleed with reference to the jurisprudential schools. I hope this explanation will be sufficient to show that Taqleed has nothing to do with Shirk or ascribing partners to Allāh ﷻ. It is in fact a simple and easy way of following the Shari'ah.

# Deducing Laws From the Holy Qur'ān and Sunnah

Q How are Masā'il (rulings) derived from the Holy Qur'ān and Sunnah? What methods are used if the Mas'alah cannot be clearly understood from the Holy Qur'ān and Ahādeeth? What is the importance of Taqleed (following a Muslim jurist) in the Shari'ah? Why are we limited to the schools of the four Imāms?

A The original source of guidance is the Holy Qur'ān but generally, it is the fundamental principles and Masā'il which are stated in the Holy Qur'ān. It was the duty of the Holy Prophet ﷺ to explain in detail these Masā'il.

Allāh ﷻ says, **"And We have revealed to you the Reminder (Qur'ān) so you may explain to mankind of what has been revealed to them so that they may contemplate." (16:44)**

The subject of how the Islamic laws are derived from the Shari'ah sources is a vast subject area. It is impossible to discuss every aspect of it due to its complex nature. However, for simplicity a few basic examples are mentioned below.

**Example No. 1**
It is stated in the Holy Qur'ān, 'Establish Salāh.' How to perform Salāh is not mentioned at all. The method of performing Salāh, the different types, and their respective rulings are all related to us by the Holy Prophet ﷺ, through Ahādeeth. For instance, we learn from the Ahādeeth only about aspects such as the number of Rak'ats in each Salāh, in which one is only Sūrah Al-Fātihah recited and in which one an additional Sūrah is recited. Furthermore, which are the ones in which Qirāt is recited quietly and in which one is Qirāt recited loudly. It is impossible to ascertain all this information from the Holy Qur'ān only. Support from the Sunnah is required.

**Example No. 2**
It is stated in the Holy Qur'ān, 'Pay Zakāt.' The Holy Qur'ān has not mentioned anything regarding this.

All the details on how the Zakāt is calculated on silver, gold, goats, cows, camels etc. have been mentioned in the Ahādeeth.

**Example No. 3**
It is stated in the Holy Qur'an, **"And pilgrimage to the house is a duty upon mankind for Allāh for those who can."** (3:97)

The details on how Tawāf should be done and how many rounds there are in one Tawāf, the Masā'il of Arafah, Minā, Muzdalifah and Ramee etc. have all been explained by the Holy Prophet ﷺ.

To understand the Holy Qur'ān, it is important to acquire the knowledge of Ahādeeth. It is impossible to understand the Holy Qur'ān whilst neglecting the Ahādeeth. The Ummah has been commanded to derive guidance from the Holy Qur'ān under the explained instructions of the Holy Prophet ﷺ. In this respect, the obedience of the Holy Prophet ﷺ means the obedience of Allāh ﷻ. **"He who obeys the Prophet has indeed obeyed Allāh."** (4:80)

Likewise it is mentioned in the Ahādeeth, "Perform Salāh in the manner that you have seen me perform." (Bukhāri) The Holy Prophet ﷺ did not say, pray the way you understand from the Holy Qur'ān.

**Different Types of Ahādeeth**
Those statements that were made verbally by the Holy Prophet ﷺ himself, are called 'Hadeeth-e-Qawli', and what the Holy Prophet ﷺ practically demonstrated are known as 'Hadeeth-e-Fe'li'. Some-

times, certain actions were done in front of the Holy Prophet ﷺ or were brought to his attention but he did not affirm nor reject them, instead he preferred to remain silent. This is taken as their confirmation. This is called 'Taqreer'. These three types of Ahādeeth are a source of guidance for the entire Ummah.

**Qiyās (Analogical Deduction)**
Qiyās is the application (Illat), also referred to as pretext or prime factor, that is found in the Holy Qur'ān, Sunnah or Ijmā (consensus) to a modern day contemporary issue. This is essentially required when the ruling of a particular contemporary issue is not clearly understood, nor is it found categorically in the Qur'ān, Sunnah or Ijmā. Thus, as a last resort, Qiyās will be used in order to determine the ruling of a contemporary matter, by carefully analysing which prime factor from the Qur'ān, Sunnah or Ijmā is similar to the current issue.

There were certain questions that the Holy Prophet ﷺ was asked. He would reply to them and to further facilitate the questioner's understanding he would sometimes give a logical reason by posing a logical question to the questioner knowing that the answer would become apparent to the questioner.

**Example:** A Sahābi ؓ once inquired that since Hajj was due upon his mother (who had passed away), would it be sufficient if he was to perform it on her behalf? The Holy Prophet ﷺ replied in the affirmative. Then he posed a (logical) question to the questioner: Suppose if your mother took a loan from somebody and you paid it off (on her behalf), would it be acceptable or not? The Sahabi ؓ replied that it would be acceptable. The Holy Prophet ﷺ then said that, paying off the loan to Allāh ﷻ is more worthy to be accepted. (Bukhāri)

In the Shari'ah this is known as Qiyās, Ijtihād, Istinbāt and I'tibār. Teachings of this nature are supported by the Holy Prophet ﷺ. Its conditions and details can be found in the books of Usool (Principles of Islamic jurisprudence).

The Holy Prophet ﷺ sent Sayyidunā Mu'āz Ibn Jabal ؓ as a judge to Yemen. Whilst he was going, the Holy Prophet ﷺ walked along-side him and gave him a lot of counsel until the Holy Prophet ﷺ came to a point to bid him farewell. During the advice, the Holy Prophet ﷺ asked him, "According to which law will you make your judgements?" He replied, "According to the Holy Qur'ān." The Holy Prophet ﷺ then inquired, "What if you do not find it in the Holy Qur'ān?" He answered, "Then according to the Sunnah of Rasūlullāh ﷺ." Then he asked, "What will you do if you do not find it in the Sunnah either?" He replied, "I will do Ijtihād." The Holy Prophet ﷺ expressed great happiness upon this reply. He was in full support of this decision and he thanked Allāh ﷻ for this selection. (Abū Dāwood)

## Ijtihād

When a Mas'alah cannot be clearly found in the Holy Qur'ān and the Ahādeeth, then a Mujtahid (jurist) will thoroughly analyse through analogy and evidences to determine its ruling. This is known as Ijtihād and Qiyās, as understood from the aforemen-tioned text. If this is agreed upon unanimously, it is called Ijmā (consensus). This is why the Ulamā of Usool (experts in the field of juristic principles) have written that, Qiyās does not establish the decree, but it just makes it evident.

A ruling that exists in the Holy Qur'ān or Ahādeeth, but is not quite apparent for a layman to understand, maybe made apparent by a Mujtahid having done Qiyās on its analogies or by analysing evidently, implicitly or by way of necessity. Imām Bukhāri ﷺ has compiled a specific chapter regarding this.

### Taqleed
The following of a Mujtahid becomes compulsory upon whoever does not have the capability of Ijtihād. This is known as Taqleed.

The greatest benefit of Taqleed is that it enables one's Deen to be systematic and easy to practice. Moreover, by practising Taqleed, there is less probability for the desires to intervene in a person's Deen. If a person is deprived of Taqleed, he will begin to pick and choose in Deen those things which are in conformity with his desires in contrast to a Muqallid (a person who practices Taqleed), for whom there is no scope to 'pick and choose'. This is why Sayyidunā Mu'ādh ﷺ was sent as a judge, so that the Masā'il and rulings he derived from the Holy Qur'ān, Ahādeeth and Ijtihād would be implemented. Following the three principles, mentioned by Sayyidunā Mu'ādh ﷺ would in fact mean obeying the Holy Prophet ﷺ.

It has been narrated from Sayyidunā Abū Hurairah ﷺ, that the Holy Prophet ﷺ said, "Whoever obeyed me has indeed obeyed Allāh

﷽ and whoever disobeyed me has indeed disobeyed Allāh ﷻ; whoever obeyed the Ameer (leader) has indeed obeyed me and whoever disobeyed the Ameer has indeed disobeyed me."

(Bukhāri)

### The Categories of Masā'il

There are two types of Masā'il. Firstly, those that have been mentioned in the Nas (Holy Qur'ān or Ahādeeth). Secondly, those which have not been mentioned in the Holy Qur'ān or Ahādeeth.

The first category will further divide into two forms; the first form is that the Nas will either have a ruling in the positive or in the negative only. The second form is, that there are two types of Nas regarding the same Mas'alah. In some we find a ruling in the positive and in others in the negative. For example, from some we find out about Āmeen-bil-Jahr (saying Āmeen loudly) and from some we find about Āmeen-bis-Sirr (saying Āmeen softly). Some inform us about Raf'ul-Yadāyn (raising the hands), whilst others tell us about Tark'ur-Raf'ul-Yadāyn (not raising the hands).

There are also another two groups of Masā'il. The first one is when historic evidence or other circumstances indicate that one Nas has preference over the other. The second type is, when it is not known which Nas has been given preference over the other and nor is it known which came first and which came later. In total there are four types of Masā'il.

### First

That type of Nas (evidence that is mentioned in the Holy Qur'ān and Hadeeth) which is so clear, that it only renders one interpretation, giving no scope for any other interpretation. No Qiyās or Ijti-hād will be done; neither would Taqleed be permissible if it oppos-es the Nas. Instead the Nas will be acted upon. All of the four Imāms are unanimous in this category because there can be no scope for differences. For instance the fundamental articles of be-lief, the prohibition of interest and alcohol etc.

**Second**

Those Masā'il which have two types of Nas and it is also known which came first and which came second. Generally, the first one will be abrogated, while the second one will be applicable. There is no need for Qiyās, Ijtihād or Taqleed in this type either.

For instance Allāh ﷻ states in the Holy Qur'ān, **"And upon those who have the strength (to fast) is Fidyah (compensation)."** (2:184) However, in another place, Allāh ﷻ states, **"So those of you that witness the month (of Ramadhān) must fast."** (2:185)

In the early days of Islām, when Ramadhān fasts were newly pre-scribed, initially a person was given the option to either fast or give Fidyah, irrespective of whether he or she was rich or poor. The for-mer verse indicates towards this option. Subsequently, this conces-sion was Mansūkh (abrogated) by the latter verse. So now, until the Day of Judgement, whoever has the strength to fast in the month of Ramadhān has to fast. The second verse clearly shows this obligation. In this case, both the Mansūkh (abrogated i.e. the former verse) and the Nāsikh (abrogator i.e. the latter verse) are known.

**Third**

Those Masā'il where there are two types of Nas and it is not known which came first and which came second. For instance, the issue of Raf'ul- Yadāyn (raising the hands during Salāh besides the Takbeer-e-Tahreemah) and Tark Raf'ul-Yadāyn (not raising the hands on other occasions besides Takbeer-e-Tahreemah).

**Fourth**

Those Masā'il regarding which there is no clear Nas at all.

In the last two categories a layman will be in one of two situations; either he is acting upon it or he is not acting upon it and wandering aimlessly. There is no permission for the latter. Allāh ﷻ says, **"Does man think that he will be left in vain?" (75:36).** This is not the case; a person is obliged to obey Allāh's ﷻ commands in every aspect. So which one will he then act upon? In the third category, which Nas does he apply? If he acts upon one, the other is omitted. He cannot prefer one Nas over the other with his own accord because he does not have the knowledge regarding which Nas came first and which came second. Likewise, he will not know which is the abrogator and which is the abrogated. In the fourth category, there is no categorical Nas at all. So without knowledge, what is he going to act upon?

Allāh ﷻ says in the Holy Qur'ān, **"Do not pursue what you have no knowledge about." (17:36)** This leaves no alternative but to do Ijtihād in the third and fourth category. This is because, in the third category one Nas has to be preferred over the other by using other contextual evidences. This must also be done in the fourth category because the ruling has to be found.

It is quite obvious that not everybody has the capability and qualification to do Ijtihād and Istinbāt (deduction of laws). The following verse of the Holy Qur'ān makes this clear; Allāh ﷻ says, **"If
they had referred it to the Messenger and to those who have authority amongst them, the proper investigators would have
known it from them (direct)." (4:83)**

Anybody can claim to make a decision, regardless of it being right
or wrong, but only he will be called a Mustanbit and Mujtahid,
who possesses the qualifications of Istinbāt (extensive analysis and
deduction) in accordance to the Shari'ah. If he cannot, then he will
be known as a Muqallid (follower).

Hence, it is important for a Mujtahid to apply Ijtihād in the third
and forth type of Masā'il. As for the Muqallid, it is important for
him to do Taqleed. Even if the Mujtahid makes an error, the Mujtahid will not be deprived of reward because his Ijtihād was according to the Shari'ah. If his Ijtihād is correct then he will be entitled to
a double reward.

A doubt might arise as to why Taqleed is restricted to the four
Imāms (Imām Abū Haneefah ﷺ, Imām Mālik ﷺ, Imām Shāfi'ee ﷺ
and Imām Ahmad ﷺ) only, despite there being many Mujtahidoon
amongst the Sahābah ﷺ, Tābi'een and Tabi'-Tābi'een? What is the
harm in doing Taqleed of anybody else, especially those Sahābah
ﷺ whose virtues have been mentioned in the Holy Qur'ān and in
many Ahādeeth? The answer to this is that, indeed the Sahābah ﷺ
have a higher status than the four Imāms.

The reason for doing Taqleed of the four Imāms in particular, is not because they are thought to be greater than the Sahābah ﷺ. Rather, when doing Taqleed, it is important to acknowledge the Masā'il in which Taqleed is done. There are three fundamental conditions for doing Taqleed of a particular Imām:

a)   That their entire Fiqh and Madhab is preserved from the chapter of purity to inheritance. This is essential so that a person or a scholar can refer to this Imām at all times regarding any aspect of life.

b)   The science of deriving laws and Usools (jurisprudential principles) have also been preserved, in order for a contemporary scholar to derive new laws on contemporary issues that emerge, based upon the Usools set by the Imām, that are extracted from the Holy Qur'ān and Sunnah.

c)   The Imām has left behind students and scholars to propagate and teach his Fiqh.

Today, there are vast amounts of detail and explanation available about the Masā'il which have been compiled and collected in the schools of the four Imāms, from the chapter of Tahārah (purity) to Kitābul-Farā'idh (chapter on inheritance), including Ibādah, dealings etc. In short, vast numbers of Masā'il, in all the fields and spheres, have been collected. This type of detailed and compiled Madhab (school) cannot be found from the Sahābah ﷺ, Tābi'een or Tabi'-Tābi'een. So, if one was to do Taqleed of anybody apart from the four Imāms, how would he do it? This is why Taqleed of the four Imāms alone has been chosen by the scholars.

Allāh ﷻ bestowed upon the four Imāms in-depth knowledge of the Holy Qur'ān and Ahādeeth and comprehensive skills of Istinbāt (deduction of laws). They also had access to the Ahādeeth of the Holy Prophet ﷺ, which were spread throughout the world by the Sahābah ﷺ.

It is possible that there will be narrations that one Imām knew about whereas another did not. However, it would be rare to find narrations that none of them knew about.

Shāh Waliullāh Muhaddith Dehlawi ﷺ has written about the spreading and circulation of Ahādeeth and about Madeenah being the headquarters of knowledge. He writes, "These four Imāms are such that their knowledge collectively encompassed the whole world and those four Imāms are Imām Abū Haneefah ﷺ, Imām Mālik ﷺ, Imām Shāfi'ee ﷺ and Imām Ahmad ﷺ."

**Note:** For further clarification on this subject please refer to reliable scholars and authentic books. It must be reminded that this subject is intricate and not easily grasped by a layman. We have merely sufficed on the important aspects of it to illustrate the complexity of this branch of learning.

# Taqleed of One Particular Imām only and not all Four Simultaneously

Q Why is it important to do Taqleed of only one Imām? What harm is there in following one Imām for one Mas'alah, then another Imām for another Mas'alah, the way it was in the time of the Sahābah ﷺ and the Tābi'een? They were not dependant on one individual in following the whole Madhab (school of thought).

A During the era of the Sahābah ﷺ, virtue and prosperity had the upper hand and generally there was no part in Deen for fulfilling personal desires. That is why when someone inquired about a Mas'alah, he asked with a good intention and acted upon it as well, regardless of whether it coincided with his desires or not.

In later times, this was not the case. Instead, people started having the urge to ask one Mas'alah from a certain Ālim (scholar) and if the answer was against their desires, they would walk off to another Ālim in search of ease. Still not content with this, there became a growing concern about how they would find a way out in every Mas'alah, which would satisfy them. It is apparent that this cannot be the motive for the search of truth.

Sometimes this can cause a lot of damage to a person's Imān. To give an example scenario, if a person made Wudhu and then touched his wife, then somebody following the Madhab (school of thought) of Imām Shāfi'ee ﷺ says to him, "Repeat your Wudhu because touching your wife breaks your Wudhu." He then replies, "I do Taqleed of Imām Abū Haneefah ﷺ and Wudhu does not break in his opinion, in this situation." Then this person vomits. So somebody following the Madhab of Imām Abū Haneefah ﷺ says to him, "Repeat your Wudhu because vomiting breaks the Wudhu, in the opinion of Imām Abū Haneefah ﷺ." He then replies, "I am following the Madhab of Imām Shāfi'ee ﷺ and in his view, Wudhu does not break by vomiting." Now, this person's Salāh is not valid in accordance with the Madhab of Imām Abū Haneefah ﷺ or that of Imām Shāfi'ee ﷺ. This is known as Talfeeq, which is not permissible by the unanimous decision of the scholars. Following in this manner is in actual fact, not doing Taqleed of any of the Imāms. Rather, he is fulfilling his personal desires by picking and choosing which is forbidden in the Shari'ah. It eventually leads a person astray from the path of Allāh ﷻ. Allāh ﷻ says in the Holy Qur'ān, **"And do not follow your personal desires, for they will lead you astray from the path of Allāh."** **(38:26)**

This is why it is important to do Taqleed of only one particular Imām. The Holy Qur'ān has associated obedience with repentance, **"And follow the path of him who turns to Me."** **(31:15)**

On this basis, any individual who had a strong presumption about Imām Abū Haneefah ﷺ, that he was repentant, and correct and that his Ijtihād was in accordance with the Holy Qur'ān and Ahādeeth, chose to do his Taqleed. Anybody who had the same thought regarding Imām Shāfi'ee ﷺ, Imām Mālik ﷺ or Imām Ahmad ﷺ began doing their Taqleed. Now, it is incorrect to leave one's own Imām whenever a person desires and start following a different Imām. Because without the permission of the Shari'ah it becomes Talfeeq and fulfilment of personal desires which ultimately leads a person astray.

Hence, Shaykh Muhammad Husain Sāhib ﷺ has written in his compilation Ishā'atus-Sunnah, after opposing Taqleed for a very long period of time and then becoming affected with a bitter experience for not doing Taqleed, "We discovered after 25 years of experience that those people who abstain from the Mujtahids and Taqleed eventually bid Islām farewell. Some leave Islām while others end up without any Madhab at all. Rebellion and disobedience of the Shari'ah is a grave result of this freedom."

This is why those learned scholars that had a deep insight of the Holy Qur'ān and countless treasures of the Ahādeeth of the Holy Prophet ﷺ and the Sahābah ﷺ, whose hearts were enriched with fear of Allāh ﷻ and whose lives were enlightened with the light of the Sunnah of the Holy Prophet ﷺ, still chose to adopt Taqleed despite having these qualities and virtues within themselves. Moreover, it is also well known that the profound scholars of the six prominent Hadeeth collections i.e. Imām Bukhāri ﷺ, Imām Muslim ﷺ, Imām Tirmizi ﷺ etc, also practiced Taqleed. For example, Imām Abū Dāwood ﷺ was a Hanbali and according to some a Shāfi'ee whilst Imām Muslim ﷺ, Imām Nasai ﷺ, Imām Tirmizi ﷺ and Imām Ibn Mājah ﷺ followed the Shāfi'ee school of thought.

Regarding Imām Bukhāri ﷺ, there are different opinions; according to some he was a Mujtahid whilst other scholars class him to be a Shāfi'ee follower. With the exemption of Imām Bukhāri ﷺ all of the scholars are unanimous that the aforementioned five Muhaddithoon (scholars of Hadeeth) would adhere to a particular Imām.

Moreover, besides the above mentioned eminent Muhaddithoon, there were many other prominent scholars in the past who adhered to a particular Imām. These are as follows:

1. From Amongst the Hanafi School of Thought:

a) Imām Yaqūb Ibn Ibrāheem, famously known as Imām Abū Yūsuf ﷺ, a renowned Faqeeh (jurist), a scholar of Hadeeth and a senior student of Imām Abū Haneefah ﷺ. He was granted the title "Qādhi-ul-Qudhāt" (The judge of judges). Demise 182 A.H.

b) Imām Muhammad Ibn Hasan Ash-Shaybāni ﷺ, also a renowned Faqeeh and a senior student of Imām Abū Haneefah ﷺ. Demise 189 A.H.

c) Muhammad Ibn Abdullāh Al-Muthannah ﷺ, who was from the progeny of a noble Sahābi, Sayyidunā Anas Ibn Mālik ﷺ. He was a Qādhi (judge) and amongst the teachers of Imām Bukhāri ﷺ, Imām Ahmad Ibn Hanbal ﷺ and others. Demise 215 A.H.

d) Imām Ahmad Ibn Muhammad Abū Ja'far At-Tahāwi ﷺ. An authority in the field of Hadeeth and also a Faqeeh. He is the author of the Hadeeth collection Sharhul Ma'āni al-Āthār. Demise 321 A.H.

e) Mahmood Ibn Ahmad Al-Badr Al-Ainee ﷺ, famously known as Allāmah Ainee ﷺ, a Muhaddith (an expert in Hadeeth) and the author of Umdatul Qāri which is a volumnous commentary of Saheeh Al-Bukhāri. Demise 855 A.H.

f) Ali Ibn Sultān Muhammad Al-Qāri Al-Harawi, famously known as Mulla Ali Qāri ﷺ, a great Muhaddith and the author of Mirqātul Mafātih which is a famous commentary of Mishkātul Masābih. Demise 1014 A.H.

2. From Amongst the Māliki School of Thought:

a) Muhammad Ibn Abdus-Salām, Ibn Suhnūn, Abū Abdullāh Al-Qairawāni ﷺ, a very high ranking scholar of Hadeeth. Demise 256 A.H.

b) Hāfiz Ibn Abdul Barr ﷺ, a great scholar of Hadeeth. Demise 463 A.H.

c) Ismāeel Ibn Ishāq Abū Ishāq, Al-Qādhi Al-Judhāmi ﷺ. Demise 282 A.H.

d) Aslam Ibn Abdul Azeez Ibn Hishām ﷺ, Chief Justice of Andalusia and also an expert in Hadeeth. Demise 319 A.H.

3. From Amongst the Shāfi'ee School of Thought:

a) Abū Bakr, Ahmad Ibnul-Husain ﷺ famously known as Imām Baihaqi ﷺ, the author of the volumnous Sunan Al-Baihaqi. Demise 458 A.H.

b) Abdullāh Ibn Muhammad, known as Abū Bakr Ibn Abi Shaibah ﷺ, a famous teacher of Imām Bukhāri ﷺ, Muslim ﷺ, Abū Dāwood ﷺ and Ibn Mājah ﷺ. Demise 235 A.H.

c) Ahmad Ibn Ali, known as Hāfiz Ibn Hajar Al-Asqalāni ﷺ, the author of Fathul Bāri a famous commentary of Saheeh Al-Bukhāri. Demise 852 A.H.

d) Ismāeel Ibn Umar Imād-ud-Deen famously known as Ibn Katheer ﷺ, an authority in the field of Tafseer, Hadeeth and Islamic History. He is the author of Tafseer Ibn Katheer (commentary of the Holy Qur'ān), Al-Bidāya Wan-Nihāya (a volumnous collection of Islamic History) and many more. Demise 774 A.H.

e) Muhi-ud-Deen Abū Zakariyyā, Yahyā Ibn Sharaf An-Nawāwi, famously known as Imām Nawāwi ﷺ, a profound scholar in Hadeeth and a famous commentator of Saheeh Muslim. Demise 676 A.H.

f) Imām Tabarāni ﷺ, the author of Tabarāni. Demise 360 A.H.

4. Followers of the Hanbali School of Thought:

a) Ahmad Ibn Abdul Haleem, known as Abul Abbās Ibn Taimiyah ﷺ, an expert in Hadeeth. Demise 728 A.H.

b) Hāfiz Ibn Qayyim Al-Jawziyah ﷺ, an expert in various fields and an author of many books. Demise 751 A.H.

c) Abdur Rahmān Ibn Ahmad, known as Ibn Rajab ﷺ, one of the commentators of Saheeh Al-Bukhāri and also Sunan Tirmizi. Demise 795 A.H.

d) Ahmad Ibn Ja'far ﷺ, a teacher of many famous Muhaddithoon such as Dārul Qutni ﷺ and others. Also one of the narrators of Musnad Ahmad. Demise 368 A.H.

The above mentioned eminent scholars are just a few; there are countless scholars up to this day that adhere to one of the Imāms. As we have cited above, it is apparent that it would not be an exaggeration if it was said that these Ulamā reached such a status only through following the Holy Prophet ﷺ and doing Taqleed of the pious servants of Deen and the great Mujtahidoon.

Shaykh Sarfrāz Sāhib ﷺ states, "O readers! This is an ocean that has no shore. Take a look into the books of biographies, the books on the categories of Muhaddithoon, the Fuqahā, the Historians, the Mufassiroon (the commentators of the Holy Qur'ān) and the grammarians and observe. You will certainly find that at least 98% of all of them were Muqallidoon i.e. followed an Imām.

**Q** If all four Madhabs were in accordance to the Holy Prophet's ﷺ way, then can I follow all four at once?

**A** Even though all the four Madhabs (schools of thought) are principally correct, in extracting their verdicts from the Holy Qur'ān and Sunnah, the juristic scholars have declared it impermissible for a layman to follow all of the four Madhabs at once. Shaykh Yūsuf Ludhyānwi ﷺ explains this point in detail in his book "Differences in the Ummah and the Straight Path". In summary, it is necessary for a layman who does not possess the qualifications of a Mujtahid to restrict himself to one Madhab only. If a person switches from one Madhab to another, with the claim that all Madhabs are correct that he follows the Holy Qur'ān and Hadeeth, then in spite of making this assertion, he will be following his own understanding and desires.

A layman is in no position to jump to conclusions and to claim what is correct and what is not, if he does not possess the basic qualifications of Ijtihād. If in the worldly affairs, no layman can draw any conclusions on a particular subject without any qualifications then how can such a person draw conclusions about religious matters?

He cannot choose to follow whosoever he wishes in a particular issue. For certain, I can say that, rather than this person adhering to the Deen in the right perspective, he in reality will be following his own desires and do what suits him best under the slogan of 'all the Imāms are correct'. Self-conceit and following ones desires are destructive for ones Deen.

Shaykh Ashraf Ali Thānwi ﷺ states, that a person who follows one Madhab, will have a Deen that is systematic and all his religious obligations will be easier to discharge; whereas a person picking and choosing from one Madhab to another, will have a Deen that is not systematic. If a person was to select all of the strictest rules from all of the Madhāhib, then he will be putting himself into unnecessary difficulty which is wrong. On the other hand, if someone selects all of the easy rulings from all of the Madhāhib, then this becomes personal interest which is also destructive. Hence, to adhere to one Imām will be systematic and free from self-interest. All of the Madhabs in their juristic verdicts and opinions are neither too strict, nor too lenient, but very moderate.

(Ashraful-Jawāb pg.161)

Shāh Waliullāh Dehlawi ۝ states, "If there was no system of re-striction to one school of thought, then every person would pick and choose rulings that conformed to their own whims and desires and Deen would become a toy (in the hands of the masses)." Thus, the only solution to suppress self-interest is to adhere to one Madhab. (Ashraful-Jawāb pg.29)

Moreover, if someone claims that all the four Imāms are right and attempts to follow all of them concurrently, then it will be impossi-ble because one may select one issue from one Imām, whereas, the other Imām may disagree. For instance, if someone bled before Salāh, then according to Imām Abū Haneefah ۝ the Wudhu will break, whereas Imām Shāfi'ee ۝ gives the verdict that the Wudhu is intact. On the other hand, if a person touches a woman, then ac-cording to Imām Abū Haneefah ۝ the Wudhu is intact, whereas according to Imām Shāfi'ee ۝, the Wudhu breaks. If someone se-lects the flexible laws from these two Madhabs, i.e. does not do Wudhu after bleeding or touching a woman and subsequently offers Salāh in this state, then according to both of the Imāms this person's Salāh is invalid. This is just one example; there are hun-dreds more examples, where there are two conflicting opinions amongst the Imāms about a particular issue, i.e. one says it is per-missible and another says it is impermissible. The question I ask is, how will such a person's Deen be systematic and easy to follow if one does not possess the qualifications to deduce laws from the Holy Qur'ān and Hadeeth, nor restrict to following one Imām?

This concept of adhering to one Imām is known as Taqleed-e-Shakhsi. This was also practiced by some people during the era of the Sahābah ﷺ, where some adhered to the opinion of one Sahābi ﷺ. Here are some examples: Ikrimāh ﷺ narrates, that the people of Madeenah during Hajj once asked Sayyidunā Abdullāh Ibn Abbās ﷺ a ruling of a particular issue. After receiving an answer, they said, "We will not practice upon your ruling and leave the ruling given by Sayyidunā Zaid Ibn Thābit ﷺ." (Bukhāri)

Imām Tāwoos ﷺ relates that I met seventy from amongst the Companions of the Holy Prophet ﷺ who would resort to the opinion of Sayyidunā Abdullāh Ibn Abbās ﷺ whenever they differed in any matter. (Fawāid-fi-Uloomil-Fiqh)

In conclusion, for the safety of ones Deen and to conduct ones obligations easily, it is necessary to follow one Imām and abstain from attempting to follow all four at once as this would involve self-interest and desire which are detrimental for one's Deen.

# Meaning of Fatwa

Q Nowadays we hear very often in the media the word Fatwa given by certain Muslim clerics. What does it mean?

A Fatwa literally means to answer a question, irrespective of whether such a question relates to an Islamic issue or not. Technically, it means to issue a legal verdict by a qualified Mufti in response to a question relating to a matter of Islām. We must remember that it is not permissible to issue a Fatwa unless a person has studied Fiqh (jurisprudence - the science of Islamic Law), in depth under the supervision and guidance of competent and qualified experts in the field. Our pious predecessors would exercise great caution in matters of Fatwa.

Imām Ahmad Ibn Hanbal ﷺ would frequently say, "I don't know." Imām Mālik ﷺ is reported to have said that the Mufti must be conscious of accountability to Allāh ﷻ before responding to any question. According to Sayyidunā Abdullāh Ibn Mas'ood ﷺ and Sayyidunā Abdullāh Ibn Abbās ﷺ, a person who answers every question is mad. Unfortunately, there are many people who claim to have the authority of issuing Fatwa, without proper training and without having acquired the necessary expertise, thereby causing confusion and misunderstanding amongst the masses.

# Meaning of Ijmā

**Q** **What does the word Ijmā mean? Has this got any basis in the Shari'ah?**

**A** The word Ijmā refers to the consensus of opinion of the Companions ﷺ and their successors on a particular matter of Shari'ah or a legal rule. It is not permissible to hold a contrary view when a matter has been unanimously agreed upon through Ijmā.

The evidence of Ijmā as a source of Islamic Law has been derived from both the Holy Qur'ān and Hadeeth. Allāh ﷻ says, **"Whoever follows a path other than the path of the Muslims, We shall assign to him what he has chosen and shall cause him to enter the Fire and it is an evil abode."** (4:115) The reference to the path of the Muslims, in this verse, is a reference to Ijmā. The Holy Prophet ﷺ said, "My nation will not unite upon error." (Mishkāt)

# The Status of Men and Women in Islām

Q In the Holy Qur'ān it states, men are a degree above women (not superior - as many men like to think), as they are supposed to be the protectors and maintainers of women and they spend from their wealth on women. In the UK, there are many men who are actually dependant on their wives, whereby the wives are providing all the financial support. Hence, the husbands are not the providers and maintainers of women and women are spending from their wealth on their husbands on everything, from providing accommodation to the food on the table. In these cases are men therefore still a degree above women?

A To understand this concept would require an elaborative answer. A crucial point must be borne in mind that, whatever command Allāh ﷻ has given, will remain as it is until the end of time. The Fuqahā (jurists) have stated that when Allāh ﷻ issues a certain command then it will fall into two categories;

1) Illat: the prime factor of the command.
2) Hikmat: it's wisdom.

The Illat will always take precedence in the command of Allāh ﷻ over wisdom. In relation to your question regarding the verse **"Men are responsible for women" (4:34)**, the prime factors (Illat) inferred from this verse are; a) That Allāh ﷻ instructs, so we cannot object, b) and that naturally men and women are not equally identical physically, biologically, psychologically, mentally and emotionally. There are certain higher degrees of capabilities that Allāh ﷻ has endowed upon a man over a woman and likewise visa versa. Mufti Shafee Sāhib ﷭ comments on this verse in the following way:

"Qawwām (translated as 'responsible') literally means to become responsible of a task and manage the overall policy of life. This is usually translated as Hākim (leader), in other words, during an occasion where people differ in the presence of a leader, the leader always has the final say, in order for matters to run smoothly. Had it not been for a leader, then people would be in a state of perpetual disparity. Similarly, he (i.e. the husband) has been appointed as a leader over his wife and children by Allāh ﷻ because he has a higher degree of advantage over his wife and children."

(Ma'āriful Qur'ān Pg.396 Vol.2)

It becomes apparent from the above cited explanation that Allāh ﷻ has naturally blessed man with many capabilities and has given him a higher degree of advantage over women in many aspects, due to his natural potential, which is why Allāh ﷻ has rendered many responsibilities to him.

It is unfortunate to say that in this day and age many men have be-come very neglectful of their responsibilities and have failed to rec-ognise them. A man should always remember that Allāh ﷻ has not privileged a man over woman out of superiority (as Allāh ﷻ Him-self will judge this), rather it is due to relativity because of his nat-ural potential, which is inevitably followed up by many responsi-bilities. A man who discards his responsibilities will become very sinful and thus will be questioned about it on the Day of Judge-ment. Sayyidunā Abdullāh Ibn Umar ؓ relates that the Holy Prophet ﷺ said, "Verily each and every one of you is a shepherd (responsible) and each and every one of you will be questioned re-garding his flock (responsibilities) and a man is responsible for his family and he will be questioned regarding his responsibilities."

(Bukhāri, Muslim)

An example of this is a principal of a school: This principal wheth-er male or female, enjoys a prestigious position compared to other employees and staff in a school. However, most of the responsibili-ties ultimately lie upon the principal in comparison to the other staff. Similar is the scenario between the husband and wife. Islām has given more responsibilities to a man, so he is liable to be ques-tioned more on the Day of Judgement regarding his responsibili-ties compared to a woman.

Allāh ﷻ in His infinite mercy, has not placed this responsibility upon a woman but has given her other responsibilities in which she has a greater potential. Even if a woman was to take up the re-sponsibilities of a man, in the eyes of Allāh ﷻ, the man is still *Qawwām* i.e. responsible and a maintainer. Hypothetically, if we alter the command of Allāh ﷻ in this scenario, i.e. that now women are *Qawwām* over men, then other instructions of Allāh ﷻ must also change in a similar manner. For instance, Allāh ﷻ has ordained upon man to be dutiful towards his parents because of the hardships they have borne for him. Now, if the parents treat their child abusively and this child after attaining adulthood, in return dedicates his service towards his parents after reaching their old age and he endures hardship for their sake, will this person now have a degree advantage over his parents? Never will this be possible! Similarly is the case with the husband and wife. What Allāh ﷻ has ordained is final and can never be altered.

Islām has not obliged a woman with such responsibilities resulting in her becoming more questionable on the Day of Judgement. A man failing to carry out his responsibilities is liable to be punished by Allāh ﷻ.

Since a man according to the book of Allāh ﷻ, is a leader of the family affairs, it is necessary to clarify at this point, the Islamic concept of leadership. Leadership in Islām does not imply that the husband becomes oppressive, abusive, violent or cruel. Such leadership is never justified in Islām. Rather, the true quality of a leader is what the Messenger of Allāh ﷺ has described in the following manner, "The (true) leader of a nation is their servant" (Kanzul Ummāl). Whenever a person is elected as a leader amongst his people, then his attributes should be that he is always watchful over his subordinates, manages their affairs according to the Shari'ah and attends to the service of people at the time of their needs.

Mufti Taqi Uthmāni Sāhib states, in reference to the above Hadeeth, that when Islām emphasises on electing a leader when undertaking a journey, then greater emphasis ought to be given when choosing a leader who would always be mindful of the family affairs (as well as an adviser), when embarking upon a lifetime journey of marriage.

Furthermore, Shaykh Ashraf Ali Thānwi ﷺ states that, indeed a man is a leader over his wife but they are also best friends. In terms of managing the affairs, he is a leader but amongst themselves, they are mutual lovers of one another.

In conclusion, a man will still remain a *Qawwām* according to the law of Allāh ﷻ however, he is ultimately responsible to manage the affairs of the family in accordance with the Shari'ah.

# Makhraj of the Letter 'ض' (Dhād)

Q **What is the Makhraj (origin of pronunciation) of the letter ض? Many people pronounce it as a دال (Dhāl). What is the correct way?**

A The letter Dhād is pronounced from the back edge of the upturned tongue, when touching the roots of the molars and the premolars. There are three ways of pronouncing the Dhād:

1. From the right side.
2. From the left side.
3. From both sides at the same time.

However, it is commonly easier to pronounce the Dhād from the left side. The letter Dhād is known as Harfe-Hāfiyah because it is pronounced from the upturned sides of the tongue. The letter Dhād has the Sifat (quality) of Istitālat. Istitālat is that quality which when pronounced, the voice of the letter will remain from the beginning of the Makhraj till the end. This quality is found only in the letter Dhād. The correct way of pronouncing the letters can only be known fully by learning from an experienced and well-versed Qāri. Practical display is essential for these matters.

# The Essential Knowledge for a Mufassir (Commentator of the Holy Qur'ān)

Q I have come across commentaries of the Holy Qur'ān which are contradictory to the commentaries of our pious predecessors. Many, even have translations of verses which are clearly wrong. Such modernists have completely ignored the status of the Holy Qur'ān and have commentated on it according to their own personal opinions. Can you mention in detail the branches of knowledge which are essential pre-requisites for a commentator?

A Specialist scholars have emphasised that anyone wanting to achieve the status of a commentator of the Holy Qur'ān, should be well versed in fifteen subjects. These are briefly given below and will show that it is not possible for everybody to understand the underlying significance and real meanings of the Holy Qur'ān, or to draw their own conclusions and commentate.

1. Lughāt - the knowledge of linguistic meanings of terms. This helps in understanding the appropriate meanings of words. Imām Mujāhid 🕮 says, "One who believes in Allāh 🕮 and the Day of Judgement should not open his lips in respect of the Holy Qur'ān, unless he is thoroughly fluent with the meaning of the Arabic language." Quite often an Arabic word has several meanings. A person may know only one or two of them, though in a given context the actual meaning may be quite different.

2. Nahw - syntax, (a branch of grammar). This helps in understanding the relationship of one sentence with another and also of I'rāb (diacritical marks) of the letters of a particular word. A change in I'rāb often renders a change in the meaning.

3. Sarf - etymology, (another branch of grammar). This helps in knowing the root words and conjugations. The meaning of a word changes with the change in the root and with a change in its conjugation. Imām Ibn Fāris 🕮 says, "One who loses the knowledge of etymology loses a great deal."

Imām Zamakhshari 🕮 mentions that a certain person sat to translate the verse, **"The Day when We shall call together all human beings with their leader." (17:71)** He ignorantly mistranslated it thus, "The Day when We shall call together all human beings with their mothers." He misunderstood the singular Arabic word 'Imām' (i.e. 'leader' which is mentioned in the verse) as being the plural of the Arabic word 'Umm' (mother). If he had been familiar with etymology, he would have known that the plural of 'Umm' is not 'Imām'.

4. Ishtiqāq - derivatives. It is necessary to have the knowledge of derivatives and their root words because if a word has been derived from two different root words, it will have two different meanings. For example, the word 'Maseeh' is derivable from 'Masah' which means to touch over, to move wet hands over. It is also from 'Masāhah' which means measurement.

5. Ilmul-Ma'āni - knowledge of semantics. This is important because phrase constructions are understood from their meanings.

6. Ilmul-Bayān - knowledge of the expression of figurative speech, like similes and metaphors.

7. Ilmul-Badee - knowledge of rhetoric, the knowledge which reveals the beauty of language and its implications.

**Note:** The last three are the branches of Ilmul Balāghah (knowledge of oration). They are considered very important subjects, which a commentator should master, because the Holy Qur'ān is a perfect miracle and its amazing constructions can only be understood after mastering these subjects.

8. Ilmul-Qirā'ah - knowledge of the art of pronunciation. This is necessary because different methods of recitation sometimes, convey different meanings and sometimes one meaning is to be preferred over the other.

9. Ilmul-Aqā'id - knowledge of the fundamentals of faith. This is necessary to explain certain analogies. The literal meaning of a cer-

tain verse referring to Allāh ﷻ may not be correct. For example, the analogy in the verse, **"The Hand of Allāh is over their hands,"** **(48:10)** will have to be explained because Allāh ﷻ has no physical hands.

10. Usūlul-Fiqh - principles of Islamic Jurisprudence. These are necessary for reasoning and finding arguments in support of statements.

11. Asbābun-Nuzool - the event which caused the revelation. The meanings of a verse will be better understood, if we know how and when it had been revealed. Sometimes the true meaning of a verse is understood only if we know the circumstances in which the verse had been revealed.

12. An-Nāsikh wal-Mansookh - knowledge of commandments that have subsequently been abrogated or changed. This is necessary so that the abrogated commandments may be distinguished from those that are applicable.

13. Ilmul-Fiqh - knowledge of Islamic Jurisprudence. This is needed because it is only through this knowledge that we arrive at a complete understanding of general principles.

14. Hadeeth - knowledge of such Ahādeeth that are a commentary on certain verses of the Holy Qur'ān and to be acquainted with the Seerah (biography) of the Holy Prophet ﷺ.

15. The last but most important is the Wahabi (bestowed) Ilm, or the gifted understanding, bestowed by Allāh ﷻ upon His selected ones. As it is referred to in the Hadeeth, "Whosoever acts upon what he knows, Allāh ﷻ bestows upon him the knowledge of things not known to him."

It is this special understanding that was implied in the reply of Sayyidunā Ali ؓ, when he was once asked by the people if he had received from the Holy Prophet ﷺ any special knowledge or instructions, which were not received by others. Sayyidunā Ali ؓ replied, "I swear by Him Who made paradise and created life that I possess nothing special, except the clear understanding which Allāh ﷻ bestows upon a person in regards to the Holy Qur'ān."

Ibn Abid Dunyā ؓ states that the knowledge of the Holy Qur'ān and that which can be derived out of it, are as vast as a boundless ocean.

The branches of knowledge described above are the tools, i.e. essential pre-requisites for a commentator. A commentary written by a person who is not thoroughly acquainted with these branches of knowledge, will be based on his personal opinion, which is prohibited. The Sahābah ؓ already had Arabic language as their mother-tongue and they reached the depth of the rest of the knowledge by means of the illuminating contact that they had with the Holy Prophet ﷺ.

Imām Jalāl-ud-Deen Suyūti ؓ states that those who think that it is beyond the capacity of a man to acquire Wahabi-Ilm (gifted understanding), are not right.

To get this knowledge from Allāh ﷻ, one should adopt the means necessary i.e. acting upon the knowledge that one has acquired and disinclination towards the world. It is stated in 'Keemiyā-e-Sa'ādat', that three people are not blessed with complete understanding of the Holy Qur'ān.

Firstly, one who is not well versed in Arabic. Secondly, one who persists in committing a major sin or indulges in an act of religious innovation, because these actions darken his heart, which in turn prevent him from understanding the Holy Qur'ān. Thirdly, one who is a rationalist, even in the matter of faith, and feels embarrassed when he reads a verse of the Holy Qur'ān, which he is not able to fully rationalise.

# Allāh ﷻ Knows Best

# 3. CHAPTER ON
# SUNNAH

# Length of the Hair

**Q** How long can a man keep his hair and what was the noble practice of the Holy Prophet ﷺ?

**A** In regards to the blessed hair of the Holy Prophet ﷺ there are various narrations as to the length of his blessed hair. Some of which are as follows:

1.    Sayyidunā Anas ؓ relates that the Holy Prophet's ﷺ hair was between the ears and the shoulders. (Bukhāri)
2.    Sayyidunā Shu'bah ؓ narrates that the blessed hair of the Holy Prophet ﷺ extended to the earlobe. (Bukhāri)
3.    In another narration, Sayyidunā Anas ؓ reports that the Holy Prophet's ﷺ hair would (sometimes) be up to shoulder length. (Bukhāri)

Mulla Ali Qāri ﷺ writes that there are various reports concerning the Holy Prophet's ﷺ noble hair:
   1. It extended to half the ear.
   2. It extended to the earlobe.
   3. It extended to between the earlobe and the shoulder.
   4. It extended to the shoulder.
   5. It was close to the shoulder.

Hāfiz Abul-Fadhl Al-Irāqi ﷺ writes the three terms used to describe the length of the Holy Prophet's ﷺ blessed hair. They are Wafrah, Jummah and Limmah. Wafrah refers to the hair that extends to the earlobes. Jummah refers to the hair that extends to the shoulders. Limmah refers to the hair that is between the earlobes and the shoulders.

Mulla Ali Qāri 🕮 further writes that the Holy Prophet's 🕮 hair generally used to be between the earlobes and the shoulders. The differences in the reports refer to the gradual growth or clipping of the hair. Both narrations refer to the time when the hair was clipped or, when it had grown to its full length. (Jam'ul-Wasā'il)

Imām Nawāwi 🕮 states that when the Holy Prophet 🕮 cut his hair, he would cut it until the earlobes. However, if he did not do so, then he would allow it to grow to shoulder length. The Sahābah 🕮 would relate the different length of the hair they had seen.

(Umdatul Qāri)

It is understood from the above that it is permissible to grow the length of hair to the earlobes or extend it up to the shoulders. To grow the hair beyond the shoulder would infringe the Sunnah and is disallowed (otherwise it will resemble women).

(Jam'ul-Wasā'il, The Sublime Conduct of Nabi 🕮)

## Length of the Beard

Q What should the length of the beard be in the light of the Shar'iah?

A It has been reported that the Holy Prophet 🕮 once cut that part of the beard that exceeded one fist length. Amr Ibn Shuaib 🕮 relates from his father, who relates from his grandfather (i.e. Abdullāh Ibn Amr Ibnul Ās ﷺ), that the Holy Prophet ﷺ used to cut his noble beard from that part which exceeded one fist length from both the sides and the length. (Tirmizi)

There is also another narration in which it is mentioned that Sayyidunā Abdullāh Ibn Umar ﷺ during Hajj and Umrah, used to cut the beard exceeding one fist. (Bukhāri)

The aforementioned narrations prove that it is permissible to cut the beard, only that which is beyond one fist. Although there are certain Ahādeeth proving that the Holy Prophet ﷺ kept a beard longer than a fist, it is conditional that one must groom and maintain it well. Sayyidunā Anas Ibn Mālik ﷺ relates that the Holy Prophet ﷺ used to oil his noble hair very frequently and groom his noble beard. (Shamā'il Tirmizi)

# Lengthy Moustache

**Q** **Nowadays, some people keep long moustaches whilst they shave their beards. What is the ruling regarding lengthening the moustache?**

**A** It is Sunnah to have the moustache trimmed and to lengthen it is not correct. Sayyidunā Abdullāh Ibn Umar ﷺ narrates that the Holy Prophet ﷺ said, "To trim the moustache is part of Fitrah (nature)." (Bukhāri)

Sayyidunā Abū Hurairah ﷺ narrates that the Holy Prophet ﷺ said,

"Five things constitute Fitrah; circumcision, shaving the pubic hair, trimming the moustache, clipping the nails and plucking the hair of the armpits. (Bukhāri)

It is narrated that Sayyidunā Abdullāh Ibn Umar ﷺ would trim his moustache so finely that the whiteness of the skin underneath would become apparent. (Bukhāri)

Sayyidunā Abdullāh Ibn Basheer ﷺ narrates that he witnessed the Holy Prophet ﷺ trimming his blessed moustache very finely. (Seerah)

Hence, it is incorrect to lengthen the moustache. Sayyidah Ā'ishah ﷺ narrates that the Holy Prophet ﷺ saw a person with a long moustache. The Holy Prophet ﷺ requested for a Miswāk and a pair of scissors. Placing the Miswāk at the edge of the lip, he trimmed his moustache. (Fathul-Bāri)

In one Hadeeth narrated by Sayyidunā Abū Hurairah ﷺ, the Holy Prophet ﷺ said, "Trim the moustache and lengthen the beard, and thereby be different to the fire worshippers."

Sayyidunā Zayd Ibn Arqam ﷺ narrates that the Holy Prophet ﷺ said, "He who does not trim his moustache is not from amongst us." (Tirmīzi)

In another Hadeeth narrated by Sayyidunā Abdullāh Ibn Umar ﷺ, the Holy Prophet ﷺ said, "Be different from the disbelievers, trim the moustache and lengthen the beard." (Bukhāri)

## Keeping a lengthy moustache is not part of the teachings of Islām

Sayyidunā Abdullāh Ibn Utbah 🌸 narrates, that a few fire-worshippers visited the Holy Prophet 🌸 and they had shaven their beards and lengthened their moustaches. When asked about it, they informed the Holy Prophet 🌸 that it was a feature of their religion. The Holy Prophet 🌸 informed them that our religion regards the lengthening of the beard and the shortening of the moustache as essentials (Ibn Abi Shaybah). Another narration says that they informed the Holy Prophet 🌸, that their Emperor Chosroes had commanded them to do so. The Holy Prophet 🌸 told them that his Lord (Allāh 🌸) had commanded him to lengthen the beard and shorten the moustache.

In the light of the Ahādeeth, jurists have extracted three methods of trimming the moustache:

1. To trim the moustache so finely that the area beneath it remains visible
2. To trim the edges so that the redness of the edge of the upper lip is exposed
3. To leave the moustache as fine as the eyebrows

Sayyidunā Abdullāh Ibn Abbās 🌸 states, that the Holy Prophet 🌸 trimmed his blessed moustache. Even when the Holy Prophet 🌸 had somebody else's moustache shortened, it was trimmed and not shaven.

Many great Sahābah 🕉 would trim their moustaches so finely that it would seem as if it was shaved (but not shaved entirely). These include Sayyidunā Abū Saeed 🕉, Sayyidunā Jābir 🕉, Sayyidunā Abdullāh Ibn Umar 🕉, Sayyidunā Rāfi Ibn Khadeej 🕉, Sayyidunā Abū Aseed 🕉, Sayyidunā Salamah Ibnul-Akwa 🕉 and Sayyidunā Abū Rāfi 🕉 (Majma).

It is evident now, that to lengthen the moustache is not permitted in Islām. Rather it should be trimmed only and not shaved.

# Most Virtuous Day for Travelling

Q Is there a particular day which is more virtuous for a person to commence his journey or is everyday equal in this matter?

A According to the Ahādeeth of the Holy Prophet 🕌, it is Sunnah and more virtuous to commence one's journey on a Thursday. Imām Bukhāri 🕉 has recorded a Hadeeth in his Saheeh, from Sayyidunā K'ab Ibn Mālik 🕉, that the Holy Prophet 🕌 departed for the expedition of Tabook on a Thursday. He further states that the Holy Prophet 🕌 loved commencing his journeys on a Thursday.

(Bukhāri)

In another Hadeeth, Sayyidah Umme Salmah 🕉 narrates that the Holy Prophet 🕌 preferred travelling on a Thursday.

Sayyidunā Abū Tāhir 🕉 narrates that whenever the Holy Prophet 🕌 despatched an army he would do so on a Thursday. Another narration mentions that Barakah (blessings) has been kept on a Thursday morning for this Ummah. (Fathul-Bāri)

**Note:** Whenever possible, the Holy Prophet 襤 would commence his journey on a Thursday and he preferred the same day for despatching armies as well. Very rarely, would he commence a journey on any other day. When departing for the farewell pilgrimage, the Holy Prophet 襤 departed on a Thursday also.

Therefore, if possible a person should arrange one's journey to commence on a Thursday as this would be closest to the Sunnah. If this is not possible then any other day will be fine.

# Musāfahah (Shaking Hands) with two hands

**Q** Is it Sunnah to shake hands with one hand or two hands?

**A** It is Sunnah to make Musāfahah with both hands. Sayyidunā Abdullāh Ibn Masood 襤 narrates that the Holy Prophet 襤 taught him the Tashahhud, whilst his palms were between the two palms of the Holy Prophet 襤. (Bukhāri)

Imām Bukhāri 襤 has presented the aforementioned Hadeeth under the chapter of Musāfahah. A few lines thereafter, Imām Bukhāri 襤 has presented another chapter: "Chapter on holding of both hands and Hammād Ibn Zaid 襤 made Musāfahah with both hands with Abdullāh Ibn Mubārak 襤". He has established from the above Hadeeth and the chapter heading, that Musāfahah should be made with two hands. In order to emphasise the importance of what was being imparted, the Holy Prophet ﷺ held Sayyidunā Abdullāh Ibn Masood's ؓ hand between both his palms. (Fatāwa Raheemiyyah)

Shaykh Abdul Hayy ؒ writes in his Majmū ul-Fatāwa, that all the jurists declare it a Sunnah to use both hands when performing Musāfahah.

**Note:** Although it is permissible to shake with one hand only, it is more closer to the Sunnah to greet with both hands because if a person shakes with only one hand, then the sins committed with that hand only will be pardoned. However, if one shakes with both hands, then the sins of both hands will be pardoned. Sayyidunā Hudhaifah ؓ narrates that the Holy Prophet ﷺ said, "When a believer meets another believer and (each one) holds the hand of the other, then both of their sins begin to fall off, just as the leaves fall from a tree." (Shuabul-Imān)

## Virtues of Shaking Hands

**Q** What is the virtue of shaking hands and when should it be done?

**A** Imām Abū Dāwood ؒ has mentioned a Hadeeth in his Sunan in which the Holy Prophet ﷺ mentions, "When two Muslims meet each other and shake hands, their (minor) sins are forgiven before they depart." (Abū Dāwood)

It is Sunnah to shake hands when a Muslim greets another Muslim with Salām. Sayyidunā Abū Dharr ؓ reports that the Holy Prophet

⚘ shook his hands every time they met. (Abū Dāwood)

According to a Hadeeth of Tirmizi, the Musāfahah is a completion of Salām. Therefore, Salām should be said before shaking hands. Many times, people make Musāfahah without doing Salām. This is contrary to the noble practice of the Holy Prophet ⚘. Shaykh Ashraf Ali Thānwi ⚘ says, "It is permissible to shake hands upon arrival and upon departure."

# Wearing a Topi (Hat)

Q Is it Sunnah to wear a hat at all times?

A In general, for a Muslim male to wear a hat is not only permissible but also the Sunnah of the Holy Prophet ⚘ and the noble Sahābah ⚘. Since then, it has always been the general practice of the pious people of the generation that followed, up until today. The evidence of wearing a hat are presented below:

Sayyidunā Abdullāh Ibn Umar ⚘ relates, that once a man asked the Messenger of Allāh ⚘ of what is permissible for a Muhrim to wear? The Messenger of Allāh ⚘ replied, "He shall not wear Qamees (shirt), nor Amāmah (turban), nor Salwār (bottoms) nor Burnus (a specific type of hat).... (Bukhāri).

In this Hadeeth, the Holy Prophet ⚘ prohibited the wearing of Burnus and likewise, other stitched clothing during Ihrām. The fact that he prohibited the wearing of Burnus during Ihrām, is an indication of the general practice of the Sahābah ⚘ of wearing a hat, just as wearing Qamees, Salwār etc was their general practice. Had it not been their practice, then surely the Holy Prophet 🌸 would not have mentioned it in the first place. Fadhālah Ibn Ubaid 🌸 relates in a lengthy Hadeeth, that Sayyidunā Umar Ibn Khattāb 🌸 once heard the Messenger of Allāh 🌸 explaining the four levels of a Shaheed. When explaining the first and the highest category of a Shaheed, he gestured with his hands upwards (indicating to the lofty status of a Shaheed), so much that his hat fell to the ground. Fadhālah 🌸 states, "I do not know whether it was the hat of the Messenger of Allāh 🌸 that fell or the hat of Sayyidunā Umar 🌸."

(Tirmizi)

The part where the narrator speaks of the falling of the hat, is a clear evidence that to wear a hat is a Sunnah practice. Sayyidah Ā'ishah 🌸 relates that when the Holy Prophet 🌸 went to relieve himself, he would cover his head and when he would approach his wives he would cover his head. (Baihaqi)

In another Hadeeth narrated in Bayhaqi, Sayyidunā Habib Ibn Sālih 🌸 reports, that when the Holy Prophet 🌸 entered the toilet he would wear shoes and cover his head. In another Hadeeth Sayyidah Ā'ishah 🌸 relates that Sayyidunā Abū Bakr 🌸 once said, "Show respect in front of Allāh 🌸, for I certainly cover my head when entering the toilet due to respect for Allāh 🌸."

(Musannaf Abdur-Razzāq)

Sayyidunā Wāthilah 🌸 relates that the Messenger of Allāh 🌸 said, "Covering the head during the day is a sign of intelligence."

(Meezānul-I'tidāl)

Sayyidunā Abdullāh Ibn Umar ﷺ relates that the Messenger of Allāh ﷺ would wear a white hat. (Tabarāni Fil Kabeer)

Hasan Al-Basri ﷺ states that the people (Sahābah ﷺ) would prostrate on their turbans and hats (Bukhāri). Those Sahābahs ﷺ that would wear a hat include; Sayyidunā Khālid Ibn Waleed ﷺ who would wear a hat whilst in the battlefield (Isābah by Ibn Hajar ﷺ). Sayyidunā Abdullāh Ibn Abbās ﷺ (Ibn Abi Shaybah) and Sayyidunā Wā'il Ibn Hujr ﷺ (Ibn Khuzaimah).

The above evidences, clearly illustrate that wearing a hat is Sunnah and has always been the general practice of the Sahābah ﷺ.

## The Amāmah (Turban)

**Q** **Did the Holy Prophet ﷺ wear the turban? Please answer in detail.**

**A** Concerning the turban, Shaykh Muhammad Zakariyya ﷺ has written the following in his commentary of 'Shamāil Tirmizi', 'Khasāil-e-Nabawi', "The tying of the turban is a 'Sunnate-Mustamirrah' (constantly adhered practice of the Holy Prophet ﷺ)."

The Holy Prophet ﷺ has enjoined the tying of the turban. It has been reported, "Tie the turban. It will increase you in patience." It is also reported that somebody enquired from Sayyidunā Abdullāh Ibn Umar ﷺ, whether the tying of the turban was Sunnah or not. He replied in the affirmative.

True love demands that you do everything as your beloved would like to see it. In fact a true devotee of the Holy Prophet ﷺ, would be prepared to give his life for the practical preservation of even one minute Sunnah. Such is the overwhelming thirst for emulation present in a true follower, that it does not matter to him whether the Sunnah is a constant act or occasional, whether the Sunnah is connected to Ibādah (the manner in which the Holy Prophet ﷺ carried out the various acts of worship) or habit or lifestyle (the manner of his speech, walking, eating, dressing etc.) As long as it can be determined that our Holy Prophet ﷺ did it, then a true Āshiq-e-Rasool (lover of the Messenger ﷺ) will go to any length to implement it in his life.

The turban is one such Sunnah which every Muslim should adhere to whether he is a scholar or not and whether he is literate or illiterate. It is a misunderstanding by many people, that the turban should be tied by the Ulamā only. There are numerous Ahādeeth that emphasize upon the tying of the turban by the Holy Prophet ﷺ:

1. Sayyidunā Amr Ibn Umayya Damri ؓ reports, "I saw the Holy Prophet ﷺ making Masah of his Kuffain (leather socks) and turban." (Bukhāri)

2. Sayyidunā Mugheerah Ibn Shu'bah ؓ reports, that the Holy Prophet ﷺ performed Wudhu and made Masah of the front portion of his head as well as of his turban and leather socks. (Muslim)

**Note:** According to the opinion of the Hanafi Fuqahā (jurists) performing Masah only on the turban, is not permissible nor sufficient

291

for absolving oneself from the compulsory act of Masah of the head in Wudhu. The minimum requirement for Masah on the head is a quarter of the head. So if a person covered at least a quarter of the head for Masah and then passed the hands over the turban, will suffice as it is apparent from the action of the Holy Prophet ﷺ in Hadeeth No. 2.

3. Sayyidunā Huraith ؓ reports that the Holy Prophet ﷺ addressed the people while wearing a black turban.

(Muslim, Ibn Abi Shaibah)

4. In another narration it is reported, "I saw the Holy Prophet ﷺ wearing a black turban." (Tirmizi, Ibn Mājah)

5. Sayyidunā Jābir ؓ reports that on the occasion of the Conquest of Makkah, the Holy Prophet ﷺ entered Makkah while wearing a black turban. (Muslim, Tirmizi, Ibn Mājah)

6. It is also reported that the Holy Prophet ﷺ said, "Wear the turban as it is a sign of Islām."

One should note that all these narrations are of the Saheeh (authentic) category.

# The Kurta (Long Shirt)

Q Did the Holy Prophet ﷺ wear the Kurta? If he did, can you tell me what the length of his sleeves were and how long the Kurta was? I have observed many people wearing the Jubba (Kurta) below the ankles. Is this correct?

A The Holy Prophet ﷺ preferred the Kurta over all other types of clothing. Sayyidah Umme Salamah ﷺ narrates that the Holy Prophet ﷺ preferred the Kurta over all types of clothing. (Tirmizi, Abū Dāwood, Nasai, Ibn Mājah)

The scholars have attributed the following qualities to the Kurta:

1. It conceals the body better than other forms of clothing such as the Chādar (a loose sheet that used to be worn) and Lungi etc.

2. It does not cost so much and is light in weight so it carries no burden on the wearer.

3. There is humility in its nature.

Shaykh Muhammad Zakariyya ﷺ says in Khasāil-e-Nabawi, "The Kurta is a wonderful concealer of the Satr (that part of the body for which concealment is obligatory), whilst fulfilling the natural demand of beauty and elegance that we have in our choice of dress."

Regarding the length, Sayyidunā Abdullāh Ibn Abbās ﷺ reports that lengthwise, the Kurta of the Holy Prophet ﷺ would be above his ankles, whilst the sleeves would reach up to his fingers. It is therefore, prohibited to wear any clothes, whether it be the Jubba, Lungi, trousers etc. below the ankles.

It is reported by Sayyidunā Abdullāh Ibn Umar ﷺ that if Isbāl (allowing clothing to be excessively long which is prohibited) occurs with the Lungi, Kurta or turban, then on the Day of Judgement, Allāh ﷺ will not look towards that individual who wore excessively long clothes (that flows beneath the ankles), due to pride.

Shu'ba ﷺ reports that he met Muhārib Ibn Dinār ﷺ, whilst the latter was riding a horse on his way to the court for a case. I asked him about this particular Hadeeth. He replied that he heard Sayyidunā Abdullāh Ibn Umar ﷺ saying that the Holy Prophet ﷺ said, "He who wears excessively long clothes (which flow below the ankles), due to pride, Allāh ﷻ will not look towards him (with mercy) on the Day of Judgement."

Shu'ba ﷺ says that he asked Muhārib ﷺ whether Sayyidunā Abdullāh Ibn Umar ﷺ had mentioned only the Lungi (i.e. does this only apply to the Lungi?). Muhārib ﷺ replied that the ruling was general and applies to all types of clothing i.e. Kurta, Lungi, turban, trousers and Jubbas etc. (Bukhāri)

Some people are of the habit of objecting to this ruling, by claiming that they wear their clothing below the ankles, but this is not done out of pride. The implication is, that they consider themselves exempt from this warning. Such people should consider the following Hadeeth of the Holy Prophet ﷺ, "Guard against lengthening your clothes (below the ankles) for such lengthening itself is an act of pride." (Abū Dāwood)

It is thus understood, that wearing the clothes below the ankles will be viewed as an act of pride in the eyes of Allāh ﷻ, whether motivated by such intentions or not. People are unaware of this and explain their wrong actions with feeble and weak excuses.

# Length of the Kurta

**Q** What is the Sunnah length of the Kurta?

**A** The Kurta should be below the knees and well above the ankles. It should be about midway between the knees and the ankles. The below ankle-length worn by many people nowadays is not permissible.

# Shaving the Head

**Q** Many people hold the view that shaving the head is a Sunnah practice. They quote the practice of Sayyidunā Ali ⚬, who habitually shaved his head. What is the correct view?

**A** Allowing the hair to grow long on the entire head is Sunnah. However, shaving or cutting the hair is Mubāh (permitted). The shaving of the head, on occasions other than Hajj and Umrah is not established from the practice of the Holy Prophet ⚬. However, there is no established Hadeeth where the Holy Prophet ⚬ prohibited men from shaving the head also. That was also the habit of the Sahābah ⚬, except for Sayyidunā Ali ⚬ who habitually shaved his head.

Sayyidunā Ali ⚬, on grounds of precaution in matters of Ghusl, used to remove his hair completely. He himself narrates that the Holy Prophet ⚬ said, "Impurity (Janābat) exists beneath every strand of hair." (Mishkāt)

Complying with the mentioned Hadeeth he states, "The one who overlooks an area equivalent to a single strand whilst performing Ghusl-Janābat (bathing after ritual impurity), will be dealt like this and like that in Hell." (A reference to strict punishment). Upon narrating this, he states, "Owing to the declaration of such threatening phrases, I chose to create enmity with my head (i.e. remove all my hair)."

It is reported in Mawāhib, "To the best of my knowledge, shaving the head is not an established practice of the Holy Prophet 🕌, except on the occasion of Umrah and Hajj. Hence, allowing the hair to grow is Sunnah. Not to keep hair is also Mubāh (permissible), without rejecting the established Sunnah."

Certain scholars support the view that both Halq (shaving of the head) and Tark (allowing hair to grow) are Sunnah practices. However, the first view is more authentic.

# Accepting Invitations

Q What is the ruling regarding accepting invitations? Many times incidents take place, which are contrary to the Shari'ah. What should one do on these occasions?

A To accept an invitation is a Sunnah of the Holy Prophet 🕌. Sayyidunā Anas 🙏 reports that once a tailor prepared food and invited the Holy Prophet 🕌. Sayyidunā Anas 🙏 says that he accompanied the Holy Prophet 🕌. In another Hadeeth, Sayyidunā Abū Moosā al-Ash'ari 🙏 relates that the Holy Prophet 🕌 said, "Free the slaves, accept the invitations of those who invite you and visit the sick." (Bukhāri)

Sayyidunā Abdullāh Ibn Umar ؓ relates a similar Hadeeth that the Holy Prophet ﷺ said, "Accept the invitation when you are invited." (Muslim)

Furthermore, in one Hadeeth the Holy Prophet ﷺ admonishes a person who does not accept invitations. Sayyidunā Abū Hurairah ؓ narrates that the Holy Prophet ﷺ said, "Whoever does not accept an invitation has disobeyed Allāh ﷻ and His Messenger ﷺ." (Bukhāri)

But we have to remember that these Ahādeeth apply only when the invitation conforms to the Sunnah and it is based on sincerity. When the objective is to show off or boast, expecting to receive something in return, making arrangements which contradict the Sunnah, or inviting only the wealthy , then it would not be permissible and in certain cases it would be compulsory to decline the invitation. For this precise reason, Islām has discouraged from attending such invitations where the laws of Islām will be violated.

Imām Nawāwi ؒ writes that if the following things occur, a person will be discouraged from attending:

1.    A person doubts if the food is Halāl.
2.    Only wealthy people are invited.
3.    Evil people will be present in the gathering.
4.    The invitation is given for show.
5.    It is an occasion where evil will take place.
6.    Alcohol will be served.
7.    People will be sitting on silky cloths.
8.    Gold or silver utensils will be used.

Nowadays, generally most invitations contain at least one of the above evils. Hence, we should be more precautious in accepting invitations.

## Drawing Lots

**Q** The Holy Prophet ﷺ drew lots before he went on any journey. Can you quote any Hadeeth regarding this matter?

**A** It is reported on the authority of Sayyidah Ā'ishah ﷺ that when the Holy Prophet ﷺ intended to go on a journey, he used to draw lots amongst his wives. Whosoever's name came out, used to accompany the Holy Prophet ﷺ in that journey. (Bukhāri, Muslim)

# Allāh ﷻ Knows Best

# 4. CHAPTER ON BID'AH
# INNOVATION

## Shaking Hands after Eid Salāh

Q After the two Eid Salāh which take place every year, people shake hands and embrace each other. Did the Holy Prophet 🌸 and his Companions 🕌 shake hands and embrace after the Eid Salāh?

A Saying Salām, shaking hands and embracing, are acts of Sunnah and are included in Ibādah (worship). However, we should remember that an act of worship will be classed as worship, when it is carried out in accordance with the Holy Qur'ān and Sunnah.

During the time of Sayyidunā Ali 🕌, when he was the Ameerul-Mu'mineen (Leader of the Muslims), a man intended to perform Nafl Salāh in the Eid-Gāh (a place designated for Eid Salāh), on Eid day. Sayyidunā Ali 🕌 forbade him. The man replied, "O' Ameerul-Mu'mineen, I know well that Allāh 🕌 will not punish me for performing Salāh." Sayyidunā Ali 🕌 replied, "I also know that Allāh 🕌 does not reward any deed or work, unless the Holy Prophet 🌸 has done it or has emphasised to do it. Hence your Salāh (at this moment) is useless and futile. So I am afraid that Allāh 🕌 may punish you for the reason that you did something against the Holy Prophet's 🌸 practice."

The Adhān is an act of Ibādah, a religious practice and an Islamic symbol. For the Friday congregational Salāh there are two Adhāns and an Iqāmah, but for the two Eid Salāh, there is neither Adhān nor Iqāmah, because they are not proven. Everyone knows that if the Adhān or the Iqāmah is given in the Eid-Gāh, it will be classed as an innovative practice.

Similarly, to consider handshaking and embracing one another necessary, instantly after the Eid or any other Salāh, is an innovation itself.

It has been stated in the book Majālisul-Abrār, "In this day and age, apart from generally meeting on other occasions, people have become accustomed to greeting one another in particularly, after the Jumu'ah Salāh and the two Eids. There is no authentic report to prove this (continuous) practice. Such practices that have not been established are rejected and not worthy of being acted upon."

It is stated in the famous book of jurisprudence 'Shāmi'; "The custom of hand shaking after Salāh (any Salāh) is disliked (Makrooh). The evidence is that the noble Companions 🐾 did not shake hands after Salāh. Hāfiz Ibn Hajar 🕌 states that the people shaking hands after the five daily Salāh, is a Bid'ah (innovation) because there is no basis for this in Islām." Furthermore, Ibnul-Hāj Makki 🕌 writes in his book, Al-Madkhal, "It is necessary for the Imām to forbid the people, who have innovated a new custom of shaking hands after the Fajr, Friday congregational and Asr Salāh, for this is a Bid'ah (innovation)."

Islāmically, the appropriate time of handshaking is at the time of meeting someone and not to restrict it to after the Salāh only. It should be done only on those occasions when Islām has prescribed e.g. when inviting someone as a guest, and returning from a journey etc. Those actions that are not Sunnah, should not be regarded as Sunnah.

Mulla Ali Qāri ﷺ (the commentator of Mishkāt) writes in his commentary, Mirqāt-Sharh-e-Mishkāt, "No doubt the time of handshaking is at the time of meeting."

People meet without shaking hands, discuss religious affairs and then shake hands after having performed the Salāh. Where is this Sunnah from? Hence some scholars have clearly confirmed that this method is Makrooh (disliked) and an innovation.

On the basis of these clarifications, it is necessary that one abstains from the customary handshaking only after Salāh. However, at the same time, one should not adopt any method whereby resentment and hatred may spread amongst the people.

On such occasions, one should keep in mind the instructions of Mulla Ali Qāri ﷺ, who says, "When a Muslim extends his hands in an inappropriate time for handshaking, one should not hurt his feelings by withdrawing one's hands and be the cause of mistrust. Instead one should politely explain and inform him of the reality of the Mas'alah (precept)."

# Shaking Hands after Salāh

**Q** Is shaking hands after each Salāh Bid'ah (innovation)?

**A** This is not an act of Sunnah and neither did the Sahābah ﷺ consider this an act of Sunnah or a continuous practice. Therefore, to practice this continuously, as a tradition and to consider it a necessary act is a Bid'ah.

# Placing the Hands on the Chest after Musāfahah (Shaking Hands)

**Q** I have noticed many brothers placing their right hands on the chests after shaking hands. Is this correct or not?

**A** There is no evidence (from the Holy Qur'ān or the Ahādeeth) regarding this practice. Hence, there is no reason to place the hand on the chest after Musāfahah, apart from it being a cultural practice. Similarly, many consider it necessary to kiss their own hands after Musāfahah and reprimanded if they do not do so. This is also disliked. In fact the famous scholar Allāmah Ibn Ābideen Shāmi ﷺ has condemned these acts and classed them as Makrooh Tahreemi (in such cases). (Shāmi)

# Accepting Money For Du'ā

**Q** Is it permissible to accept money for making Du'ā? It has become customary in many places, that at the time when Du'ā for the deceased or sick is made, a sum of money regarded as Hadyah (gift) is given to the Imām etc. Is this permissible? Can the Imām accept that money?

**A** It is not permissible to accept money for making Du'ā because Du'ā is an act of pure Ibādah (worship), just as it is not permissible to accept money for reciting the Holy Qur'ān, due to it being an act of pure Ibadāh. It is not permissible to accept or charge money for Du'ā, nor is it permissible to give the Imām etc. money for having made a Du'ā. This customary practice is in the category of an arranged practice. It is not acceptable to perform acts of Ibādah for monetary gain. Such Du'ās, accompanied by customary payment, are devoid of Ikhlās (devotion) and are carried out for worldly motives, not for the sake of Allāh 靈.

# Using the Words 'Qiblah or Ka'bah' for Spiritual Guides

**Q** Many disciples nowadays write the word Qiblah or Ka'bah with the names of their spiritual guides. Is this permissible?

**A** It is not permissible to write or utter such words of praise for any person, even though he may be a renowned spiritual guide. Allāh 靈 informs us in the Holy Qur'ān, disapproving the ways of the people of the Book who exaggerated in the matter of their religion. **"O People of the Book! Do not commit excesses in your religion and speak only the truth about Allāh. The Maseeh, Eesā, the son of Maryam was but the Messenger of Allāh and His Word." (4:171)**

It is mentioned in the most authentic book of Ahādeeth, Saheeh Al-Bukhāri, "Do not exaggerate in praising me as the Christians did regarding Sayyidunā Eesā 靈. Listen carefully, I am the servant of Allāh 靈, so proclaim that I am the servant and Messenger of Allāh 靈. (Do not cross the limit of praises as the People of the Book did)."If the Holy Prophet 靈 did not tolerate such words of praise, then how can it be acceptable for his followers? Hence the words Qiblah and Ka'bah should not be used in writing, nor in calling the spiritual guides.

# Performing Lengthy Salāh on the Night of Barā'at

**Q** On Laylatul Barā'at (15th night of Sha'bān), many people perform very lengthy Salāh which include a specific amount of Sūrahs e.g. 25 times Sūrah Ikhlās in the 1st Rak'at, 50 times in the 2nd Rak'at etc. They greatly emphasise on performing these Salāh and quote the sayings of pious people. Should we perform these Salāh? Are there any Ahādeeth regarding these Salāh?

**A** There is no specific Salāh that is prescribed for the night of Barā'at. A person should perform Nafl as usual and because of the special virtue of the night of Barā'at, every person should seek Allāh's ﷻ Mercy and Forgiveness.

1. It is reported from Sayyidunā Mu'ādh Ibn Jabal ؓ that the Holy Prophet ﷺ said, "On the 15th night of Sha'bān, Allāh ﷻ bestows His special attention on His entire creation. He then pardons His entire creation, except an idolater and the one who harbours enmity." (Tabarāni has recorded this Hadeeth in Awsat, Ibn Hibbān in his Saheeh, Baihaqi and Targheeb-Wath-Tarheeb)

2. It is narrated from Sayyidunā Abdullāh Ibn Amr ؓ, that the Holy Prophet ﷺ said, "Allāh ﷻ looks with special attention towards His creation on the fifteenth night of Sha'bān and forgives all His servants except two categories of people; the person who harbours enmity and a murderer." Imām Ahmad ﷺ reports this Hadeeth with a slightly weak chain of narrators. (Targheeb-Wath-Tarheeb)

3. It is related from Makhool ﷺ, who narrates from Khatheer Ibn Murrah ﷺ, that the Holy Prophet ﷺ said, "On the 15th night of Sha'bān, Allāh ﷻ forgives all the inhabitants of the earth except an idolater and the one who harbours hatred for others." (Baihaqi)

**Note:** In the Islamic calendar, the night precedes the day. Hence, the night between the fourteenth and fifteenth of Sha'bān is implied.

From these Ahādeeth, we can realise the importance of this night but nowhere in the Ahādeeth can we find any mention of these Salāh. Shaykh Anwar Shāh Kashmiri ﷺ writes that the significance of the night of Barā'at is proven. However, there is no proof for those weak and unacceptable narrations mentioned in certain books.

Shaykh Yūsuf Binnouri ﷺ writes in Ma'ārifus-Sunan, that Shaykh Abū Tālib Makki ﷺ recorded these narrations in his book, "Qootul-Quloob". Imām Ghazāli ﷺ following Shaykh Abū Tālib ﷺ did the same and Shaykh Abdul Qādir Jilāni ﷺ has followed them in his book, "Ghunyatut-Tālibeen". They mention a narration of Sayyidunā Ali ﷺ that discusses a Salāh of one hundred Rak'ats. However, Imām Ibnul-Jawzee ﷺ and others declared the narration to be Mowdhu (fabrication).

Imām Dhahabi, Ibnul-Arrāq, Imām Suyooti, Mulla Ali Qāri ﷺ and other scholars of Hadeeth (Muhaddithoon) have strongly refuted such Salāh.

**Note:** Imām Dhahabi ❀ states regarding the book, "Ghunyatut-Tālibeen", that although it is the work of Shaykh Abdul Qādir Jīlāni ❀, many additions were made to his book after his death. The above book cannot be relied upon. As far as Ahādeeth are concerned, the opinion of the scholars of Hadeeth are always considered and not those of Wā'izeen (lecturers) and Sūfis.

Furthermore, with all due respect towards the Mashāikh of Tasawwuf, the point to mention is that the opinions of the scholars specialising in a particular field, is always given preference over others when that field is under discussion. Therefore, in the matter of the acceptance or rejection of narrations, the opinion of the Muhaddithoon will always take precedence.

Mulla Ali Qāri ❀ has discussed the matter under a particular chapter regarding the prescribed Salāh of the night of Barā'at. After mentioning the Salāh, he declares them to be baseless and therefore, concludes that these Salāh were first introduced in the fourth century in Baitul-Maqdis. Thus, some Ahādeeth were fabricated in order to support these baseless methods.

# Celebrating the Birth of the Holy Prophet ﷺ

Q On the 12th of Rabeeul Awwal, Muslims around the world celebrate the birth of the Holy Prophet ﷺ. What is the ruling in the Islamic teachings for this celebration?

A Shaykh Mufti Taqi Uthmāni Sāhib discusses this topic at length in one of his famous works, 'Islamic Months.' In summary he states as follows. The month of Rabeeul-Awwal is the most significant month in Islamic history because humanity has been blessed in this month, with the birth of the Holy Prophet ﷺ. Prior to the birth of the Holy Prophet ﷺ, not only the Arabian Peninsula but also the so-called civilised nations of Rome and Persia, were drowned in the darkness of ignorance, superstitions, oppression and unrest. The Holy Prophet ﷺ came with the eternal truth of Tawheed (oneness of Allāh ﷻ), the only faith which provides a firm basis for the real concept of knowledge, equity and peace. It was this faith which delivered humanity from ignorance and superstition and spread the light of true knowledge all over the world.

Thus, the birth of the Holy Prophet ﷺ was the most significant and most remarkable event to occur in human history. Had there been any room in the Islamic teachings for the celebration of birthdays or anniversaries, the birth of the Holy Prophet ﷺ would have undoubtedly deserved it more than the birthday of any other person.

However, the nature of Islamic teachings is such, that it primarily directs towards practicalism instead of formalism. The dates of the two Eids do not correspond to the birthday of any outstanding or prominent person of Islamic history, nor can their origin be attributed to any particular event of history that occurred on these dates.

Both of the two Eids have been prescribed for expressing gratitude towards Allāh ﷻ upon the completion of two significant acts of worship. The first is the completion of the fasting of Ramadhān and the second is the completion of Hajj. These two forms of worship are regarded to be amongst the five pillars of Islām.

The manner prescribed for the celebration of these two Eids (festivals) is also different from non-Islamic festivals. There are no formal processions, illuminations or other activities showing formal happiness. On the contrary, congregations of prayer have been prescribed and informal mutual visits to each other is practiced, which can give real happiness, rather than mere representation of symbols.

Islām has not prescribed any festival for the birthday of any person, however great or significant he may be. The Prophets of Allāh عَلَيْهِم السلام are the people of the highest status amongst all human beings and the best of Allāh's ﷻ creation. Nevertheless, the Holy Prophet ﷺ and his noble Companions رضي الله عنهم never observed the birthday or anniversary of any of them. Even the birth of the Holy Prophet ﷺ, the most spectacular event to occur in the history of mankind, was never celebrated by the Holy Prophet ﷺ himself, nor by his noble Companions رضي الله عنهم and nor the generation that followed them. So what legal right does it give us to celebrate his birthday? The Companions of the Holy Prophet ﷺ remained alive after him for approximately a century. However, despite their unparalleled and profound love towards the Holy Prophet ﷺ, they never celebrated the birthday or the death anniversary of the Holy Prophet ﷺ. They devoted their lives for promoting the cause of Islām, implementing his noble teachings, conveying his message all around the world and establishing the Islamic order in every walk of life.

In fact, commemorating the birth of a distinguished person has never been prescribed by any religion attributing itself to divine revelation. It was originally a custom prevalent in pagan commu-

nities only. Even Christmas, the famous Christian feast commemorating the birth of Jesus Christ, finds no mention in the Holy Bible
or in the early Christian writings. It was only in the 4th century,
after the ascension of Jesus Christ, that Christmas was recognised
as a Christian festival. To quote from the Collier's Encyclopaedia:
"It is impossible to determine the exact date of the birth of Christ,
either from the evidence of the gospels, or from any sound tradition. During the first three centuries of the Christian era there was
considerable opposition in the Church to the pagan custom of celebrating birthdays, although there is some indication that a purely
religious commemoration of the birth of Christ was included in the
feast of Epiphany.

Clement of Alexandra mentions the existence of the feast in Egypt
around the year 200 A.D and we have some evidence that it was
observed on various dates in scattered areas. After the triumph of
Constantine, the Church at Rome assigned December 25th as the
date for the celebration of the feast, possibly about 320 or 353 A.D.
By the end of the fourth century the whole Christian world was
celebrating Christmas on that day, with the exception of the East-
ern Churches, where it was celebrated on January 6th. The choice
of December 25th was probably influenced by the fact that on this
day the Romans celebrated the Mithraicism feast of the Sun-God,
and that the Saturnalia also came at this time." (Collier's Encyclopaedia 1984 ed. V.6, P. 403).

A similar description of the origin of Christmas is found in the Encyclopaedia Britannica with some more details. Its following passage will throw more light on the point:

"Christmas was not among the early festivals of the Church and before the 5ᵗʰ Century there was no general consensus of opinion as to when it should come in the calendar, whether on January 6th, March 25th or December 25th. The earliest identification of December 25th with the birthday of Christ is in a passage, otherwise unknown and probably spurious, of the philos of Antioch (c.180), preserved in Latin by the Magdeburyg Centuriators (i.3, 118), to the effect that the Gauls contended that since they celebrated the birth of Lord on December 25th, so they ought to celebrate the resurrection on March 25th. A passage, almost certainly interpolated, in 'Hippelates' (c.2002) commentary on Daniel iv, 23, says that Jesus was born at Bethlehem on Wednesday, December 25th, in the 42ⁿᵈ year of Augustus, but he mentions no feast, and such a feast, indeed, would conflict with the then orthodox ideas. As late as 245 Origin (hom.viii on Leviticus) repudiated the idea of keeping the birthday of Christ "as if he were a King Pharaoh." (Britannica, 1953 ed. V. 5, P.642)."

The above two extracts are more than sufficient to prove the following points:

1. The commemoration of the birthdays was originally a pagan custom, never recognised by a divine scripture or a prophetic teaching.

2. The exact date of the birth of Sayyidunā Eesā عليه السلام is unknown and impossible to be ascertained.

3. The commemoration of the birth of Sayyidunā Eesā عليه السلام was not a recognised practice in the early centuries of the Christian history.

4. It was in the 4ᵗʰ or 5ᵗʰ century that it was recognised as a reli-

gious feast and that too under the influence of the pagans who worshipped a 'Sun-God'.

5. There was a strong opposition to commemorating the birthday by the early Christian scholars, like Origen, on the ground that it was originally a custom of pagans and idolaters.

In the original Islamic sources, we cannot find any instructions about the celebration of birthdays or death anniversaries. Many Companions of the Holy Prophet ﷺ passed away during his life-time. His beloved wife Sayyidah Kadeejah ﷺ passed away in Mak-kah. His beloved uncle Sayyidunā Hamzah ﷺ was brutally mar-tyred during the battle of Uhud. But the Holy Prophet ﷺ never ob-served their birthdays or their death anniversaries, nor did he ever advise his followers to celebrate his own birthday in Rabeeul-Awwal.

The reason for abstaining from such celebrations is because they divert the attention of people from the real teachings of Islām. Ini-tially, such commemorations start off as an act of piety and with a sincere devotion to pay tribute to a pious person. However, experi-ence shows that the celebration ultimately constitutes elements of merrymaking, festivity and rejoicing. The example of Christmas will again be relevant. This Christian feast was originally innovat-ed to commemorate the birth of Jesus Christ and of course, to re-member his teachings. But once the occasion has been recognised as a festival, all the secular elements of public festivals infiltrated. The following quotation from the Encyclopaedia Britannia is worth attention: "For several centuries Christmas was solely a church an-niversary observed by religious services. But as Christianity spread among the people of pagan lands, many of the practices of the winter solstice were blended with those of Christianity because of the liberal ruling of Gregory I, the great, and the co-operation of the missionaries. Thus, Christmas became both religious and secular in its celebration, at times reverent, at other gay."

The kinds of activities that have been implemented to celebrate Christmas is mentioned in the following paragraph:

"Merrymaking came to have a share in Christmas observance through popular enthusiasm even while emphasis was on the religious phase. In the wholly decked great halls of the feudal lords, whose hospitality extended to all their friends, tenants and household were sailing, feasting, singing and games, dancing, masquerading and mummers presenting pantomimes at masques were all part of the festivals." (Encyclopaedia Britannica, 1953 V. 5, P.64)

The above discussion is sufficient to illustrate how a feast of reverence was subsequently converted into a secular festival whereby merrymaking and seeking enjoyment took precedence over the religious and spiritual activities. This was merely to explain the danger of introducing new practices and traditions into religion and what would be the final repercussion. We Muslims should take heed from this example.

Therefore, being fully aware of this human psychology, Islām has never prescribed, nor encouraged the observance of birthdays and anniversaries. Such celebrations to be included as part of religion is totally forbidden. The Holy Qur'ān has clearly pronounced on the occasion of the last Hajj of the Holy Prophet 🦋: **"Today, I have completed (the teachings of) your religion"** (5:3).

This implies that all the teachings of Islām have been disseminated to the Muslims through the Holy Qur'ān and the Sunnah of the Holy Prophet 🦋. No one is permitted thereafter, to introduce anything extra as a part of religion. What was initially not part of religion during the lifetime of the Holy Prophet 🦋, can never become part of it until the Day of Judgement. Such additions added are termed by the Holy Prophet 🦋 as Bid'ah or innovation.

Thus, the observance of the 12th of Rabeeul-Awwal as a religious feast has not been prescribed by any verse of the Holy Qur'ān or by any teaching of the Holy Prophet 🦋. Had it been a part of the religion it would have been clearly ordered or practiced by the Holy Prophet 🦋 and his blessed Companions 🦋, or at least, by their students. Nevertheless, no example of such celebrations can be traced back in the early centuries of Islamic history. It was centuries later that some monarchs started observing the 12th of Rabeeul-Awwal as the birthday of the Holy Prophet 🦋, without a sound religious basis. Initially congregations in the name of Mawlood or Meelād were held, narrating the historical event of the Holy Prophet's 🦋 birth.

To observe 12th of Rabeeul-Awwal as the birthday of the Holy Prophet 🦋 is not only an innovation having no basis in the Islamic teachings, but the accuracy of the real birthday of the Holy Prophet 🦋 is also very much doubted. There are different dates suggested in different traditions and the majority of the authentic scholars are inclined to hold that the Holy Prophet ﷺ was born on the 9th of Rabeeul-Awwal. This difference of opinion is another evidence to suggest that the observance of the birthday is not a part of religion; otherwise, its exact date would have been preserved with accuracy.

The life of the Holy Prophet ﷺ is without doubt, an important source of guidance for all the Muslims. Every Muslim is under an obligation to learn and study the events of his life and follow the pragmatic example set by him in every sphere of life. The narration of his pious biography (the Seerah) in itself is a pious act which invites the divine blessings, but the Holy Qur'ān and the Sunnah have not prescribed a particular time or method for it. This pious act should be performed in all the months and at all times. The Shari'ah has not prescribed the month of Rabeeul-Awwal for holding such congregations to commemorate the birth or life of the Holy Prophet ﷺ. It is thus an innovation to restrict the Seerah meetings to the month of Rabeeul-Awwal only, or to believe that the meetings held in this month are worthy of more reward than the meetings held on any other date during the year.

In fact, the Companions ﷺ of the Holy Prophet ﷺ used to commemorate the life of the Holy Prophet ﷺ daily. Not only by studying and conveying his message to others, but also by following his way of life and acting upon his teachings in each and every branch of their activities. This is exactly what a Muslim is required and supposed to do. By this we do not mean that the Seerah meetings should not be held in the month of Rabeeul-Awwal. The main point is, that they should not be restricted to a particular month, nor should it be viewed that Shari'ah emphasised on holding such meetings in this particular month. To hold such beliefs is misguidance.

Another point which I would like to mention, is that while holding such meetings, they must completely conform with the rules of Shari'ah. A Muslim is supposed to abide by the rules of Shari'ah in all his activities. However, at least the meetings held in the memory of the Holy Prophet 鑫, should be free from all the acts forbidden by the Shari'ah.

It is often observed that the people hold the Seerah meetings where men and women freely intermingle and the laws of Hijāb are overlooked. This is not allowed in Shari'ah. If practices such as this take place, then how can Seerah meetings transpire reward where such fundamental teachings of the Shari'ah are openly violated?

In some meetings the Nāts (poems) in the memory of the Holy Prophet 鑫 are recited by the women before the male audience and sometimes include music. This has been clearly prohibited in Shari'ah. Apart from this, it violates the sanctity of the Seerah of the Holy Prophet 鑫.

All other activities, often practiced on the 12th of Rabeeul-Awwal, like holding processions, constructing the artificial tombs of the Holy Prophet 鑫 and illumination of the buildings and the roads are a clear violation of the Shari'ah. Such gatherings are based on the imitation of other religions; no example of such activities can be traced from the earlier Islamic history.

What is really important, with regards to the Holy Prophet 鑫, is to follow his teachings, to make his pious Seerah available to every Muslim, to preserve it in the hearts of the Muslims from childhood, to educate the family members to live their lives according to it and to hold it as the best example of human conduct the universe has ever witnessed. All this should be done with utmost love and reverence, not manifested by some formal activities only but also through the actual behaviour of following the Sunnah. True love of the Holy Prophet 🌙 and adhering to his Sunnah cannot be achieved by merely holding gatherings of celebration.

## The Ruling of Saying 'Yā Rasūlallāh'

Q Is it permissible to call the Holy Prophet 🌙 by saying 'Yā Rasūlallāh'?

A Shaykh Yūsuf Ludhyānwi 🌙 writes in his book, 'Differences in the Ummah', Amongst this, is the one important question as to whether it is permissible to say, 'Yā Rasūlallāh' or not? My opinion on the matter is, that there are numerous occasions and manners in which one says, 'Yā Rasūlallāh', and the ruling for each one differs. For example, one way is when a poet who in his poetical imagination addresses things, such as the mountains, a jungle, or some animal, etc., he is not really talking to the thing he is addressing nor does he believe that the addressee is listening to him or will answer him. This is merely a way of expressing his emotions. If in such circumstances, the poet remembers the name of the Holy Prophet 🌙 and addresses him, then my opinion is that it will be permissible and correct.

The second way, is when a person addresses his beloved. In this manner a person may call out to the Holy Prophet ﷺ, to express his love for him, where his objective is not to actually call the Holy Prophet ﷺ, as though he is speaking to him. This is like a mother who had lost her child, calls out his/her name, knowing full well that the child will not hear her call in the grave, but this is merely her way of giving expression to her emotions. This is like an instinctive and involuntary action, spurred by love and emotion. In a similar manner, if a person calls out to the Holy Prophet ﷺ, then such a call will be permissible, provided there is no disorder in his Aqā'id.

Another way is when a person says Durood (supplication) in the specific form of 'As-Salātu was-Salāmu alaika Yā Rasūlallāh', believing that the specially appointed angels of Allāh ﷻ will convey this Durood to the Holy Prophet's ﷺ grave. This act would also not be regarded as impermissible, because the Holy Prophet ﷺ said, "Whosoever sends Durood at my grave side, I hear him, and whoever sends Durood on me from afar, it is conveyed to me." (Mishkāt)

It is reported in another Hadeeth, "Indeed there are some angels of Allāh ﷻ who traverse the earth and convey to me the Salāms of my Ummah." (Mishkāt)

Another Hadeeth states, "Do not make your homes graves and do not make my grave an object of festivities. Send Durood upon me, because indeed your Durood is conveyed to me wherever you are." (Mishkāt)

The correct way is to recite Durood in the methods and words taught to us by the Holy Prophet ﷺ and not to use the terms of addressing him directly. However, if one uses the words 'Yā Rasūlallāh' in this context, without there being any fear of one's Aqā'id corrupting, or that of another who is listening becoming corrupt, then such words cannot be regarded as impermissible.

The fourth way is to say 'Yā Rasūlallāh' and to harbour the belief that just as Allāh ﷻ listens to every word all the time, since He is Omnipresent, so too, one believes the Holy Prophet's ﷺ condition (that he is Hāzir-o-Nāzir). In such a case, I regard this to be totally impermissible.

Such a belief, as mentioned before is incorrect and there is neither consent nor leeway for it in the Holy Qur'ān, nor the Sunnah, nor the beliefs of Ahle Sunnah. Since the general masses have scant regard for the limits of the Shari'ah, the Salaf-e-Sāliheen (pious predecessors) have exercised great caution in such matters. It is reported from Sayyidunā Abdullāh Ibn Mas'ood ﷺ in Bukhāri, "As long as the Holy Prophet ﷺ was present in our midst, we used to say 'Assalāmualaika Ayyuhan Nabi', when reciting 'Attāhiyyāt'. However, after his demise we replaced these words with 'Alan Nabi ﷺ'." (Vol.2, Pg.926)

The objective of the Sahābah-e-Kirām ﷺ, was to show that in the 'Attāhiyyāt', the words which indicate to the Holy Prophet ﷺ being directly addressed was not indicative or based on the belief that he was omnipresent and that he heard the word of every person. In fact, this Salām (in 'Attāhiyyāt') refers to the Speech of Allāh ﷻ, which He spoke when the Holy Prophet ﷺ went to Mi'rāj.

The fifth way is when one who visits the grave of the Holy Prophet ﷺ says, 'As-Salātu Was Salāmu Alaika Yā Rasūlallāh'. Since the Holy Prophet ﷺ is alive in his grave and he hears and replies to every visitor who makes Salām to him, only in this situation is it permissible to say this; in fact it is commendable.

These are the few ways and manners of saying 'Yā Rasūlallāh' which I have enumerated upon and given my view upon. Now, for those people who say 'Yā Rasūlallāh', what are their intention when they are saying it and what is their motive? The conclusion to this you can draw for yourself.

One important point to note is that just as in Du'ā and to gain nearness to Allāh ﷻ, one calls out to Him and recites Wazeefahs (prayers) using His Pure Names, similarly, some people use the names of some pious people, call to them and recite invocations. This is completely impermissible in Islām. The reason being that such actions fall under the scope of Ibādah and all Ibādah are purely for the sake of Allāh ﷻ. Neither the Holy Prophet ﷺ, nor the Sahābah ﷺ, nor any pious predecessors used the name of any other being besides Allāh ﷻ for the recitation of any invocation. Qādhi Thanāullāh Pāni Patti ﷺ states, "It is not permissible to make Dhikr with the name of any of the pious, as a Wazeefah or as a means of achieving an objective or need as the ignorant do." (Al-Jannatu Li Ahlis-Sunnati)

# Kissing & Rubbing the Thumbs onto the Eyes

**Q** I have observed some people kiss and rub the thumbs onto their eyes when the noble name of the Holy Prophet ﷺ is mentioned? Is there any evidence of this practice in the light of Ahādeeth?

**A** There is no authentic narration regarding the notion that we have Noor on our thumbs and neither was it required or recommended, by the Holy Prophet ﷺ to kiss them and rub them in the eyes, upon hearing his blessed name at the time of Adhān. What is required from us, however, is to send Durood (salutations) upon hearing the blessed name of the Holy Prophet ﷺ and furthermore, to recite Durood Shareef (preferably Durood-e-Ibrāheem) frequently to the best of one's ability.

The Hadeeth which is commonly presented in order to justify this act is as follows; On a Friday the Holy Prophet ﷺ came to the Masjid before Salāh and reclined against a pillar. Thereafter, Sayyidunā Bilāl ؓ called out the Adhān. When he said, "Ash-hadu anna Muhammadar-Rasūlullāh", Sayyidunā Abū Bakr ؓ rubbed his thumbs on his eyes saying, "The coolness of my eyes is in you, O' Messenger of Allāh ﷺ." (Tafreehul Azkiyā fi Ahwālil Ambiyā)

According to the earlier Hanafi scholars, this Hadeeth is unacceptable, on the grounds of either fabrication or being extremely weak and furthermore this Hadeeth is not mentioned in any of the main authentic books of Ahādeeth. What is instructed by the Holy Prophet ﷺ is to send Durood upon him, when hearing his blessed name. This is understood from the following Hadeeth, Sayyidunā Ali ⚬ relates that the Holy Prophet ﷺ said, "A miser is the one before whom I am mentioned but he does not send blessings (Durood) upon me." (Tirmizi)

## Decorating the Masjid

**Q** In our locality, the trustees and the committee members decorate the Masjid on the Holy Prophet's ﷺ birthday. Please comment.

**A** It is a Bid'ah (innovation) to decorate the Masjid with lights etc. on any occasion. It is not permissible to adopt this practice.

# Allāh ﷻ Knows Best

# 5. CHAPTER ON TAHĀRAH
# PURITY

# Hadath (Impurity)

**Q** What is Hadath?

**A** Hadath literally means impurity. Hadath is of two types, Hadath Akbar and Hadath Asgar. Hadath Akbar is that impurity which makes Ghusl compulsory and Hadath Asgar is that impurity which makes Wudhu compulsory.

# Age of Puberty

**Q** When is a child considered a Bāligh (mature)?

**A** According to the Shari'ah, when a child attains puberty he/she is said to have become Bāligh. A boy becomes Bāligh (mature) if he experiences any of the following:

1. He has a wet dream and semen is discharged.
2. He is able to make a woman pregnant.

A girl becomes Bāligh (mature) if she experiences any the following:

1. She experiences a monthly period - Haidh (menstruation).
2. She has a dream (and she ejaculates).
3. She becomes pregnant.

If the above signs are not evident but he/she reaches the age of 14 years and 7 months then he/she will be regarded as having reached the age of puberty. On reaching the age of puberty all the principles of Islām such as Salāh and fasting becomes Fardh (obligatory). If he/she disobeys or neglects any of these, then he/she becomes a sinner.

## Exposing the Satr (Private Parts)

**Q** If a person exposes his Satr (the parts of the body which are necessary to cover) after performing Wudhu (ablution) in front of someone or in solitude, does it break his Wudhu?

**A** It will not break the Wudhu in both circumstances, but it is a grave sin to expose one's Satr in front of someone else. The Satr of a man is from below the navel up to below the knees. A woman has three categories of Satr;

1.  A woman to a woman - below the navel up to below the knees.
2.  A woman to her Mahram - Above her chest up to below her knees.
3.  A woman to a Ghair-Mahram (stranger) - The entire body apart from her face, hands and feet. However, in the case of Hijāb she must cover those parts also.

## Prohibited Things in the State of Major Impurity

**Q** When a person is in the state of Janābat (impurity), what things are not permissible to carry out?

**A** The following things are prohibited in the state of Janābat (Hadath-Akbar):

1.  Performing Salāh
2.  Touching the Holy Qur'ān
3.  Reciting the Holy Qur'ān

4.    To enter a Masjid
5.    To make Tawāf of the Ka'bah

# Using the Miswāk

**Q** What is the ruling regarding using Miswāk when doing **Wudhu and what are its benefits?**

**A** The Holy Prophet ﷺ emphasised greatly on the use of Miswāk, so it is Sunnah to use it during Wudhu. Its importance is such, that the Holy Prophet ﷺ on one occasion, was under the impression that Allāh ﷻ might ordain the use of the Miswāk to be Fardh upon the Ummah. Sayyidunā Abū Umāmah ؓ narrates that the Holy Prophet ﷺ said, "Use the Miswāk, for verily it purifies the mouth and pleases the Lord."

"Jibreel عليه السلام continuously exhorted me to use the Miswāk until I feared it would be decreed as obligatory upon me and upon my Ummah."

He also said, "If I did not fear imposing hardship on my Ummah, then I would have surely made its use obligatory upon my Ummah. "

"Verily, I use the Miswāk so much that I fear the front part of my mouth being peeled, with the constant and abundant brushing with it."

When a Miswāk is available but not used, the complete reward of

Wudhu is not achieved. Miswāk was also used for cleaning and brushing the teeth by the people of the past including the Prophets ﷺ. There are many Ahādeeth indicating that Miswāk was the Sunnah of all the Prophets ﷺ. Sayyidunā Abū Ayyūb Al-Ansāri ؓ narrates that the Holy Prophet ﷺ said, "Four things are amongst the practices of the Prophets ﷺ; circumcision, applying perfume, Miswāk and marriage." (Ahmad, Tirmizī)

Apart from the above, there are many other Ahādeeth that mention the Miswāk to be the practice of the previous Prophets ﷺ. We can deduce from the above Hadeeth, that the practice of using the Miswāk is not something new or specific for this Ummah, rather it was used in the past nations also. Therefore, one of its greatest benefits is the good fortune of being associated with the Prophets ﷺ in this meritorious practice. On the other hand, those who neglect the use of the Miswāk, are very unfortunate by depriving themselves from the tremendous reward which this noble practice carries.

There are numerous benefits of using the Miswāk. Sayyidunā Abdullāh Ibn Umar ؓ narrates that the Holy Prophet ﷺ said, "Make a regular practice of the Miswāk, for verily it cleanses the mouth and pleases the Lord."(Bukhāri)

In this Hadeeth it mentions the worldly benefit (i.e. it cleanses the mouth) as well as the benefit of the Hereafter, which is attaining Allāh's ﷻ pleasure. The prime motive of a true believer, in his use of the Miswāk, is his desire to obtain the reward of the Hereafter.

# Method of Using the Miswāk

**Q** What is the correct method of using a Miswāk?

**A** The Miswāk or Siwāk is a kind of toothbrush made of fibrous wood, about a hand span long. The correct method of using the Miswāk is to hold it with the right hand, the thumb at one end and the little finger below the other end. The remaining fingers should be on the upper portion of the Miswāk and held with the fist. First, brush the upper teeth on the right side length wise and then on the left side.

In the same manner, brush the lower teeth beginning with the right side. After using it once, dry it by squeezing it, after removing it from the mouth. Then wet it again with water and brush the teeth a second time. Repeat a third time in the same way. Finally wash the Miswāk and place it upright against a wall etc. Do not place it on the ground directly.

# Using the Finger as a Substitute for Miswāk

**Q** Can one use his fingers if he does not have a Miswāk?

**A** In the case where a Miswāk is not available, then the fingers can be used as a substitute. This method will serve a similar purpose as the Miswāk far as the reward is concerned. So if a Miswāk is not available, the reward of using the Miswāk will be obtained by using the fingers as a substitute, provided that the intention of Miswāk is made and a Miswāk is not available. In the famous book of Jurisprudence, 'Muheet', it states, "Rubbing the teeth with the forefinger and the thumb is Miswāk."

Imām Tahtāwi 🕮 says, "The promised reward (of using the Miswāk) shall be obtained in the event of the absence of the Miswāk and not in the event of its availability."It is also mentioned in Fatāwa Hindiyyah, "If a Miswāk is not available, then the finger from the right hand will serve as a substitute."

**Note:** A toothbrush will not serve as a substitute in terms of reward when a Miswāk is available. The same applies for tooth powder or any other means of cleansing.

# Facing the Qiblah whilst Answering the Call of Nature

**Q** What should one do if one's toilet is facing the Qiblah?

**A** It is impermissible and sinful to sit with one's front or back facing the Qiblah. The Holy Prophet 🕮 said, "When you go to relieve yourself then do not sit with your front or back facing the Qiblah." (Bukhāri, Muslim)

Thus, if the toilet is such that one's front or back will face the Qiblah, it will be impermissible and sinful to use it. It is thus necessary to correct the direction of the toilet as soon as possible.

It is mentioned in the famous book of jurisprudence, Shāmi, "It is Makrooh Tahreemi (near forbidden) to sit facing your front or back towards the Qiblah even if it is in a built up area (i.e. bathroom). Thus, if the direction of the toilet is not changed then one should try his best to sit at an angle away from the Qiblah."

# Covering the Head When Relieving Oneself

Q Should a person cover his head before entering the toilet?

A To cover the head when entering the toilet to relief oneself is Sunnah. Sayyidah Ā'ishah ﷺ relates that when the Holy Prophet ﷺ went to relieve himself he would cover his head. (Bayhaqi)

In another Hadeeth of Bayhaqi, Sayyidunā Habib Ibn Sālih ﷺ reports that when the Holy Prophet ﷺ entered the toilet, he would wear shoes and cover his head.

Sayyidah Ā'ishah ﷺ also relates that Sayyidunā Abū Bakr ﷺ once said, "Show respect in front of Allāh ﷻ, for I certainly cover my head when entering the toilet due to respect for Allāh ﷻ." (Musannaf Abdur-Razzāq)

Apart from the above Ahādeeth, to cover the head with a Topi (hat) when entering the toilet has also been narrated from other Sahābahs ﷺ, such as Sayyidunā Anas Ibn Mālik ﷺ and Sayyidunā Abū Moosa Al-Ash'ari ﷺ.

# Saliva of a Dog

Q What is the Shari'ah ruling regarding a dog's saliva? If a dog touches you with its tongue, are the clothes clean or unclean?

A   The saliva of a dog is impure. Sayyidunā Abū Hurairah ﷺ relates that the Holy Prophet ﷺ said, "If a dog was to drink from
your bowl then he should wash it seven times." (Bukhāri)

So if it touches the body or clothes, then only the affected part
must be washed thoroughly and not the entire clothes. The same
ruling also applies to pigs and all carnivore animals. Their saliva is
Najāsat Ghaleezah (major impurity). (Durrul-Mukhtār)

# Wudhu after Ghusl

Q Is it necessary to perform Wudhu after having taken a bath?

A No, it is not necessary.

# Doubt Regarding Wudhu

Q Frequently it happens, that I perform complete Wudhu but
later on, a doubt occurs in my mind that my Wudhu is broken.
Should I perform fresh Wudhu or shall I overlook my doubt?

A   Mere doubt will not break the Wudhu. Sayyidunā Abū
Hurairah ﷺ relates that the Holy Prophet ﷺ said, "If anyone
amongst you feels anything in his stomach and questions whether
anything has come out or not, then he should not exit the Masjid
until he hears either a sound (of passing wind) or smells
it." (Muslim)

The above Hadeeth clearly explains that mere doubt will not nullify the Wudhu. So if one is certain that he has made Wudhu, but doubts regarding the breaking of Wudhu, then such doubt will not break the Wudhu and it will still remain intact. (Hindiyyah)

# Performing Wudhu while Wearing Contact Lenses

**Q** Is the Wudhu valid if performed whilst wearing contact lenses?

**A** Wudhu will be valid since it will suffice for Wudhu and Ghusl to wash the outer part of the eye. It is not necessary to wash the inside of the eyes. In fact, it is not even recommended because of the fear of potential harm to the eye. (Al-Mughni)

# Performing Wudhu whilst Standing

**Q** Almost all homes in the UK have wash basins where the people usually perform Wudhu standing. Is the Wudhu valid if it is done in such a manner?

**A** Wudhu performed whilst standing at a wash basin is valid. However, from the etiquettes of Wudhu, is that it should be done whilst seated at an elevated place, facing the Qiblah. Thus, where there is an appropriate arrangement, it is best to perform Wudhu whilst seated, facing the Qiblah otherwise it will be against the preferred method. Where there is no appropriate facilities, then to stand and make Wudhu at a wash basin will not be contrary to the preferred method. (Marāqil-Falāh)

# Washing Beneath the Beard in Wudhu

**Q** I have a thick beard and I want to know if it is Fardh for the water to reach the skin beneath it during Wudhu.

**A** If the beard is so thick that the skin under it cannot be seen, then it is not Fardh for the water to reach the skin. However, if the beard grows sparsely, such that the skin under it can be seen, then it is Fardh for the water to reach the skin as well. (Durrul Mukhtār)

# Removing Earrings for Wudhu

**Q** Should a woman remove her earrings for Wudhu? Is it necessary to wet the earlobes?

**A** It is not necessary to wet the earlobes in Wudhu as Masah (wiping) is sufficient. Hence removing them will not be necessary.

# Holy Qur'ān Text on Touch Screen Devices

**Q** If someone has no Wudhu, can they touch a screen which has the Holy Qur'ān written on it i.e. computer, touch screen mobile phones?

**A** If on the computer, mobile phone etc., the Holy Qur'ān application is activated and Qur'anic verses appear on the screen, then it would not be permissible for a person who is not in the state of Wudhu to touch the screen.

333

It is stated in Durrul-Mukhtār: "It is prohibited for him who is in the state of Hadath-Akbar (in the state of a compulsory bath) and Hadath-Asgar (not in the state of Wudhu) to touch the Mushaf."

Allāmah Ibn Ābideen Ash-Shāmi ﷺ states the following: "It is lawful (to touch) any part of the Mushaf (Holy Qur'ān) except that area where the verses are inscribed."

# Dripping of Urine

**Q** I have a severe problem of retaining my Wudhu due to the constant dripping of urine. How shall I perform my Salāh?

**A** A person who is unable to retain or renew his Wudhu due to continuous dripping of urine, bleeding, flowing of pus, passing of wind etc. and he remains in this condition for the complete duration of a Fardh Salāh time, then such a person is referred to as a Ma'zoor. A person will remain a Ma'zoor as long as that illness continues for the duration of one complete Fardh Salāh time, from the first time the illness began. If it continues thereafter for the following Fardh Salāh, or the illness occurs even once during the next Salāh time, then the person will continue to remain a Ma'zoor.

The ruling is that a Ma'zoor should perform his Wudhu at the beginning time of every Fardh Salāh. The Wudhu of this Salāh will remain intact irrespective of the continuous illness which a person is suffering from until the time that Fardh Salāh ends. Thereafter, the Ma'zoor's Wudhu will break upon the expiry time of a Fardh Salāh. However, if any other acts which break the Wudhu occur during the Salāh time other than the actual illness, then it will break the Wudhu of a Ma'zoor.

He will no longer be regarded a Ma'zoor if the illness does not occur at least once, from the beginning to the end time of a particular Fardh Salāh.

# Noticing Blood after Wudhu

**Q** I was blowing my nose when I noticed blood on my handkerchief. Does that affect my Wudhu in any way?

**A** If dry blood comes out of the nose while blowing it, then the Wudhu is not broken. Wudhu will only break if the blood is in a fluid state.

# Wetting the Head due to Injury or Illness

**Q** My brother suffered a head injury due to which he is unable to pour water over his head. Is his Ghusl (bath) valid without wetting the head?

**A** Due to some sickness, illness or injury, if it is harmful to pour water over the head, then one should do Masah over the head. If Masah is harmful for the head, then it is permissible to wash the entire body apart from the head. However, upon recovery, it becomes necessary to wash the head and there is no need to renew the Ghusl.

# Fluid Flowing from the Ears

**Q** I often have ear-aches which causes the flowing of fluid from the ears. I do not remember having a sore or pimple in my ear. What is the ruling regarding my Wudhu?

**A** Fluid flowing from a painful ear will break the Wudhu even if there is no sore or pimple in the ear.

# Fluid Flowing from the Eyes

**Q** Does the fluid that flows out of the eye whilst yawning, break the Wudhu?

**A** The liquid that comes out of the eye whilst yawning does not break the Wudhu.

# Alcohol Touching the Body

**Q** Is Ghusl necessary prior to performing Salāh if alcohol or any other Harām substance touches the body?

**A** No, Ghusl is not necessary. Only that portion of the body or clothes which is impure should be washed by water thrice.

We should remember that dealing with alcohol is Harām. It is very disrespectful and sinful to deal with alcohol (whether it is buying, selling or drinking) and then proceed to the Masjid to stand before Allāh ﷻ.

# Talking whilst Having a Bath

**Q** Is it permissible to speak whilst having a bath?

**A** It is Makrooh (undesirable) to talk unnecessarily whilst having a bath with the Satr uncovered.

# Pubic Hair

**Q** What is the maximum period that pubic hair could be left on the body?

**A** Unwanted hair should preferably be removed once a week. If this is not possible, then every second week. Care should be taken that it is not left for more than 40 days. Beyond 40 days, the neglector will be sinful. (Fatāwa Hindiyyah)

# Method of Clipping the Nails

**Q** Is there a certain method for clipping the nails?

**A** Imām Nawāwi ﷺ, Hāfiz Ibn Hajar ﷺ and Allāmah Aynee ﷺ have written in their respective commentaries, that the following method is Mustahab and should be adopted when pairing the nails. Commencing with the right hand nails, one should firstly pare the nail of the index finger, then the middle, ring finger, little finger and lastly, the thumb. Going onto the left hand, one should commence with the little finger and continue all the way until the thumb. However, Imām Ghazāli ﷺ has written that one should leave the thumb of the right hand for last, when following the above-mentioned sequence. A third method has also been mentioned by Hāfiz Ibn Hajar 🏵, which commences with the little finger on the right hand, and continues all the way through to the little finger on the left hand.

As far as the feet are concerned, Hāfiz Ibn Hajar 🏵 has written that one should commence with the small toe of the right foot and continue all the way until the big toe of the right foot. Thereafter, commencing with the big toe of the left foot until the small toe.

(Fathul-Bāri)

The author of Ithāf, which is the most popular commentary of Ihyā-ul-Uloom, states that no matter which procedure is adopted when pairing the nails, one will inevitably gain the reward for adhering to the Sunnah. (Vol 2 Pg 412)

# Finger and Toe Nails

**Q** Is there any sequence to be followed when cutting the finger and toe nails?

**A** Cutting the fingernails should begin at the Shahādat finger (index finger of the right hand). Then the nails of the next three fingers (of the right hand) should be cut in order. Thereafter, continue with the small finger of the left hand and complete the remaining three fingers and thumb, in sequence. Lastly, cut the nail of the right thumb. Cutting the toe nails should begin at the small toe of the right foot and end at the small toe of the left foot, in order.

**Note:** The above sequence is desirable, not compulsory.

# Long Fingernails

**Q** How often should a person cut their nails?

**A** It is preferable to cut the nails of the fingers and toes once a week. If this is not possible then every ten days (or two weeks). Care should be taken not to leave it for more than 40 days. Beyond 40 days the neglector will become sinful. (Fatāwa Hindiyyah)

Nowadays, it is considered fashionable for women to keep long fingernails. Dirt can accumulate under such long nails and obstruct the moistening of the parts covered by the dirt, which is contrary to Islamic hygiene. Apart from this, if the dirt is of a non-porous nature, which does not allow water to seep through, then the Wudhu and Ghusl will remain incomplete, thus, not valid.

# Cutting the Nails after Wudhu

**Q** If after performing Wudhu, nails are cut or dead skin of a wound is scratched, will the Wudhu remain valid?

**A** The Wudhu will remain valid and it will not be necessary to wash those parts again.

# Nail Polish and Wudhu

Q Is it compulsory to remove nail polish or lip stick when performing Wudhu or Ghusl?

A It is compulsory to remove nail polish, lipstick or any other substance which does not allow water to penetrate through to the skin before performing Wudhu or Fardh Ghusl. Otherwise, the Wudhu and Ghusl will not be valid.

# Vomit

Q Does vomiting break Wudhu?

A If the vomit is less than a mouthful then it will not break the Wudhu. However, if the vomit is a mouthful (i.e. the quantity which prevents the person from speaking when in the mouth) or more, whether the mouthful is of blood, food or water, then the Wudhu will be broken. But if only phlegm comes out, the Wudhu is not broken. (Durrul Mukhtār)

# Vomit of a Baby

Q Is the vomit of a baby pure or impure with regards to clothes for Salāh?

A If it is a mouthful or more, then the vomit and the clothes soiled by the vomit will become impure, otherwise not. (Fatāwa Hindiyyah p11 vol 1)

# Emission of Milk

**Q** Does the emission of milk from a woman's breasts break the Wudhu?

**A** Emission of milk from a woman's breasts does not break the Wudhu.

# Vomiting Phlegm

**Q** If someone vomits but only phlegm comes out from ones mouth, does it affect the Wudhu?

**A** Wudhu does not break if only phlegm comes out of the mouth.

# Changing the Nappy of a Baby

**Q** It is commonly believed that by changing the nappy of a baby, the Wudhu breaks. Is this correct?

**A**. Changing the nappies of a baby or an ill adult does not break Wudhu.

# Touching the Private Parts

**Q** If someone touches his private parts, will that break his Wudhu? Is there any difference if it is touched over a cloth or not?

**A** Touching one's private parts does not break the Wudhu. There is no difference if it is touched over a cloth or with bare hands. In both circumstances the Wudhu will remain intact (unbroken). (Durrul Mukhtār)

# Wudhu Breaks whilst Performing Wudhu

**Q During Wudhu, if the Wudhu breaks due to passing wind or bleeding, then what should one do?**

**A** Whilst performing Wudhu or Tayammum if any breakers of Wudhu occur, i.e. passing wind or blood comes out, then the Wudhu should be re-started or at least the Fardh (compulsory) parts should be washed again. (Munyatul-Musalli)

# Blood Flowing from the Gums

**Q I felt blood come out of my gums which I accidentally swallowed. Does this in any way affect my Wudhu?**

**A** If blood comes out of the gums and it is swallowed but its quantity cannot be determined, then it would be preferable to make fresh Wudhu. If any blood is noticed in the saliva but it is very small in quantity and the colour of the saliva is white or yellowish, then the Wudhu is intact. However, if it is red in colour then the Wudhu is broken.

# Masah (Passing Wet Hands) Over Ordinary Socks

**Q** Why is it not permissible to do Masah over ordinary socks (i.e. nylon, cotton)?

**A** It is not permissible to do Masah over ordinary socks because it is contrary to the commandment of the Holy Qur'ān. Allāh ﷻ says, "O you who believe! When you intend to offer Salāh, wash your faces and hands up to the elbows, wipe (by passing wet hands over) your heads, and (wash) your feet up to the ankles." (5:6)

All the Ahādeeth which show the permissibility of doing Masah on ordinary socks are weak and there is no Saheeh Hadeeth to prove its permissibility. This is confirmed by authentic and reliable scholars. As there is no Saheeh Hadeeth, it is not permissible to perform Masah on ordinary socks nor is it permissible to prove its permissibility by such weak Ahādeeth. When the purpose of Masah on socks is to keep water out, how could Masah be permissible on ordinary socks, since doing so allows the water to reach the feet?

# Masah Over Leather Socks

**Q** What is the ruling regarding Masah on leather socks? Can you explain in detail the method of Masah and the compulsory acts?

**A** It is from the acts of Sunnah for males and females to make

Masah on leather socks. The Farāidh (compulsory) acts of Masah are:

1. The Masah has to be made on the upper section of the leather socks and not on the sole of the socks.
2. To pass at least the three small wet fingers of the hand on the upper section of the leather socks.

The Sunnah method of Masah is as follows:
1. Wet at least three (i.e. the index, middle and ring) fingers of both hands with clean water. (If more than three fingers are used it is permissible. However, if less than three fingers are used, Masah will not be done).
2. Thereafter place these three wet fingers on the leather socks and pass them from the toes stretching towards the ankles and also the area above it, thus forming wet lines on both the leather socks.

## Q Why is it permissible to do Masah on leather socks when this is also contradictory to the commandment of the Holy Qur'ān ?

A. The Ahādeeth which proves the permissibility of doing Masah on Khuffain are all Saheeh (rigorously authentic). Its permissibility is a consensus of the four great Imāms (Jurists of the Ummah), as well as the Muslim Ummah. The Ahādeeth of allowing to perform Masah over leather socks has been transmitted from each generation as Tawātur. Tawātur means that there be such an overwhelming number of transmitters, that there is no possibility of fabrication or lying. The knowledge attained from such transmission is Qat'i (absolute certainty). The scholars of Hadeeth have ruled that a Tawātur Hadeeth is equal in status to the Holy Qur'ān.

**Note:** There are so many Ahādeeth on this subject that according to Imām Abū Haneefah ﷺ and Imām Mālik ﷺ, to acknowledge the permissibility of performing Masah on Kuffain is a sign of the people of Ahlus-Sunnah Wal-Jamā'at. Imām Abū Haneefah ﷺ is reported to have said, "I was not convinced (of the permissibility of performing Masah on Kuffain) until the Ahādeeth reached me in such vast numbers like the bright morning light."

# Masah Over Cotton or Cloth Socks

**Q** Is it permissible to do Masah over any particular type of cotton or cloth socks?

**A** Yes, according to the four Imāms it is permissible to do Masah over those socks (cloth, cotton etc.) that fulfil the following conditions:

1. The socks are so thick that if water was sprinkled on top of them it does not reach the feet.

2. The socks would stay on without tying them to the foreleg (shin).

3. The socks are such that it is suitable to walk continuously in them without shoes and without them tearing (for at least 1 mile). The permissibility of performing Masah on the above mentioned socks is not on the basis that they are ordinary socks. Rather if

they fulfil the aforementioned criteria, they would be classed in the same category as Khuffain (leather socks). Thus, it would be permissible to perform Masah over such socks. There are also two other types of socks on which Masah is permissible:

1. Those cotton or cloth socks which are covered top to bottom in leather.

2. Those cotton or cloth socks which have their soles covered in leather.

From the aforementioned points it is clear that it is not permissible to perform Masah on ordinary socks. This is the view held by the four Imāms and the majority of scholars.

# Allāh ﷻ Knows Best

# Other titles from JKN PUBLICATIONS

## Marriage - A Complete Solution

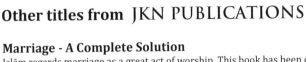

Islām regards marriage as a great act of worship. This book has been designed to provide the fundamental teachings and guidelines of all what relates to the marital life in a simplified English language. It encapsulates in a nutshell all the marriage laws mentioned in many of the main reference books in order to facilitate their understanding and implementation.

**UK RRP: £5.00**

## Pearls of Luqmān

This book is a comprehensive commentary of Sūrah Luqmān, written beautifully by Shaykh Mufti Saiful Islām. It offers the reader with an enquiring mind, Abūndance of advice, guidance, counselling and wisdom.

The reader will be enlightened by many wonderful topics and anecdotes mentioned in this book, which will create a greater understanding of the Holy Qur'ān and its wisdom. The book highlights some of the wise sayings and words of advice Luqmān ﷺ gave to his son.

**UK RRP: £3.00**

## Arabic Grammar for Beginners

This book is a study of Arabic Grammar based on the subject of Nahw (Syntax) in a simplified English format. If a student studies this book thoroughly, he/she will develop a very good foundation in this field, Inshā-Allāh. Many books have been written on this subject in various languages such as Arabic, Persian and Urdu. However, in this day and age there is a growing demand for this subject to be available in English .

**UK RRP: £3.00**

## A Gift to My Youngsters

This treasure filled book, is a collection of Islāmic stories, morals and anecdotes from the life of our beloved Prophet ﷺ, his Companions ﷺ and the pious predecessors. The stories and anecdotes are based on moral and ethical values, which the reader will enjoy sharing with their peers, friends, families and loved ones.

"A Gift to My Youngsters" – is a wonderful gift presented to the readers personally, by the author himself, especially with the youngsters in mind. He has carefully selected stories and anecdotes containing beautiful morals, lessons and valuable knowledge and wisdom.

**UK RRP: £5.00**

## Travel Companion

The beauty of this book is that it enables a person on any journey, small or distant or simply at home, to utilise their spare time to read and benefit from an exciting and vast collection of important and interesting Islamic topics and lessons. Written in simple and easy to read text, this book will immensely benefit both the newly interested person in Islām and the inquiring mind of a student expanding upon their existing knowledge. Inspiring reminders from the Holy Qur'ān and the blessed words of our beloved Prophet ﷺ beautifies each topic and will illuminate the heart of the reader.                                    **UK RRP: £5.00**

## Pearls of Wisdom

Junaid Baghdādi ﷺ once said, "Allāh ﷻ strengthens through these Islamic stories the hearts of His friends, as proven from the Qur'anic verse,
**"And all that We narrate unto you of the stories of the Messengers, so as to strengthen through it your heart." (11:120)**
Mālik Ibn Dinār ﷺ stated that such stories are gifts from Paradise. He also emphasised to narrate these stories as much as possible as they are gems and it is possible that an individual might find a truly rare and invaluable gem among them.                                             **UK RRP: £6.00**

## Inspirations

This book contains a compilation of selected speeches delivered by Shaykh Mufti Saiful Islām on a variety of topics such as the Holy Qur'ān, Nikāh and eating Halāl. Having previously been compiled in separate booklets, it was decided that the transcripts be gathered together in one book for the benefit of the reader. In addition to this, we have included in this book, further speeches which have not yet been printed.

**UK RRP: £6.00**

## Gift to my Sisters

A thought provoking compilation of very interesting articles including real life stories of pious predecessors, imaginative illustrations, medical advices on intoxicants and rehabilitation and much more. All designed to influence and motivate mothers, sisters, wives and daughters towards an ideal Islamic lifestyle. A lifestyle referred to by our Creator, Allāh ﷻ in the Holy Qur'ān as the means to salvation and ultimate success.

**UK RRP: £6.00**

## Gift to my Brothers

A thought provoking compilation of very interesting articles including real life stories of pious predecessors, imaginative illustrations, medical advices on intoxicants and rehabilitation and much more. All designed to influence and motivate fathers, brothers, husbands and sons towards an ideal Islamic lifestyle. A lifestyle referred to by our Creator, Allāh ﷻ in the Holy Qur'ān as the means to salvation and ultimate success.

**UK RRP: £5.00**

## Your Questions Answered

An outstanding book written by Shaykh Mufti Saiful Islām. A very comprehensive yet simple Fatāwa book and a source of guidance that reaches out to a wider audience i.e. the English speaking Muslims. The reader will benefit from the various answers to questions based on the Laws of Islām relating to the beliefs of Islām, knowledge, Sunnah, pillars of Islām, marriage, divorce and contemporary issues.

UK RRP: £7.50

## Hadeeth for Beginners

A concise Hadeeth book with various Ahādeeth that relate to basic Ibādāh and moral etiquettes in Islām accessible to a wider readership. Each Hadeeth has been presented with the Arabic text, its translation and commentary to enlighten the reader, its meaning and application in day-to-day life.

UK RRP: £3.00

## Du'a for Beginners

This book contains basic Du'ās which every Muslim should recite on a daily basis. Highly recommended to young children and adults studying at Islamic schools and Madrasahs so that one may cherish the beautiful treasure of supplications of our beloved Prophet ﷺ in one's daily life, which will ultimately bring peace and happiness in both worlds, Inshā-Allāh.

UK RRP: £2.00

## How well do you know Islām?

An exciting educational book which contains 300 multiple questions and answers to help you increase your knowledge on Islām! Ideal for the whole family, especially children and adult students to learn new knowledge in an enjoyable way and cherish the treasures of knowledge that you will acquire from this book. A very beneficial tool for educational syllabus.

UK RRP: £3.00

## Treasures of the Holy Qur'an

This book entitled "Treasures of the Holy Qur'ān" has been compiled to create a stronger bond between the Holy Qur'ān and the readers. It mentions the different virtues of Sūrahs and verses from the Holy Qur'ān with the hope that the readers will increase their zeal and enthusiasm to recite and inculcate the teachings of the Holy Qur'ān into their daily lives.

349

UK RRP: £3.00

## Heroes of Islām

"In the narratives there is certainly a lesson for people of intelligence (understanding)." (12:111)

A fine blend of Islamic personalities who have been recognised for leaving a lasting mark in the hearts and minds of people.

A distinguishing feature of this book is that the author has selected not only some of the most world and historically famous renowned scholars but also these lesser known and a few who have simply left behind a valuable piece of advice to their nearest and dearest. **UK RRP: £5.00**

## Should I Follow a Madhab?

Taqleed or following one of the four legal schools is not a new phenomenon. Historically, scholars of great calibre and luminaries, each one being a specialist in his own right, were known to have adhered to one of the four legal schools. It is only in the previous century that a minority group emerged advocating a severe ban on following one of the four major schools.

This book endeavours to address the topic of Taqleed and elucidates why it is necessary to do Taqleed in this day and age. It will also, by the Divine Will of Allāh ﷻ dispel some of the confusion surrounding this topic. **UK RRP: £5.00**

## Advice for the Students of Knowledge

Allāh ﷻ describes divine knowledge in the Holy Qur'ān as a 'Light'. Amongst the qualities of light are purity and guidance. The Holy Prophet ﷺ has clearly explained this concept in many blessed Ahādeeth and has also taught us many supplications in which we ask for beneficial knowledge.

This book is a golden tool for every sincere student of knowledge wishing to mould his/her character and engrain those correct qualities in order to be worthy of receiving the great gift of Ilm from Allāh ﷻ. **UK RRP: £3.00**